THE LIFE
OF
HIUEN-TSIANG

THE LIFE OF HIUEN-TSIANG

BY THE SHAMAN
HWUI LI

WITH AN INTRODUCTION CONTAINING
AN ACCOUNT OF THE WORKS OF I-TSING

SAMUEL BEAL

WITH A PREFACE BY
L. CRANMER - BYNG

GYAN

Published by

Gyan Publishing House
5, Ansari Road
Daryaganj, New Delhi-110002
Phone: 011-47034999, 9811692060
E-mail: books@gyanbooks.com

Distribution Network
gyanbooks.com
India, USA, Canada, UK, Australia, France

ISBN : 978-81-2120-036-3 (HB)
First Published, London, 1911

2nd Impression 2020

Printed at: Gyan Press, Delhi.

The Life of Hiuen-Tsiang
Author: Samuel Beal

THE
LIFE OF HIUEN-TSIANG

BY THE

SHAMAN HWUI LI

WITH AN INTRODUCTION CONTAINING AN ACCOUNT OF THE WORKS OF I-TSING

BY

SAMUEL BEAL, B.A., D.C.L.

PROFESSOR OF CHINESE, UNIVERSITY COLLEGE, LONDON
RECTOR OF GREENS NORTON, NORTHAMPTONSHIRE, ETC. ETC.

WITH A PREFACE BY

L. CRANMER-BYNG

POPULAR EDITION

LONDON
KEGAN PAUL, TRENCH, TRÜBNER & CO. LTD
BROADWAY HOUSE, 68-74 CARTER LANE, E.C.

PREFACE

CENTURIES before biography became a business, before the peccadilloes of Royal mistresses and forgotten courtesans obtained a "market value," the writing of the Master's life by some cherished disciple was both an act of love and piety in the Far East. The very footprints of the famous dead became luminous, and their shadows shone in dark caves that once withheld them from the world. Memory looking back viewed them through a golden haze; they were merged at last in ancient sunlight; they were shafts of God rayed in the tangled forests of time. In this spirit, then, the man of compassionate feeling (such is the rendering of the Sanscrit Shama), the Shaman Hwui-li, took up his tablets and wrote the life of Hiuen-Tsiang. The Master had already written his immortal *Si-yu-ki* or Record of Western Countries, yet the sixteen years of that wonderful quest in far-off India, of cities seen and shrines visited, of strange peoples and stranger customs, cannot be crowded into one brief record. And so we watch the patient disciple waiting on those intervals of leisure when the task of translation from Sanscrit into Chinese is laid aside, when the long routine of a Buddhist day is ended, waiting for the impressions of a wandering soul in the birthland of its faith. The Life is supplement to the Record. What is obscure or half told in the one is made clear in the other.

Hwui-li begins in the true Chinese manner with a grand pedigree of his hero, tracing his descent from the Emperor Hwang Ti, the mythical Heavenly Emperor.

This zeal for following the remotest ancestors over the borders of history into the regions of fable may be largely ascribed to a very human desire to connect the stream of life with its divine source. We are chiefly concerned to know that he came of a family which had already given notable men to the State, and was launched "in the troublous whirl of birth and death" but a little distance from the town of Kou-Shih, in the province of Honan, in the year 600 A.D. Here and there biography leaves us a glimpse of his outward appearance as boy and man. We are told that "at his opening life he was rosy as the evening vapours and round as the rising moon. As a boy he was sweet as the odour of cinnamon or the vanilla tree." A soberer style does justice to his prime, and again he comes before us, "a tall handsome man with beautiful eyes and a good complexion. He had a serious but benevolent expression and a sedate, rather stately manner." The call of the West came early to Hiuen-Tsiang. From a child he had easily outstripped his fellows in the pursuit of knowledge, and with the passing of the years he stepped beyond the narrow limits of Chinese Buddhism and found the deserts of Turkestan between him and the land of his dreams. Imperfect translations from the Sanscrit, the limited intelligence of the Chinese priesthood, the sense of vast truths dimly perceived obscurely set forth, the leaven of his first Confucian training—all contributed to the making of a Buddhist pilgrim. The period of his departure, 629 A.D., was an eventful one for China. T'ai-Tsung, the most powerful figure of the brilliant T'ang dynasty, sat on the throne of his father Kaotsu, the founder of the line. The nomad Tartars, so long the terror of former dynasties, succumbed to his military genius, and Kashgaria was made a province of the Empire. Already the kingdom of Tibet was tottering to its fall, and Corea was to know the devastation of war within her boundaries. Ch'ang-an was now the capital, a city of floating pavilions and secluded gardens, destined to become the centre of a literary movement that would leave its mark for all time. But the days were not yet when the terraces of Teng-hiang-ting would see the butterflies alight on the flower-crowned locks of Yang-kuei-fei, or the green vistas re-echo to the voices of poet and emperor joined in praise of her. Only two wandering monks emerge furtively through the outer gates of the city's triple walls, and one of them looks back for a glimpse of Ch'ang-an, the last for sixteen eventful years of exile.

Others had crossed the frontier before him, notably Fa-hian and Sung Yun, others in due course would come and go, leaving to posterity their impressions of a changing world, but this man stands alone, a prince of pilgrims, a very Bayard of Buddhist enthusiasm, fearless and without reproach. As we read on through the pages of Hwui-li the fascination of the Master of the Law becomes clear to us, not suddenly, but with the long, arduous miles that mark the way to India and the journey home.

Take the Master's tattered robes, let the winds of Gobi whistle through your sleeve and cut you to the bone, mount his rusty red nag and set your face to the West. In the night you will see "firelights as many as stars" raised by the demons and goblins; travelling at dawn you will behold "soldiers clad in fur and felt and the appearance of camels and horsemen and the glittering of standards and lances; fresh forms and figures changing into a thousand shapes, sometimes at an immense distance, then close at hand, then vanished into the void." The time comes when even the old red steed avails not, the Great Ice Mountains loom in front of you, and you crawl like an ant and cling like a fly to the roof of the world. Then on the topmost summit, still far away from the promised land, you realise two things—the littleness of human life, the greatness of one indomitable soul.

But the superman is also very human. With the vast bulk of his encyclopædic knowledge he falls on the pretentious monk Mokshagupta, he flattens him and treads a stately if heavy measure on his prostrate body. And withal clear-sighted and intolerant of shams, he is still a child of his age and religion. With childish curiosity he tempts a bone to foretell the future, and with childish delight obtains the answer he most desires. In the town of Hiddha is Buddha's skull bone, one foot long, two inches round. "If anyone wishes to know the indications of his guilt or his religious merit he mixes some powdered incense into a paste, which he spreads upon a piece of silken stuff, and then presses it on the top of the bone: according to the resulting indications the good fortune or ill fortune of the man is determined." Hiuen obtains the impression of a Bôdhi and is overjoyed, for, as the guardian Brahman of the bone explains, "it is a sure sign of your having a portion of true wisdom (Bôdhi)." At another time he plays a kind of religious quoits by flinging garlands of flowers on the sacred image of Buddha, which, being caught on its hands and arms, show that his desires will be fulfilled. In simple faith he tells Hwui-li how Buddha once cleaned his teeth and flung the fragments of the wood with which he performed the act on the ground; how they took root forthwith, and how a tree seventy feet high was the consequence. And Hiuen saw that tree, therefore the story must be true.

But it is not with the pardonable superstitions of a human soul of long ago that we need concern ourselves. The immense latent reserve, the calm strength to persist, is the appeal. It comes to us with no note of triumph for the thing accomplished or the obstacle removed, but rather underlies some simple statement of fact and is summed up in these few trite words: "We advanced guided by observing the bones left on the way." The little incidents of life and death are as nothing to one who looks on all men as ghosts haunted by reality. And so the Master of the Law resigns himself to the prospect of a violent end at the hands of the river pirates of the Ganges, to the miraculous interposition of a timely storm, with the same serenity with which he meets the long procession streaming out of Nâlanda in his honour, with its two hundred priests and some thousand lay patrons who surround him to his entry, recounting his praises, and carrying standards, umbrellas, flowers, and perfumes.

Yet there are moments of sheer delight when scenes of physical beauty are fair enough to draw even a Buddhist monk from his philosophic calm, when even Hiuen-Tsiang must have become lyrical in the presence of his recording disciple. Who would not be the guest of the abbot of Nâlanda monastery with its six wings, each built by a king, all enclosed in the privacy of solid brick? "One gate opens into the great college, from which are separated eight other halls, standing in the middle (of the monastery). The richly adorned towers, and the fairy-like turrets, like pointed hilltops, are congregated together. The observatories seem to be lost in the mists (of the morning), and the upper rooms tower above the clouds.

"From the windows one may see how the winds and the clouds produce new forms, and above the soaring eaves the conjunctions of the sun and moon may be observed.

"And then we may add how the deep, translucent ponds bear on their surface the blue lotus intermingled with the Kanaka flower, of deep red colour, and at intervals the Amra groves spread over all, their shade.

"All the outside courts, in which are the priests' chambers, are of four stages. The stages have dragon-projections and coloured eaves, the pearl-red pillars, carved and ornamented, the richly adorned balustrades, and the roofs covered with tiles that reflect the light in a thousand shades, these things add to the beauty of the scene."

Here ten thousand priests sought refuge from the world of passing phenomena and the lure of the senses.

Wherever our pilgrim goes he finds traces of a worship far older than Buddhism. He does not tell us so in so many words, yet underneath the many allusions to Bôdhi-trees and Nāgas we may discover the traces of that primitive tree and serpent worship that still exists in remote corners of India, as, for instance, among the Nāga tribes of Manipur who worship the python they have killed. In Hiuen's time every lake and fountain had its Nāga-râja or serpent-king. Buddha himself, as we learn from both the *Si-yu-ki* and the Life, spent much time converting or subduing these ancient gods. There were Nāgas both good and evil. When Buddha first sought enlightenment he sat for seven days in a state of contemplation by the waters of a little woodland lake. Then this good Nāga "kept guard over Tathâgata; with his folds seven times round the body of the Buddha, he caused many heads to appear, which overshadowed him as a parasol; therefore to the east of this lake is the dwelling of the Nāga." In connection with this legend it is interesting to remember that Vishnu is commonly represented as reposing in contemplation on the seven-headed snake. Even after the passing of the Buddha the Nāgas held their local sway, and King Asoka is foiled in his attempt to destroy the Nāga's *stûpa*, for, "having seen the character of the place, he was filled with fear and said, 'All these appliances for worship are unlike anything seen by men.' The Nāga said, 'If it be so, would that the king would not attempt to destroy the *stûpa!*' The king, seeing that he could not measure his power with that of the Nāga, did not attempt to open the *stûpa* (to take out the relics)." In many instances we find the serpent gods not merely in full possession of their ancient haunts, but actually posing as the allies and champions of the new faith and its founder. In the *Si-yu-ki* we are told that "by the side of a pool where Tathâgata washed his garments is a great square stone on which are yet to be seen the trace-marks of his robe. . . . The faithful and pure frequently come to make their offerings here; but when the heretics and men of evil mind speak lightly of or insult the stone, the dragon-king (Nāga-râja) inhabiting the pool causes the winds to rise and rain to fall."

The connection between Buddhism and tree-worship is even closer still. The figure of the Master is for ever reclining under the Bôdhi-tree beneath whose shade he dreamed that he had "the earth for his bed, the Himalayas for his pillow, while his left arm reached to the Eastern Ocean, his right to the Western Ocean, and his feet to the great South Sea." This Bôdhi-tree is the *Ficus Religiosa* or peepul tree, and is also known as Rarasvit or the tree of wisdom and knowledge. The leaves are heart-shaped, slender and pointed, and constantly quivering. In the *Si-yu-ki* it is stated of a certain Bôdhi-tree that although the leaves wither not either in winter or summer, but remain shining and glistening throughout the year, yet "at every successive *Nirvâna*-day (of the Buddhas) the leaves wither and fall, and then in a moment revive as before." The Buddha sat for seven days contemplating this tree; "he did not remove his gaze from it during this period, desiring thereby to indicate his grateful feelings towards the tree by so looking at it with fixed eyes." Hiuen-Tsiang himself and his companions contributed to the universal adoration of the tree, for, as that impeccable Buddhist the Shaman Hwui-li rather baldly states, "they paid worship to the Bôdhi-tree."

How did Buddhism come to be connected in any way with tree and serpent worship? The answer is, through its connection with Brahmanism. As Buddhism was Brahmanism reformed, so Brahmanism in its turn was the progressive stage of tree and serpent worship. Siva the destroyer is also Nág Bhushan, "he who wears snakes as his ornaments." Among the lower classes in many districts the worship of the serpent frequently supplants or is indistinguishable from the worship of Siva. In the Panma Purána, the Bôdhi-tree is the tree aspect of Vishnu, the Indian fig-tree of Pudra, and the Palasa tree of Brahma. Again, Vishnu is also Hari the Preserver —Hạri who sleeps upon a coiled serpent canopied by its many heads. The Laws of Manu lay down the worship to be offered both to the water-gods (Nāgas) and the tree spirits:—"Having thus, with fixed attention, offered clarified butter in all quarters . . . let him offer his gifts to animated creatures, saying, I salute the Maruts or Winds, let him throw dressed rice near the door, saying, I salute the *water-gods* in water; and on his pestle and mortar, saying, I salute *the gods of large trees.*"

The tree and the serpent coiled at its roots are the two essential symbols of primitive religion, whether the tree is the peepul and the serpent a Nāga-râja, or the serpent be the Tiamat of the Babylonians and the tree the date-palm. There are the serpent-guarded fruits of the Hesperides; there is the serpent beneath the tree of knowledge in the garden, or rather grove, of Eden; there is Yggdrasill, the sacred ash tree of Norse mythology, with Nidhögg the great serpent winding round its roots. The first mysteries of religion were celebrated in groves, as those of Asher and Baal and the groves of the early Romans.

Serpent-worship has universally been the symbol-worship of the human desire for life, the consequent reproduction of the species, and hence the immortality of the race. To-day the barren women of Bengal pay reverence to the person of the Nāga mendicant. But the worship of trees takes its rise from the emotions of primæval man, inspired in the forest. Fear and awe and the passions all dwelt in its shade. The first god of man emerging from the animal is Pan, and his the woodnote that, calling through the sacred grove, causes the new-found conscience to start and the guilty to hide their shame.

But in pointing out the survivals of ancient faith so naïvely testified to by Hiuen-Tsiang, I have intended no disparagement to the gentle, compassionate Master of the Eastern World. Buddha could not have planted any tree that the jungles of India would not have swiftly strangled in one tropic night. He sought for Brahmanism, that giant of the grove, the light and air for which it pined, he cleared the creepers that would have closed it in, he cut away the dead and dying branch and gave the tree of ancient faith its chance of attainment. And if he left the old wise Nāgas to their woodland lakes, or paid silent recognition to the spirit of the Bôdhi-tree, who shall blame him? Man the primitive, with his fresh mind brought to bear upon the mysteries around him, with all senses alert to catch the rhythmic pulses of life and view the silent growth that soared beyond him, with his imagination unfettered and his garb of convention as yet unsewn, was nearer to the great dawn than all the book-bound philosophers that followed him.

But Hiuen-Tsiang or Yüan Chwāng, for such is the latest rendering of his name in the modern Pekinese, was born into a world that beheld the tree of Buddhism slowly dying from the top. He bore witness, if unconsciously, to a time of transition and a noble faith in decay, and the swift, silent growth of jungle mythology around the crumbling temples of Buddha. His record of these sixteen years of travel is a priceless one, for through it we are able to reconstruct the world and ways of Buddhist

India of the centuries that have passed. Yet far more priceless still is that record, read between the lines, of a human soul dauntless in disaster, unmoved in the hour of triumph, counting the perils of the bone-strewn plain and the unconquered hills as nothing to the ideal that lay before him, the life-work, the call of the Holy Himalayas and the long toil of his closing years. It is difficult to over-estimate his services to Buddhist literature. He returned to his own country with no less than 657 volumes of the sacred books, seventy-four of which he translated into Chinese, while 150 relics of the Buddha, borne by twenty horses, formed the spoil reverently gathered from the many lands we call India.

And so we leave him to his rest upon Mount Sumeru, where once his venturous soul alighted in the dreams of youth, with the serpents coiled beneath its base, with its seven circling hills of gold and the seven seas between, and the great salt ocean encompassing them all. There, as Mr. Watters has finely said, "he waits with Maitreya until in the fulness of time the latter comes into this world. With him Yuan-chuang hoped to come back to a new life here and to do again the Buddha's work for the good of others." Till then we leave him to the long interval of bliss transcending all planes of human ecstasy.

> "Around his dreams the dead leaves fall;
> Calm as the starred chrysanthemum
> He notes the season glories come,
> And reads the books that never pall."

L. CRANMER-BYNG.

May 16th, 1911.

CONTENTS.

[*For a detailed Index of Proper Names the reader is referred to the Second Volume of the "Records of the Western World."*]

BOOK I.

Begins with the (birth of Hiuen-Tsiang) in Kow-shi, and ends with the account of his arrival at Kau-Chang.

BOOK II.

Commencing with O-ki-ni, and ending with Kie-jo-kio-she (Kanauj).

BOOK III.

BOOK IV.

BOOK V.

CONCLUSION.

HISTORY

OF THE

EARLY LIFE OF HIUEN-TSIANG.

INTRODUCTION.

1. The present volume is intended to supplement the "History of the Travels of Hiuen-Tsiang" (*Si-yu-ki*), already published by Messrs. Trübner in two volumes, and entitled "Buddhist Records of the Western World."

The original from which the translation is made is styled "History of the Master of the Law of the three Piṭakas of the 'Great Loving-Kindness' Temple." It was written, probably in five chapters, in the first instance by Hwui-li, one of Hiuen-Tsiang's disciples, and afterwards enlarged and completed in ten chapters by Yen-thsong, another of his followers.[1] Yen-thsong was selected by the disciples of Hwui-li to re-arrange and correct the leaves which their master had written and hidden in a cave. He added an introduction and five supplementary chapters. The five chapters added by Yen-thsong are probably those which follow the account of Hiuen-Tsiang's return from India, and relate to his work of translation in China. I have not thought it necessary to reproduce

[1] *Julien*, Preface to the Life of Hiouen-Tsiang, p. lxxix.

this part of the original; my object has been simply to complete the "Records" already published relating to India.

2. It will be found that Hwui-li's history often explains or elucidates the travels of Hiuen-Tsiang. Yen-thsong evidently consulted other texts or authorities. This is especially the case in reference to the history of the Temple of Nâlanda, in the third chapter of the book, compared with the ninth book of the "Records."[1]

3. I may also notice the interesting statement found in the fourth book, referring to King Sadvaha (*So-to-po-ho*), and the rock temple he excavated for Nâgârjuna.[2]

Nâgârjuna is now believed to have flourished as late as 100 years after Kanishka,[3] *i.e.*, towards the end of the second century A.D. This would also be the date of Sadvaha. Who this king was is not certain. He is said to have reigned over Shing-tu, which may simply mean *India*. He was surnamed *Shi-yen-to-kia* (Sindhuka?). He probably had resided on the Indus, and by conquest had got possession of the Southern Kôsala. Was he a Pallava? and was *Alamana*, where Nâgârjuna knew him, the same as *Aramana* on the Coromandel Coast, between Chôḷa and Kaliṅga?[4] Be that as it may, we know that Nâgârjuna was so closely acquainted with the king that

[1] With respect to Tathâgata-Râja, *e.g.*, the phrase used in the original does not mean "*his son*," but "*his direct descendant*," and this goes far to reconcile this account with that found in the *Si-yu-ki*.

Again, with reference to the remark of Hwui-li found on page 112 *infra*, that the Nâlanda monastery was founded 700 years before the time of Hiuen-Tsiang, this, as I have observed (in the note), clears up the date of Śakrâditya, who is described as a *former* king of the country, living after the Nirvâna of Buddha; the expression "not long after," found in the *Si-yu-ki*, must be accepted loosely. The foundation of the convent would be about 80 B.C.

[2] I think it is abundantly clear from the evidence of Chinese traditions that the Patriarch Nâgârjuna and the Bhikshu Nâgasena (who disputed with Menander) are distinct persons. The first (as I have shown in some papers written for the *Indian Antiquary*) was an innovator, and more or less given to magical practices; the latter was a learned Bhikshu engrossed in metaphysical studies.

[3] So says Taou-Sün in his history of the Sâkya family.

[4] For some remarks on this point, *vide Indian Antiquary*, May 1888, p. 126, c. 1. *Cf.* also Schiefner's *Taranatha*, p. 303.

he sent him a friendly letter exhorting him to morality of life and religious conduct. The king in return prepared the cave-dwelling for him of which we have the history in the tenth book of the "Records." This cave-dwelling was hewn in a mountain called *Po-lo-mo-lo-ki-li*, *i.e.*, Bhramarâgiri, the mountain of the *Black bee* (Durgâ).[1]

Dr. Burgess has identified this mountain with the celebrated Śri Śailas, bordering on the river Kistna, called by Schiefner Çri-Parvata. Doubtless it is the same as that described by Fa-hian in the 35th chapter of his travels. He calls it the *Po-lo-yue* Temple, which he explains as "the Pigeon" (*Pârâvat*) monastery. But a more probable restoration of the Chinese symbols would be the *Parvatî*, or the *Parvata*, monastery. The symbol *yue* in Chinese Buddhist translations is equivalent to *va* (or *vat*).[2]

We may therefore assume that the *Po-lo-yue* monastery of Fa-hian was the Durgâ monastery of Hiuen-Tsiang, otherwise called *Śri-parvata*. This supposition is confirmed by the actual history of the place; for Hiuen-Tsiang tells us that after the Buddhists had established themselves in the monastery, the Brahmans by a stratagem took possession of it. Doubtless, when in possession, they would give it a distinctive name acceptable to themselves; hence the terms Bhramarâ or Bhramarâmba.

4. With respect to Fa-hian's restoration of *Po-lo-yue* to

[1] M. Julien restores these symbols to Baramoulagiri, and accepts the interpretation given by Hiuen-Tsiang, viz., "the black peak." Before I had been able to consult any parallel record I was satisfied that this restoration was wrong, and in a paper read before the Royal Asiatic Society, J. R. A. S., vol. xv. part 3, I ventured to assert that the Chinese character "fung," "a peak," was a mistake for "fung," "a bee," and that the name of the hill was Bhramarâgiri, *i.e.*, the hill of the "Black-bee" or of Durgâ. I was gratified some months afterwards to find in Taou-Sün a complete confirmation of my opinion, as he in his account of this district speaks of the Black-bee Mountain, using the symbol "fung," "a bee," for "fung," "a peak."

[2] Thus in Fa-hian's account of the five-yearly religious assembly (*Pañcha-vassa-parishad*), the Chinese symbols are *pan-cha-yue-sse* (*hwui*), where *yue* evidently corresponds to *va*. Again, throughout Taou-Sün's work on the history of the Sâkyas, the symbols for Chakkavat are *cha-ka-yue*, where again *yue* is equivalent to *vat*. And so again, when Taou-Sün describes the inhabitants of Vaisâlî in the time of Buddha, he always calls them *yue-chi*, *i.e.*, Vajjis or Vaṭis (the symbol *chi* is used for *ṭi*, as in *Kiu-chi* for Koṭi).

Pârâvata, "a pigeon," there need be no difficulty. It may have been called the "Pigeon monastery" in pre-Brahman times. The highest storey was probably decorated with pigeon-emblems,[1] or, like the top beams of the gateways at Sanchi, adorned with the trisul emblem. This emblem, in all probability, originally denoted the three rays of the rising sun.[2] These three rays, by the addition of a simple stroke at the base, were converted into a representation of a descending pigeon or dove. This would be sufficient to account for the name the *Pigeon* monastery. But there is no need to press this matter; for whether the symbol *yue* be equal to *va* or *vat*, in this particular case, there can be no doubt as to its true restoration.

5. This remark leads me to allude briefly to the people named *Yue-chi* or *Yue-ti* in Chinese Buddhist literature. There is frequent mention made of the Yue-chi in Chinese books *previous* to the Turushka invasion of North-West India by the predecessors of Kanishka. The inhabitants of Vaisâlî are, *e.g.*, in Buddha's lifetime, called *Yue-chi*.[3]

These people we know were *Vajjis* or *Vaṭis*;[4] they are represented as a proud and arrogant race, and remarkable for personal display and the equipment of their chariots.[5] I should argue then that as the Amardi are called Mardi, and the Aparni are called Parni, so the Vaṭis were the same as the Avaṭis. But in the Scythic portion of the Behistun inscription we have distinct mention of the Afarṭis or Avarṭis as the people who inhabited the high lands bordering on Media and the south shores of the Caspian. Were the Vajjis or Vaṭis, then, a people allied to

[1] I cannot suppose that he meant to say that the different storeys were constructed in the *shape* of the animals denoted, but that they were decorated by emblems of these animals.

[2] *Cf.* the figure of Mithra in Dr. Bruce's *Itinerarium Septentrionale*, and also "Abstract of Four Lectures," p. 159.

[3] Viz., in many passages in the works of Sang-yui and Taou-Sün.

[4] The symbol *chi* is convertible with *ṭi* (as before noticed).

[5] I have called attention to the equipment, &c., of the Liććhavis in vol. xix., *Sacred Books of the East*, p. 257, n. 2.

these Medes or Scyths, who at an early date had invaded India? The question at any rate is worth consideration.[1]

6. Arising from this is a still more interesting inquiry, although perhaps more speculative, touching the origin of the name "Liććhavis," given to the inhabitants of Vaiśâlî. Mr. Hodgson speaks of these people as Scyths;[2] and if we remember that the Vajjians, otherwise Liććhavis, were a foreign people, and throughout their history regarded as unbelievers, having *chaityas* consecrated to Yakshas, &c., it will not be unreasonable to derive their name from the Scythic race known as *Kavis* or *Kabis*, by whose aid Feridun was placed on the throne of Persia.[3] These *Kavis* or *Kabis* were unbelievers,[4] and their blacksmith's flag,[5] which was adopted by the Persians as their national banner, was finally taken and perhaps destroyed by the Arabs. Is the flag (Plate xxviii. fig. 1, *Tree and Serpent Worship*) this flag of the Kavis? There is another scene in which a similar flag may be observed (surmounted, as the former, by a trisul), I mean in Plate xxxviii. If this Plate represents the siege of Kuśinagara by the Vajjis, to recover a portion of the relics of Buddha, then the procession on the left, in which the relic-casket is carried off in triumph, accompanied by the flag, is probably intended to represent the Vajjians proceeding to Vaiśâlî for the purpose of enshrining the relics, as already noticed and represented in Plate xxviii.

7. But again, the followers of the Turushka invaders under Kanishka and his predecessors were deeply imbued with Zoroastrian conceptions, as is evident from their coins,[6] and these too were Yue-chi or Vaṭis. They must have derived their Zoroastrian proclivities from residence

[1] In confirmation, I would again refer to the testimony of the sculptures at Sanchi; *vide* my short and uncorrected paper, J. R. A. S., January 1882.

[2] *Collected Essays*, Trübner's edition, p. 17.

[3] Cf. Sir H. Rawlinson, J. R. A. S., xv. p. 258.

[4] "Blind heretics;" *vide Zendavesta* by Darmesteter and Mills, *pass.*

[5] Derefsh-i-Kavani.

[6] *Vide* paper by M. Aurel Stein, *Ind. Antiq.*, April 1888.

among, or connection with, people professing this religion; and so again we argue that these Yue-chi or Kushans[1] were a Northern people from the borders of the Caspian. The entire argument appears to be confirmed by the fact that Hiuen-Tsiang[2] places a district called Vaṭi in this very neighbourhood, where also dwelt the Mardi, a term equivalent to Afarṭi or Avaṭi, as already shown by Norris.

8. This leads me to observe, lastly, that the plates in "Tree and Serpent Worship," in which Nâgas and their female attendants are represented as worshipping the various thrones or seats on which was supposed to reside the spiritual presence of Buddha, do in fact denote the effect of the preaching of the Master on these emigrant Medes or Afarṭis. The Medes, as is well known, were called Mars, *i.e.*, Snakes; and in the *Vendîdad*, Ajis Dahaka, "the biting snake," is the personification of Media. When, therefore, Buddha converted the people of Vaiśâli and the Mallas of Kuśinagara (who were Kushans),[3] the success of his teaching was denoted in these sculptures by representing the Nâgas (remarkable for their beauty, as were the Medes) in the act of paying worship before him, as he was supposed to be spiritually present on the seats or thrones in places he had occupied during his career in the world.

It will be sufficient for my purpose if these remarks lead to a consideration of the point as to the probability of an early migration (or, perhaps, *deportation*) of a northern people allied to the Medes into India, who made Vaiśâlî their capital.

9. There is an interesting point to be noticed respecting the council of Patna under Aśôka. On page 102 of

[1] The Kushans are constantly mentioned by Ferdusi as the aboriginal race of Media. J. R. A. S., xv. p. 205; *vide* p. 46, *infra*, n. 5.

[2] *Records*, vol. i. p. 35.

[3] It is curious that the *Mallas* are called in Chinese *Lih-sse*, *i.e.*, *Strong-lords*. But does the symbol *lih* correspond with the Accadian *lik* or *lig*, a lion? In this case we should gather that the Liċċhavis were *lik*+*Kavis*. *i.e.*, powerful, or lion, Kavis.

the translation following, it will be observed that Aśôka is said to have convened 1000 priests in the Kukkutârama, *i.e.*, the "Garden of the cock." By comparing this passage with Dipavaṁsa, vii. 57, 58, 59, it will be plain that this convent is the same as the Asokârama, and that the allusion in my text is to the third council at Patna. But it appears from the corresponding account in the *Si-yu-ki*[1] that the members of this council were all Sthaviras or Theras, and therefore that it did not include any members of the other schools. We may hence understand why this council takes such a leading place in the records of the Ceylonese Buddhist Church, but is almost entirely ignored in the Northern books.

II. I come now to notice very briefly the records left us by I-tsing respecting other pilgrims after Hiuen-Tsiang, who, leaving China or neighbouring places, visited sacred spots in India consecrated by association with Buddha's presence or connected with his history.

1. It will be remembered that Hiuen-Tsiang returned to China after his sojourn in India in the year 645 A.D., and that he died in the year 664 A.D. It was just after this event, viz., in the year 671 or 672, that I-tsing, then a mere stripling, resolved, with thirty-seven other disciples of Buddha, to visit the Western world to pay reverence to the sacred vestiges of their religion. Taking ship at Canton, he found himself deserted by his companions, and so proceeded alone by what is known as the southern sea-route to India. This route, as we shall notice hereafter, was by way of Condore[2] to Śribhoja (*Palembang*, in

[1] *Records, &c.*, vol. ii. p. 96.*

[2] It is curious to find that the inhabitants of the Condore Islands at this time were of the Negro type, with thick woolly hair, and that their language was used in all the neighbouring districts. I-tsing speaks of himself as interpreting this language at Śribhoja. We learn too from other sources that these Condore negroes were largely used as servants or slaves at Canton and Southern China about this time.

* The expression *chief-priests*, on the page referred to, is equal to *Sthaviras*.

Sumatra), and thence to Quedāh; then to Nagapatam and Ceylon, or by way of Arakan and the coast of Burmah to Tamralipti (*Tatta*), where stood a famous temple called Varâha (*the wild boar*), in which most of the pilgrims stopped awhile to study Sanskrit. It was in this temple that I-tsing translated the "friendly letter" which Nâgârjuna had composed and sent to his patron King Sadvaha. He dwelt here for three years.

After visiting more than thirty countries, I-tsing returned to Śribhoja, from which place, having accidentally missed his passage in a homeward-bound ship, he sent one of his treatises, viz., his "History of the Southern Sea Religious (Law) Practices," in four chapters, to China (*the inner land*), and himself remained for some time longer at Śribhoja. Finally, he returned to Honan towards the close of the seventh century A.D. (viz., 693–694 A.D.), bringing with him nearly 400 distinct volumes of original copies of the Sûtras and the Vinaya and Abhidharma Scriptures. He translated during the years 700–703 A.D. twenty volumes, and afterwards in 705 A.D. four other works. Altogether, between the years 700–712 A.D. he translated (with others) fifty-six distinct works in 250 chapters. Of these, the *Kau-fă-kao-sang-chuen* (in two parts) is an account of fifty-six priests or Buddhist converts who visited India and the neighbourhood from China and bordering districts during the latter half of the seventh century A.D. A part of these pilgrims proceeded by the southern sea-route, and a part across the deserts and mountains by the northern route to India. With respect to the former, I will call attention to the incident recorded on p. 188 of the present work, from which we gather that this route was known and used at any rate as early as Hiuen-Tsiang's time. And it would appear that Bhâśkaravarman, the king of Kâmarûpa, and probably former kings of that kingdom, had this sea-route to China under their special protection. In fact, so early as the time of Fa-hian it appears to have been well established, as he returned from Ceylon to China by sea. We learn from I-tsing's account that in his time there was a flourishing mercantile and religious establishment on the coast of Sumatra, probably on the site of the present Palembang (as before suggested), where the merchants were accustomed to find shelter and ship their spices for Canton. I have alluded to this point in the Journal of the Royal Asiatic Society, October 1881, and also in Trübner's *Record;* there is no need therefore to repeat the arguments in this place. But I will place down here a brief *resumé* of I-tsing's notices concerning some of these pilgrims, in the order of his book, referred to above.

KAU-FA-KAO-SANG-CHUEN.

(*Nanj. Cat.* 1491.)

III. The author in the preface having alluded to the journeys of Fa-hian and Hiuen-Tsiang, who proceeded to the western countries to procure books and pay reverence to the sacred relics, passes on to notice the hardships and dangers of the route, and the difficulty of finding shelter or entertainment in the different countries visited by their successors, pilgrims to the same spots, and *that* in consequence of there being no temples (monasteries) set apart for Chinese priests. He then goes on to enumerate the names of the pilgrims referred to in his memoirs.

1. The Shaman *Hiuen-Chiu,* master of the law, a native of Sin-chang, in Ta-chau. His Indian name was *Prakâsamati.* At a very early age he became a disciple of Buddha, and when arrived at manhood, he purposed in his mind to set out to worship the sacred traces of his religion. Accordingly, in the course of the Chêng-Kwan period (627–650 A.D.), taking up his residence in the capital, he first applied himself to the acquisition of the Sanskrit (*Fan*) language. Then, staff in hand, travelling westward, he got beyond *Kin-fu,* and passing across the desert of

drifting sands, he arrived by way of the Iron Gates,[1] over the Snowy Peak, through Tukhâra and Tibet into North India, and finally reached the Jâlandhar country, having narrowly escaped death at the hands of robbers. He remained in Jâlandhar four years. The king of the *Mung*[2] country caused him to be detained, and gave him all necessary entertainment. Having gained proficiency in Sanskrit literature, after a little delay, he gradually went southward and reached the Mahabôdhi (*convent*). There he remained four years. After this he went on to Nâlanda, where he remained three years. After this he followed the Ganges' northern course, and received the religious offerings of the king of the country. He remained here in the *Sin-che* and other temples, then, after three years, he returned to Loyang by way of Nepal and Tibet, after a journey of some 10,000 *li*.

Hiuen-Chiu after this, in the year 664 A.D., returned to Kaśmir, where he found an aged Brahman called Lokayata, with whom he returned to Loyang. And now being pressed to set out again, he passed by way of the piled-up rocks (*asmakûta*) along the steep and craggy road that leads across rope-bridges into Tibet. Having escaped with his life from a band of robbers, he arrived at the borders of North India. Here he met with the Chinese envoy,[3] who accompanied him and Lokayata to the Marâthâ country in Western India. Here he met the Mung king, and, in obedience to his instruction, remained there for four years. Proceeding to South India, he purposed to return to Tangut, taking with him various sorts of medicines. He reached the Vajrasâna, and passed on to Nâlanda, where I-tsing met him. And now, having fulfilled the purpose of his life, he found the way through Nepal blocked by Tibetan hordes, and the road

[1] *Vide Buddhist Records*, &c., p. 36, n. 119.

[2] There is much mention of the *Mung* king in *I-tsing;* is he the same as the Balá-rai who seems to have succeeded the last Śilâditya? *Vide Records*, p. 176 n., and p. 242.

[3] This is probably the envoy who was sent from China, and arrived in India after the death of Śilâditya.

through Kapiśa in the hands of the Arabs. Then he returned to the Grihdṛakûta peak and the Bamboo garden, but could find no solution of his doubts; so retiring to the Amrâvat country in Mid-India, he died there, aged sixty odd years.[1]

2. *Taou-hi*, a doctor of the law, of the district of Lih-Shing, the department Tsa'i-chau. He was called by the Sanskrit name Śrideva. He went by the northern route through Tibet towards India, visited the Mahâbôdhi, and paid respect to the sacred traces, and during some years dwelt in the Nâlanda monastery and in the Kuśi country. The Mung king of Amrâvat paid him great respect. Whilst in the Nâlanda monastery he studied books of the Great Vehicle; whilst in the Chu-po-pun-na (*Dâvavâna*) temple (*the temple of the cremation*) he studied the Vinaya piṭaka, and practised himself in the *Śabdavidyâ*, a synopsis of which he drew up in the square and grass characters. Whilst in the Mahâbodhi temple he engraved one tablet in Chinese, giving an account of things new and old in China. He also wrote (copied?) some four hundred chapters of sûtras and śâstras whilst at Nâlanda. I-tsing, although in the west, did not see him, but whilst dwelling in the Amrâvat country, he sickened and died, aged fifty years.

3. *Sse-pin*, a doctor of the law, a man of Ts'ai-chau, well versed in the Sanskrit forms of magic incantation. He accompanied Hiuen-chiu from North India to Western India. Arrived at Amarakova (?), he dwelt in the Royal Temple, where he met with *Taou-Hi;* they remained here for one year together, when Sse-pin sickened and died, aged thirty-five years.

4. *Aryavarman*, a man of Sin-lo (*Corea*), left Chang'an A.D. 638. He set out with a view to recover the true teaching and to adore the sacred relics. He dwelt in the

[1] With respect to the other priests named by I-tsing, we can only here give an abstract of his notices. For the Amâravatî country *vide Records*, ii. 209, n. 70.

Nâlanda Temple, copying out many Sûtras. He had left the eastern borders of Corea, and now bathed in the Dragon pool of Nâlanda. Here he died, aged seventy odd years.

5. *Hwui-nieh*, a Corean, set out for India 638 A.D., arrived at the Nâlanda Temple, and there studied the sacred books and reverenced the holy traces. I-tsing found some writing he had left in the temple, where also he had left his Sanskrit MSS. The priests said he died the same year, about sixty years of age.

6. *Hiuen-Ta'i*, a doctor of the law, a Corėan, called by the Sanskrit name of Sarvajñanadeva. In the year *Yung-hwei* (650 A.D.) he went by the Tibetan road through Nepal to Mid-India; he there worshipped the relics at the Bôdhi Tree. Afterwards going to the Tukhâra country, he met Taou-hi, with whom he returned to the Ta-hsio Temple (*Mahâbôdhi*). Afterwards he returned to China, and was not heard of again.

7. *Hiuen-hau*, a doctor of the law, a Corean, went with Hiuen-chiu, in the middle of the *Chêng-kwan* period, to India, and reaching the Ta-hsio Temple, he died there.

8. Two priests of Corea, names unknown, started from Chang'an by the southern sea-route and came to Śribhoja. They died in the country of *Po-lu-sse*, to the westward (the western portion of Sumatra).

9. *Buddhadharma*, a man of To-ho-shi-li (*Tushara* or *Turkhâra*), of great size and strength. He became a priest, and being of a gentle disposition, he wandered through the nine provinces of China, and was everywhere received. Afterwards he went to the west to worship the sacred traces. I-tsing saw him at Nâlanda; afterwards he went to the north when about fifty years old.

10. *Taou-fang*, a doctor of the law, of Ping-chau, went by way of the Sandy Desert and the *Tsih* rock to Nepal, and afterwards came to the Ta-hsio Temple, where he remained several years; he then returned to Nepal, where he still is.

11. *Taou-sing*, a doctor of the law, of Ping-chau, called

in Sanskrit Chandradeva, in the last year of the *Chêng-kwan* period (649 A.D.) went by the Tu-fan (*Tibetan*) road to Mid-India; he arrived at the Bôdhi Temple, where he worshipped the *chaityas;* afterwards he went to Nâlanda. After that, going twelve stages to the eastward, he came to the *King's Temple,* where they study only the Little Vehicle. He remained here many years, learning the books of the *Tripiṭaka* according to the Hinayâna. Returning to China through Nepal, he died.

12. *Shang-tih,* a contemplative priest, of Ping-chau. He longed for the joys of the Western Paradise, and, with the view of being born there, he devoted himself to a life of purity and religion (*reciting the name of Buddha*). He vowed to write out the whole of the *Prajña-Sûtra,* occupying 10,000 chapters. Desiring to worship the sacred vestiges, and so by this to secure for himself the greater merit, with a view to a birth in that heaven, he travelled through the nine provinces (*of China*), desiring wherever he went to labour in the conversion of men and to write the sacred books. Coming to the coast, he embarked in a ship for Kaliṅga.[1] Thence he proceeded by sea to the Malaya country, and thence wishing to go to Mid-India, he embarked in a merchant-ship for that purpose. Being taken in a storm, the ship began to founder, and the sailors and merchants were all struggling with one another to get aboard a little boat that was near. The captain of the ship being a believer, and anxious to save the priest, called out to him with a loud voice to come aboard the boat, but Shang-tih replied, "I will not come; save the other people." And so he remained silently absorbed, as if a brief term of life were agreeable to one possessed of the heart of Bôdhi. Having refused all help, he clasped his hands in adoration, and looking towards the west, he repeated the sacred name of Amita, and when the ship went down these were his last words. He was about fifty

[1] The coast of Annam.

years of age. He had a follower unknown to me, who also perished with his master, also calling on the name of Amita Buddha.

13. *Matisiṁha*, a man of the capital, his common name being *Wong-po*. This man accompanied the priest Sse-pin, and arriving at the Middle Land, dwelt in the *Sin-ché* Temple. Finding his progress little in the Sanskrit language, he returned homewards by way of Nepal, and died on the way there, æt. 40.

14. *Yuan-hwui*, a doctor of the law, according to report offspring of the commander-in-chief *Ngan*. Leaving North India, he dwelt in Kaśmir, and took charge of the royal elephants. The king of this country delighted day by day in going to the different temples, the *Dragon-Lake* Mountain Temple, the *Kung Yang* Temple. This is where the 500 Rahats received charity. Here also the venerable Madyantika, the disciple of Ananda, converted the Dragon King. Having remained here some years, he went southwards and came to the great Bôdhi Temple, where he worshipped the Bôdhi Tree, beheld the Lake of "Mu-chin" (Muchhalinda), ascended the Vulture Peak, &c. After this he went back to Nepal and died there.

15. Again, there was a man who accompanied the envoy by the northern route to the Baktra country, and lodged in the Nâva-vihâra in Balkh. In this establishment the principles of the Little Vehicle were taught. Having become a priest, he took the name of Chittavarma. Having received the precepts, he declined to eat the three pure things, on which the master of the convent said, "Tathâgata, our Great Master, permitted five things (*as food*); why do you object to them?" He answered, "All the books of the Great Vehicle forbid them; this is what I formerly practised; I cannot now bring myself to change." The superior answered, "I have established a practice here in agreement with the three sacred collections, and you follow your own interpretation, which is contrary to mine. I

cannot permit this difference of opinion; I cease to be your master." Chittavarma was thus reluctantly obliged to yield. Then having learned a little Sanskrit, he returned by the northern route. I know no more about him.

16. Again, there were two men who lived in Nepal; they were the children of the wet-nurse of the Duke-Prince of Tibet (Tufan). They both were ordained, but one went back to lay life. They lived in the Temple of the Heavenly Kings. They spoke Sanskrit well and understood Sanskrit books.

17. *Lung*, a doctor of the law; I know not whence he came. In the *Chêng Kwan* period (627–650 A.D.) he went by the northern route to North India, wishing to visit the sacred spots. In Mid-India he got a Sanskrit copy of the *Fă-hwa* (Lotus of the Good Law), and having gone to Gandhâra, he died there.

18. *Ming-Yuen*, a man of Yih-chau, a doctor of the law, whose Sanskrit name was Chinta-deva. He embarked in a ship of Cochin-China, and came to the Kaliṅga country, and thence to Ceylon.

19. *I-long*, a priest of Yih-chau, well versed in the *Vinaya Piṭaka*, and in the interpretation of the *Yoga*, set forth from Chang'an with a priest, Chi-ngan, of his own province, and an eminent man called I-hiuen, and after travelling through the southern provinces came to Niau-Lui, and there embarked on board a merchant-ship. Having arrived at Langkia (Kamalanka?), Chi-ngan died. I-long, with his other companion, went on to Ceylon, where they worshipped the Tooth, and having obtained various books, returned through Western India. It is not known where he is now residing. He has not been heard of in Mid-India.

20. I-tsing next refers to a priest of Yih-chau named *Huining*. He left China by sea for the south in the year 665 A.D., and passed three years in the country called Ho-ling.[1]

[1] Kaliṅga.

21. The next notice is of the life of a priest called *Wan-ki* of Kiau-chau, who spent ten years in the Southern Sea, and was very learned in the language of *Kun-lun* (Condore), and partly acquainted with Sanskrit. He afterwards retired to a lay life and resided at *Shi-lo-fo-shi* (Sribhôja).

22. Another priest called *Mocha-Deva*, a Cochin-Chinese, went to India by the southern sea-route, and having visited all the countries of that part, arrived at the Mahâbodhi Temple, where he adored the sacred relics, and died æt. 24.

23. *Kwei-chung* (the disciple of *Ming-yuen*, No. 18), another priest of Cochin-China, went by the Southern Sea with his master, *Ming-yuen*, to Ceylon; afterwards in company with him proceeded to the Bôdhi Tree, and afterwards to Râjagṛiha, and being taken sick in the Bamboo garden (Veluvana), he died there, aged thirty years.

24. *Hwui Yen*, a doctor of the law, of Kwai-chau, was a pupil of Hing-Kung; he went to Siṁhala, and remained there. Whether he is dead or alive I know not.

25. *Sin-chiu*, a doctor of the law, his country not known. His Sanskrit name Charita-varma. Taking the northern route, he arrived in the Western country, and after the customary reverence, he lived in the Sin-ché Temple. In an upper room of this temple he constructed a sick chamber, and left it for ever for the use of sick brothers. He himself died here. Some days before his death, in the middle of the night, he suddenly exclaimed, "There is Bôdhisattva, with outstretched hand, beckoning me to his lovely abode;" and then, closing his hands, with a long sigh he expired, æt. thirty-five.

26. *Chi Hing*, a doctor of the law, of Ngai-Chau, his Sanskrit name Prajña-Deva, went to the Western region, and afterwards dwelt in the Sin-che Temple, north of the river Ganges, and died there, aged about fifty years.

27. We next read of a priest of the Mahâyana school

called *Tang*, or "the lamp" (*dipa*), who went with his parents when young to the land of *Dvârapati* (Sandoway in Burmah), and there became a priest. He returned with the Chinese envoy to the capital. Afterwards he went by the southern sea-route to Ceylon, where he worshipped the Tooth; and then proceeding through South India and crossing into Eastern India, arriving at *Tamralipti*: being attacked by robbers at the mouth of the river, he barely escaped with his life; he resided at Tamralipti for twelve years, having perfected himself in Sanskrit; he then proceeded to Nâlanda and Buddha Gayâ, then to Vaiśâli and the Kuśi country, and finally died at Kuśinagara, in the Pari-Nirvâṇa Temple.

28. *Sañghavarma*, a man of Samarkand, when young crossed the Sandy Desert and came to China. Afterwards, in company with the envoy, he came to the Great Bôdhi Temple and the Vajrâsana, where he burnt lamps in worship for seven days and seven nights continuously. Moreover, in the Bôdhi Hall, under the Tree of Aśoka, he carved a figure of Buddha and of *Kwan-tseu-tsai* Bodhisattva. He then returned to China. Afterwards, being sent to *Kwai-chau* (Cochin-China), there was great scarcity of food there. He daily distributed food, and was so affected by the sorrows of the fatherless and bereaved orphans, that he was moved to tears as he visited them. He was on this account named the *weeping Bodhisattva.* He died shortly afterwards from infection caught there, which soon terminated fatally, æt. about sixty.

29. Two priests of *Kao-chang* went to Mid-India, and died on the voyage. Their Chinese books are at Śribhoja.

30. *Wan-yun*, a doctor of the law, of Loyang, travelling through the southern parts of China, came to Cochin-China, thence went by ship to Kaliñga, where he died.

31. *I-hwui*, a man of Loyang, of eminent ability, set out for India to recover some copies of Sanskrit (*Fan*) books. He died æt. 30.

32. Three priests set out by the northern route for Udyâna, and also for the place of Buddha's skull-bone. They are said to have died there.

33. *Hwui Lun*, a Corean, otherwise called Prajñavarma, came by sea from his own country to *Fuchau*, and proceeded thence to Chang'an. Following after the priest *Hiuen-chiu* (No. 1, p. xiii.), he reached the West, and during ten years dwelt in the Amrâvat country and in the *Sin-ché* Temple (north of the Ganges). Passing through the eastern frontiers, and thence proceeding northward, he came to the Tu-ho-lo (*Tukhâra*) Temple. This temple was originally built by the Tukhâra people for their own priests. The establishment is called *Gandhârasanda.* To the west is the Kapiśa Temple. The priests of this establishment study the Little Vehicle. Priests from the north also dwell here. The temple is called *Guṇacharita.*

Two stages to the east of the *Mahâbhôdi* [1] is a temple called *Kiu-lu-kia.*[2] It was built long ago by a king of the Kiu-lu-ka country, a southern kingdom (*Kurukshetra ?*). Although poor, this establishment is strict in its teaching. Recently, a king called Sun-Army (*Adityasena*), built by the side of the old temple another, which is now newly finished. Priests from the south occupy this temple.

About forty stages east of this, following the course of the Ganges, is the *Deer Temple*, and not far from this is a ruined establishment, with only its foundations remaining, called the *Tchiṇa* (or *China*) Temple. Tradition says that formerly a Mahârâja called Śrigupta built this temple for the use of Chinese priests. He was prompted to do so by the arrival of about twenty priests of that country who had travelled from Sz'chuen to the Mahâbhôdi Temple to pay their worship. Being impressed by their pious de-

[1] It is doubtful whether the Mahâbhôdi named here does not refer to the *Tu-ho-lo* Temple mentioned above.

[2] This may be restored to Kuruka, and may possibly refer to the *Kuru* country.

meanour, he gave them the land and the revenues of about twenty villages as an endowment. This occurred some 500 years ago. The land has now reverted to the king of Eastern India, whose name is *Devavarma*, but he is said to be willing to give back the temple-land and the endowment in case any priests come from China. The Mahâbhôdi Temple, near the *Diamond Throne* (*i.e.*, at *Gayâ*), was built by a king of Ceylon for the use of priests of that country. The Nâlanda Temple, which is seven stages north-east of the Mahâbhôdi, was built by an old king, Śri-Śakrâditya, for a Bhikshu of North India called *Râja-Bhâja*. After beginning it he was much obstructed, but his descendants finished it, and made it the most magnificent establishment in Jambudvîpa. This building of Nâlanda stands four-square, like a city precinct. The gates (*porches*) have overlapping eaves covered by tiles. The buildings (*gates ?*) are of three storeys, each storey about twelve feet in height.

Outside the western gate of the great hall of the temple is a large stûpa and various châityas, each erected over different sacred vestiges, and adorned with every kind of precious substance.

The superior is a very old man; the *Karmadâna* or *Vihâraswâmi* or *Vihârapâla* is the chief officer after the superior, and to him the utmost deference is paid.

This is the only temple in which, by imperial order, a water-clock is kept to determine the right time. The night is divided into three watches, during the first and last of which there are religious services; in the middle watch, as the priests may desire, they can watch or repose. The method in which this clock determines the time is fully described in the "*Ki-kwei-ch'uen.*"

The temple is called *Śri Nâlanda Vihâra*, after the name of the Nâga called Nanda.

The great temple opens to the west. Going about twenty paces from the gate, there is a stûpa about 100 feet hig

This is where the Lord of the World (*Lokanâtha*) kept *Wass* (the season of the rains) for three months; the Sanskrit name is *Mûlagandhakoti.* Northwards fifty paces is a great stûpa, even higher than the other; this was built by *Balâditya*—very much reverenced—in it is a figure of Buddha turning the wheel of the law. South-west is a little *châitya* about ten feet high. This commemorates the place where the Brahman, with the bird in his hand, asked questions; the Chinese expression *Su-li fau-to* means just the same as this.

To the west of the *Mûlagandha* Hall is the tooth-brush tree of Buddha.

On a raised space is the ground where Buddha walked. It is about two cubits wide, fourteen or fifteen long, and two high. There are lotus flowers carved out of the stone, a foot high, fourteen or fifteen in number, to denote his steps.

Going from the temple south to *Râjagriha* is thirty *li.* The *Vulture Peak* and the *Bambu Garden* are close to this city. Going S.W. to the Mahâbôdhi is seven stages (*yojanas*). To *Vaisâli* is twenty-five stages north. To the *Deer Park* twenty or so stages west. East to *Tamralipti* is sixty or seventy stages. This is the place for embarking for China from Eastern India and close to the sea. There are about 3500 priests in the temple at *Nâlanda,* which is supported by revenues derived from land (villages) given by a succession of kings to the monastery.

34. *Taou-lin,* a priest of King-chau (in *Hupeh*), whose Sanskrit name was *Silaprabha,* embarked in a foreign ship, and passing the copper-pillars, stretched away to *Lanka* (Kamalanká); after passing along the *Kalinga* coast he came to the country of the naked men. He then proceeded to Tamralipti, where he passed three years learning the Sanskrit language. After visiting the Vajrâsana and worshipping the Bôdhi Tree, he passed to *Nâlanda,* where he studied the *Kosha,* and after a year or two went

to the ... ure Peak, near Râjagriha, and finally proceeded to South India.

35. *Tan-Kwong*, a priest of the same district in China, went to India by the southern sea-route, and having arrived at *A-li-ki-lo* (Arakan ?), he was reported to have found much favour with the king of that country, and to have got a temple built and books and images; in the end, as was supposed, he died there.

36. *Hwui-ming*, another priest from the same district, set out to go to India by the southern sea-route, but the ship being baffled by contrary winds, put in at *Tung-chu* (copper pillars), erected by Ma-yuen, and after stopping at *Shang-king*, returned to China.

37. *Hiuen-ta*, a priest of Kung-chow and the district of Kiang Ning, was a man of high family. He appears to have accompanied an envoy in a Persian ship to the southern seas. Having arrived at Fo-shai (*Sribhôja*), he remained there six months studying the *Sabdavidyâ;* the king was highly courteous, and on the occasion of his sending a present to the country of *Mo-lo-yu* (Malaya), *Hiuen-ta* proceeded there, and remained two months. He then went on to Quĕdàh, and then at the end of winter went in the royal ship towards Eastern India. Going north from Quĕdàh, after ten days or so they came to the country of the naked men. For two or three *lis* along the eastern shore there were nothing but cocoa-nut trees and forests of betel-vines. The people, when they saw the ship, came alongside in little boats with the greatest clamour; there were upwards of one hundred such boats filled with cocoa-nuts and plantains; they had also baskets, &c., made of rattan; they desired to exchange these things for whatever we had that they fancied, but they liked nothing so much as bits of iron. A piece of this metal two fingers' length in size would buy as many as five or ten cocoa-nuts. The men here are all naked, the women wear a girdle of leaves; the sailors in joke offered

them clothes, but they made signs that they did not want any such articles. This country, according to report, is south-west of Sz'-ch'uan. The country produces no iron and very little gold and silver; the people live on cocoa-nuts and some esculent roots, but have very little rice or cereals. Iron is very valuable; they call it *Lu-a.* The men are not quite black, of middling height, they use poisoned arrows, one of which is fatal. Going for half a month in a north-west direction, we come to Tamralipti, which is the southern district of East India. This place is some sixty stages or more from Nâlanda and the Bôdhi Tree. Meeting the priest called "Lamp of the Great Vehicle" (*Mahâyana dipa*) in this place, they remained together there one year, learning Sanskrit and practising themselves in the *Śabda-śâstra.* They then went on with some hundred or so merchantmen towards Central India. When about ten days' journey from the Mahâbôdhi, in a narrow pass, the road being bad and slippery, *Hiuen-ta* was left behind and attacked by robbers, who stripped him and left him half dead. At sundown some villagers rescued him and gave him a garment. Going on north, he came to Nâlanda, and after visiting all the sacred spots in the neighbourhood, he remained at Nâlanda ten years, and then going back to *Tamralipti,* he returned to Quĕdàh, and with all his books and translations, amounting in all to 500,000 ślokas, enough to fill a thousand volumes, he remained at Śribhôja.

38. *Shen-hing,* a priest of Sin-Chow, also went to Śribhoja, where he died.

39. The priest *Ling-wan,* having gone through Annam, came to India, and erected under the Bôdhi Tree a figure of *Mâitreya Bodhisattva* one cubit in height, and of exquisite character.

40. *Seng-chi,* a priest and companion of the former, went to India by the southern sea-route, and arrived at *Samotata.* The king of that country, named Râjabhata

(or *patu*), a Upâsaka, greatly reverenced the three objects of worship, and devoted himself to his religious duties.

41. A priest, *Chi-sz*, is mentioned, who went to the south and resided at *Shang-king*, near Cochin-China. He then went south to Śribhôja, and afterwards proceeded to India.

42. A priest, *Wou Hing* (*Prajñadeva*), in company with the last, left Hainan with an easterly wind; after a month he arrived at Śribhôja. He then went in the royal ship for fifteen days to Malaya, in another fifteen days to Quedàh, then waiting till the end of winter, going west for thirty days he arrived at *Naga-vadana* (Nagapatam ?), whence after two days' sea-voyage he came to Simhapura (*Ceylon*). He there worshipped the sacred tooth, and then going N.E. for a month, arrived at the country of *O-li-ki-lo*. This is the eastern limit of East India. It is a part of Jambudvîpa. After this he proceeded to the Mahâbôdhi Temple. Having rested here, he returned to Nâlanda and studied the *Yoga*, *Kosha*, and other works. Moved with a desire to find copies of the *Vinaya*, he repaired to the Tiladaka Temple. In the end he died at Nâlanda.

43. *Fa-shin* also started by the southern route, and after passing Shang-king (Saigon), Ku-long, Kaling, and Quĕdàh, he died.

Putting together these notices, we may conclude that the sea-route between China and India in the early years of the *Tang* dynasty was by way of Java, Sumatra, the Straits of Malacca, the coast of Burma and Arakan, to Tamralipti, or else by the more adventurous way of Ceylon from Quĕdàh. It seems that the Condore Islands were a centre of trade, and that the language of the natives of these islands was used generally through the Southern Seas; at least *I-tsing* speaks of himself as interpreting the language at Śribhôja (*vide* p. xv. n.).

We have one or two points of some certainty in the

itinerary of these pilgrims. For instance, in the *Si-yu-ki*, Hiuen-Tsiang (*Records*, ii. 200) says that to the N.E. of *Samotata* is the country called *Śrikshetra*, to the S.E. of this is *Kamalangka*, to the east of this is *Dârapati* (read Dvârapati). This country has been identified by Captain St. John (*Phœnix*, May 1872) with old Tung-oo and Sandoway in Burma, lat. 18° 20′ N. long. 94° 20′ E.; it is, in fact the "door land" between Burma and Siam; this latter being called Champa or Lin-I. Hiuen-Tsiang remarks that to the S.W. of *Lin-I*, or Siam, is the country of the *Yavanas*, or, as they are called in his text, the *Yen-mo-na*. We do not read of this country in *I-tsing*; it may perhaps represent Cambodia.

IV. Another work of some importance written by I-tsing is the following:—

Nan-hae-ki-kwei-niu-fa-ch'uen.

(*Nanj. Cat.* 1492.)

This work, in four chapters, was compiled by I-tsing, and forwarded to China "by one returning to the inner land," to be arranged and published. It relates to matters connected with the religious customs of India and some other districts (Southern Sea islands) visited by I-tsing, or gathered from others who had visited these places, during the time of his absence on foreign travel.

Passing by the introduction, which refers to the origin of the world and its orderly arrangement, I-tsing (*or his editor*) next alludes to the number of the Buddhist schools (*Nikâyas*), and the various countries in which they flourished. The chief schools of independent origin—but depending on distinct tradition—he names, are these:—

1. The Aryamahâsanghiti, divided into seven branches.
2. The Aryasthaviras, divided into three branches, the Tripiṭaka more or less like the former.

3. Âryamûlasarvâstavâdins, divided into four branches, the Tripiṭaka more or less like the former.

4. The Âryasammatiyas, divided into four branches. The Tripiṭaka differs in its number of stanzas from the former, and the school has other divergences.

These schools, with their sub-branches, compose the eighteen sects into which Buddhism was divided at an early date (the century following the Nirvâna).

In the country of Magadha, he observes, each of the four schools is in a flourishing condition. In the Marâṭha country and in Sindh the Sammatîya school is chiefly followed. In the north the Sarvâstavâdins and Mahâsaṅghikas are met with; in the southern borders the Mahâsthaviras are principally found. The others are little known. On the eastern outskirting countries the four schools are intermingled. [From Nâlanda, five hundred stages east, is the frontier land referred to. For these countries *vide Records*, ii. 200.]

In Ceylon the Sthavira school alone flourishes; the Mahâsaṅghikas are expelled.

With respect to the ten countries known as the Southern Sea islands,[1] the Mûlasarvâstavâdins and the Sammatîyas are principally found; the other two schools at the present time are seldom met with. The teaching of the Little Vehicle is principally affected; in *Mo-lo-yau*, however, the Great Vehicle is studied also. Some of these islands may be perhaps 100 *li* in circuit, others several hundred *li*, and some 100 stages round. It is difficult to calculate distances on the great ocean, but the best skilled merchantmen know that they first arrive at *Kiu-lun* (called by the Cochin-China ambassadors Kwan-lun).[2]

[1] Reckoning from the west, the names of the islands are, *Po-lu-sse*, *Mo-lo-yau* (the same as *Shi-li-fo-yau*), *Mo-ho-siu*, *Ho-ling*, *Tan-Tan*, *Pw'an-pw'an*, *Po-li*, *Kiu-lun*, *Fo-shi-po-lo*, *O-shen*. *Mo-kia-man*, and other little islands not catalogued.

[2] The people of this country alone have woolly hair and black skins. With this exception, the people of all the other countries are like those of China.—*Ch. Ed.*

In Châmpa (otherwise called *Lin-I*), the Sammatîya school is chiefly found, with a few Sarvâstavâdins. A month's voyage south-west is Annam. Formerly the people sacrificed to Heaven, but afterwards the law of Buddha flourished; now a wicked king has destroyed the priests, and all the heretics live mixed together. This is the southern point of Jambudvîpa.

Speaking generally, the Great Vehicle prevails in the north, the teaching of the Little Vehicle in the south. In some parts of China the Great Vehicle is in favour, but with these exceptions the Great and Little Vehicle are intermingled without distinction. In both cases the rules of moral conduct and the four truths are taught, but in the Great Vehicle they worship the Bodhisattvas, but not in the teaching of the Little Vehicle.

With respect to the Great Vehicle, there are only two branches, viz., (1) the Chung-kwan (*Mâdyamîkas?*); (2) the Yôga system. The Mâdyamîkas regard all outward phenomena as empty and substantially unreal. The Yôgas regard outward things as nothing, inward things as everything. Things are just what they appear to cognition. And so with respect to the sacred doctrine, it is true to one and false to another; there is no positive certainty for all. The great aim is to reach *that shore*,[1] and to stem the tide of life.

After some further remarks, I-tsing proceeds to say that his records are framed on the teaching of the Mûlasarvâstavâdin school, divided into three branches:—1. The Dharmagûptas; 2. the Mahîsâsakas; 3. the Kâsyapîyas.

In Udyâna, Karashar, and Khotan there is a mixture of doctrine.

We will now pass on to give the headings of the chapters in the work under notice:—

[1] *That shore*, *i.e.*, the other side of the stream of transmigration.

THE NAMES OF THE FORTY CHAPTERS OF THE NAN-HAE-KI-KWEI-NIU.

1. The evil of disregarding the observation of the season of rest (*Vass*).
2. Right decorum in the presence of the honoured one (*images or paintings of the honoured one or ones*).
3. The diminutive seats to be used whilst eating or reposing.
4. On the necessary cleansing of food vessels and personal preparation.
5. On cleansing after meals.
6. On the two sorts of water-pitchers.
7. On the early inspection with regard to insects.
8. On the early tooth-cleansing wood (*brush*).
9. Rules on undertaking religious fasts.
10. On special requirements as to raiment and food.
11. As to the different kinds of vestments.
12. On special rules as to female clothing.
13. Rules as to sacred (*pure*) enclosures.
14. The resting-time of the community (*the five grades*).
15. The period called Pravârana (*relaxation after Vass*).
16. On the mode of eating food (with *chop-sticks*).
17. On proper rules as to the seasons or hours of religious worship.
18. On articles of private property.
19. Rules and regulations for ordination.
20. The proper occasions for ablutions.
21. On seats used, and personal accommodation whilst seated.
22. On rules concerning apartments for sleeping and resting.
23. On the advantage of proper exercise to health.
24. Worship not mutually dependent.
25. On the way of personal behaviour to a teacher.

26. On the way of conduct towards strangers (priests).

27. On symptoms of bodily illness.

28. On medical rules.

29. On exceptional medical treatment (*for offensive ailments*).

30. On turning to the right in worship.

31. On rules of decorum in cleansing the sacred objects of worship.

32. On chanting in worship.

33. On reverence to sacred objects.

34. On rules for learning in the West.

35. On the propriety of long hair.

36. On disposing of the property of a deceased monk.

37. On property allowed to the fraternity.

38. On cremation.

39. On charges brought by low or depraved men.

40. The unselfish character of the old worthies.

So far the headings of the chapters of this most important but obscure work. It is to be hoped that the promised translation by a Japanese scholar may soon appear; the contents of the various chapters, as I have summarised them for my own reference, show me that the book, when clearly translated, will shed an unexpected light on many dark passages of Indian history.

The entire number of books translated by I-Tsing, as we have before remarked, amounted to fifty-six. I need allude to none of these on the present occasion, except to say that their names may be found in Mr. Nanjio's Catalogue of the Buddhist Tripiṭaka (Appendix II., p. 441) With respect, however, to the small tract numbered 1441 in the Catalogue, I may add that I am now printing the original text, which I hope to publish shortly with an F lish translation and notes.

commending the present rather laborious work to the e of the public, I must regret its many defects, and at the same time apologise both to the Publishers and my Readers for the long delay in completing the task I undertook. Responsibilities which have increased with increasing years, and flagging energies, the result of long sickness, must be my excuse.

But I may not conclude without sincerely thanking those who have supported me in my labours, and especially his Lordship the Secretary of State for India and his Grace the Duke of Northumberland, from both of whom I have received material assistance.

GREENS NORTON RECTORY.

HISTORY

OF THE

EARLY LIFE OF HIUEN-TSIANG

AND OF

HIS TRAVELS IN THE WESTERN WORLD.

BOOK I.

Begins with the birth (of Hiuen-Tsiang) in Kow-shi, and ends with the account of his arrival at Kau-Chang.

THE infant name of the Master of the Law [1] was Hiuen-Tsiang; his ordinary family name was Chiu: he was a native of Chin-Liu. He descended from Chang-Kong, who during the Han dynasty was lord of Tai-K'iu. His great-grandfather, whose name was Kin, was prefect of Shang-Tang, under the after-Wei dynasty. His grandfather Kong, by his distinguished scholarship, obtained employment in the public service. During the Ts'i dynasty he was appointed president of the Imperial College,[2] having, as endowment, the revenues of the town of Chow-nan: he thus founded the fortunes of his descendants: he also was born in the district of Kow-shi. His father Hwui was distinguished for his superior

[1] This title, which corresponds to the Chinese *Fa-sse,* will be applied to *Hiuen-Tsiang* throughout the present work.

[2] Old University at Peking.

abilities, the elegance of his manners and his moderation. At an early age he (*i.e., the father of Hiuen-Tsiang*) began to recite the Sacred Books;[1] in figure he was eight feet[2] in height, with finely lined eyebrows, and bright eyes. He wore his dress large, and his girdle was full, loving to be recognised as a scholar. Born in those times, and a man of a remote district, he was simple in his manners and contented—and sought neither honour nor preferment.

Anticipating the decay and fall of the Sui dynasty, he buried himself in the study of his books. Many offers of provincial and district offices were pressed on him, which he persistently refused; he declined all magisterial duties on the plea of ill-health; so he remained in retirement, much to the admiration of his acquaintances.

He had four sons, of whom the Master of the Law was the fourth. Even when a child he (*i.e., the Master of the Law*) was grave as a prince, and of exceptional ability. When he was eight years old his father sitting near his table was reading aloud the Hiau classic (*on filial piety*), and coming to the passage when Tsang-tseu rose (*before his master*), suddenly the boy arranged his dress and got up. His father asking him why he did so, he replied: "Tsang-tseu hearing the command of his master, rose up from his seat; surely then Hiuen-Tsiang dare not sit at ease whilst listening to the loving instruction (*of his father*)." His father was much pleased by this reply, and perceived that his child would become a distinguished person. Then calling together the members of his family, he narrated the incident to them, on which they congratulated him, and said: "There is here promise of high nobility." Even at this early age his wisdom was of such a remarkable kind.

From this age he took to reading the Sacred Books,[1] and was charmed with the writings of the ancient sages

[1] That is, the Classics and other religious treatises.

[2] The *foot* here referred to is equal to about 9½ inches. *Vide* Julien's Translation, p. 468, l. 31.

A book without elegance and propriety he would not look at; he would have no intercourse with those whose ways were opposed to the teaching of the holy and wise. He did not mix with those of his own age, nor spend his time at the market-gates. Although cymbals and drums, accompanied by singing, resoùnded through the public streets, and the girls and boys congregated in crowds to assist in the games, singing and shouting the while, he would not quit his home. Moreover, when he was still young he applied himself with diligence to the duties of piety and gentleness at home.

His second brother Chang-tsi had previously become a disciple of Buddha, and dwelt in the convent of Tsing-tu at Loyang (*the Eastern capital*). Observing that the Master of the Law was deeply given to the study of religious doctrine, he therefore took him to his convent (*seat of sacred wisdom*) and taught him the method and practice of the Sacred Books (*of Buddhism*).

At this time there was an unexpected Royal mandate for the election at Loyang of fourteen priests, to be supported free of charge. There were several hundred applicants. The Master of the Law, owing to his youth, could not be a candidate, but he took his stand close by the Hall gate. At this time the high-commissioner, Ch'ing-Shen-Kwo, having an aptitude for recognising talent in those whom he met, observing Hiuen-Tsiang, addressed him and said: "My friend, who are you?" Replying he said: "I am so-and-so." Again he asked: "Do you wish to be elected?" He replied, "Yes! certainly; but not being sufficiently advanced in years, I am excluded." Again he asked: "And what is your motive in becoming a disciple?" He replied: "My only thought in taking this step is to spread abroad the light of the Religion[1] of Tathâgata, which we possess." Shen-Kwo was deeply gratified with the sentiment, and

[1] Transmitted Law.

as the outward appearance of the youth was prepossessing, he selected him and took him to the officers and said: "To repeat one's instruction is easy, but true self-possession and nerve are not so common; if you elect this youth, he will without doubt become an eminent member of the religion of Śâkya. Only I fear that neither I (*Kwo*) nor your Excellences will live to see the day when the soaring clouds shall distil the sweet dew (*of Buddha's doctrine*). But nevertheless, the illustrious character of this honourable youth will not be eclipsed, as I regard the matter."

And so the words of the noble Ch'ing prevailed.

Having been admitted as a recluse, he dwelt with his brother.

At this time there was in the convent a Master of the Law, called *King*, who recited and preached upon the Sûtra of the Nirvâna. Hiuen-Tsiang having got the book, studied it with such zeal that he could neither sleep nor eat. Moreover he studied under the direction of *Yen*, doctor of the law, the *Sâstra* of the Great Vehicle (*Mahâyâna Sâstra*); and thus every day his love for such studies increased. By hearing a book only once, he understood it thoroughly, and after a second reading he needed no further instructions, but remembered it throughout. All the assembly of priests were astonished, and when at their direction he mounted the pulpit, he expounded with precision and clearness the deep principles of Religion to the bottom. The Masters and honourable body of priests listened with attention; he thus laid the foundation of his renown. At this time he was thirteen years old.

After this the Sui dynasty lost the Empire, and the whole kingdom was in confusion. The capital became a rendezvous for robbers, and the *Ho* and *Lo*[1] a resort of wild beasts. The magistrates were destroyed and the

[1] Or, the district between the rivers *Ho* and *Lo*.

body of priests either perished or took to flight. The streets were filled with bleached bones, and the burnt ruins of buildings. Since the rebellion of Wang-tong, and dreadful riots of Liu-shih, when massacre and ruin prevailed everywhere, no such calamity had happened to the Empire. The Master of the Law, although he was young, yet understood thoroughly the nature of these vicissitudes; and so he affectionately addressed his brother and said: "Though this were our native city, yet how could we, during the present state of things, avoid death? Now I understand that the Prince of Tang has repulsed the people of Tsin-Yang, and established himself at Chang'an. The empire relies on him, as on father and mother; let my brother go there with me!"

The brother agreeing with this advice, they went both together.

It was now the first year of Wu-Têh.[1] At this time the country was without regular government, and all the troops were under arms. The books of Confucius, and the sacred pages of Buddha were forgotten, every one was occupied with the arts of war. There were therefore no further religious conferences in the capital, and the Master of the Law was greatly afflicted thereat.

Yang-ti, the emperor,[2] in the first year of his reign had founded four Religious Houses in the Eastern capital, and had invited renowned priests of the empire to dwell therein. Those who were summoned were men of very superior merit, and so it followed that crowds of eminent religious teachers (*aiders of religion*) resorted to these establishments, of whom King-tu and Sai-tsin were the chief. In the last year of his reign, the country being in confusion, the necessaries of life began to fail: in consequence many people travelled into the territory of

[1] A.D. 618. [2] The second Emperor of the Sui dynasty, A.D. 605-617.

Min and Shuh,[1] and amongst the rest the body of the priests (*in question*).

And now the Master of the Law addressed his brother and said: "There is no religious business being attended to, and we cannot be idle, let us pass into the country of Shuh (*Sz'chüen*) and pursue our studies."

His brother having consented, they traversed together the valley of Tseu-wu and entered Han-chüen; and there they met the two Doctors *Kong* and *King*, the principal priests of their convent. At the sight of these persons they were moved to tears with joy, and they abode with them a month and some days, receiving instruction; after this they went on together to the town of Shing-tu. As there were many priests assembled in this town they founded there a religious place of assembly.[2] Thus they listened once more to Sai-tsin explaining the Shi-lun (*Mahâyâna Samparigraha Sâstra*) and the Pi-tan (*Abhidharma Sâstra*), whilst the Master Chin expounded the works of Kia-yen (*Kâtyâyana*). Studying thus without loss of a moment, and with great earnestness, after two or three years, they had thoroughly mastered the teaching of the different schools.

At this time the Empire was visited with famine and riot; in Shuh alone there was abundance and peace; priests from every quarter therefore flocked there, and hundreds of men ever assembled under the pulpit of the Preaching Hall. The Master of the Law by his profound wisdom and eminent talent in discussion, surpassed them all; so that throughout Wu and Shuh and Khing and Tsuh there was no one but had heard of him, and desired to witness his skill, as those of old respected the names of Li and Kwoh.[3]

The Master of the Law for the sake of being with his brother took up his abode in the Hung-hwui Temple of

[1] North-West and South-West China.

[2] Or, *they established Religious meetings.* [3] *Vide* Mayers, 379 and 304.

Shing-tu; he too (*i.e., his brother*) was remarkable for his saintly appearance, and was of a noble and commanding presence like that of his father. He loved both the esoteric and exoteric doctrine.[1] He was accustomed to preach on the Nirvâna Sûtra and the Sâstra called Shi-ta-shing,[2] and the Abhidharma (*Sâstra*): he was versed also in literature and history, but he excelled principally in the study of Lau (*tseu*) and Chwang.[3] The people of Shuh so much loved him that the Governor of the Province, Tsan-Kung, gave him particular marks of his high respect. When he undertook to write or speak on a subject his manner was so dignified and his discourse so free from embarrassment, that he was in no way inferior to his brother.

As to the latter, he was grave and dignified, living apart from the crowd, and avoiding worldly concerns. He traversed the eight expanses (*heavens?*), and penetrated the hidden secrets of nature. Possessed of a noble ambition he desired to investigate thoroughly the meaning of the teaching of the Holy ones, and to restore the lost doctrine and to re-establish the people. He was prepared to face wind and weather, and his mind, even if he stood by chance in the presence of the Emperor, would only gather strength and firmness: certainly in these respects he surpassed his brother. But both of them were distinguished by their singular talents and a certain sweetness of manner; they were renowned among their associates and of noble character; so that the brothers of *Lu-Shan* could not add to their fame.

When the Master of the Law had completed his twentieth year, that is, in the fifth year of the period Wu-têh, he was fully ordained in Shing-tu. During the Rain-retreat he studied the Vinaya according to the Rule of the five divisions and seven sections;[4] after

[1] *i.e.*, Buddhism and other literature.

[2] Named before.

[3] Mayers, 92.

[4] This is obscure. It may refer to the Vinaya of the *Mahîsâsaka School*, and to the seven sections of "Moral Science" referred to by Mr. Alwis, Lecture II., p. 19, *as reprinted* by the *Pali-Text* Society.

mastering this at one time, he then turned his attention to the Sûtras and Śâstras, and having investigated these he once more thought of going to the Capital, to inquire from the most celebrated masters concerning some difficulties he had met with (*in his studies*). However, being restrained from effecting his purpose by his brother's influence, he secretly embarked with some merchants, and passing down the river through the three gorges [1] he arrived at Hang-chow, where he retired into the temple called Tien-hwang. The clergy and laity of that place had for a long time known of him by report, and now they came together and prayed him to explain the Sacred Books. The Master of the Law on their account preached on the Shi-lun, and the Abhidharma. From the summer to the winter, he went through each of these three times.

At this time the King of Han-yang, by his highly virtuous character and his affectionate kindness, held his country in constraint and obedience. Hearing of the arrival of the Master of the Law, he was exceedingly rejoiced, and went in person to salute him. On the day when he stated the theme of the religious discussion, the king and his officers and a great number of lay and religious people came together to see him and hear him. And now they pressed forward in vast bodies to raise a discussion.[2] The Master of the Law answered them in turn and gave them the desired explanations. They soon confessed themselves to be surpassed in argument—whilst the more learned were grieved to think that they were not able to gain the victory.

The king then spoke of him in admiration without bounds: and offered him abundant presents, which he declined to accept. After the conferences he proceeded again northwards, seeking the most renowned priests. Arriving at Siang-chow, he began to place his difficulties

[1] *Vide* Mayers, No. 873.
[2] *Vide* Julien, *in loc.*

before *Hiu*, a Master of the Law, and ask for explanations of his doubts.

From this he came to Chiu-chow, and there he visited *Shin*, a Master of the Law, and studied the Shing-shih-lun (*Satyasiddha-vyâkaraṇa-śâstra*). After this he entered Chang'an and took up his abode in the Ta-hioh[1] Temple. There he studied with *Yoh*, a Master of the Law, the Kiu-she (*Kôsha*) Śâstra. After one reading he was perfected, and he retained the whole treatise in his memory. Neither young nor old could surpass him. Even in the most extremely difficult passages, beyond the comprehension of all the others, he alone could penetrate the meaning of these mysteries, and discover the sense.

At this time there were at Chang'an two great teachers, *Shang* and *Pin*; they had thoroughly explained the Two Vehicles, and investigated the Three Systems: they were the leaders of the religious people in the Capital. Both clergy and laity resorted to them; the entire district resounded with their praises, and their reputation spread beyond the sea; moreover their disciples were as numerous as the clouds. Although they had mastered all the Sûtras, they loved to discourse principally on the *Shi-ta-lun*. The Master of the Law had already distinguished himself in the land of Wu and Shuh; from the time he arrived at Chang'an, he persistently inquired of these teachers, and in a moment perceived the meaning of the deepest truths that they could explain. They were filled with admiration and overwhelmed him with praise. "Master," they said, "you can be well styled in the religion of Śâkya, 'a courier who traverses a thousand *li* in a day.' You are called to make the sun of wisdom shine again; but as for us, worn out by age, we fear that we shall not see the day!"

From this time the disciples all looked up to him with reverence, and his renown filled the capital.

[1] The Chinese form of *Mahâbôdhi*.

The Master of the Law having visited the celebrated Masters all round, devoured their words and examined their principles; and so he found that each followed implicitly the teaching of his own school; but on verifying their doctrine he saw that the holy books differed much, so that he knew not which to follow. He then resolved to travel to the Western world in order to ask about doubtful passages. He also took the treatise called Shi-tsih-ti-lun[1] to explain his various doubts; this treatise is now called Yu-kia-sse-ti-lun.[2] "Moreover," he said, "Fa-hien and Chi-yen, the first men of their age, were both able to search after the Law for the guidance and profit of the people; should I not aim to preserve their noble example (*traces*) so that their blameless character may not be lost to posterity? The duty of a great Teacher should be to follow in their steps."

On this he agreed to go in company with others and present a petition; but there was an imperial rescript forbidding (*the project of going abroad*). On this the others gave up the plan; the Master of the Law alone did not abandon his purpose, and resolved to travel alone. Again, hearing of the obstructions and dangers of the Western road, he considered with himself and resolved that as he had been able to bear and overcome so many calamities common to men, he could not withdraw from his present purpose. Then he entered a sacred building and made known his undertaking, and requested permission to carry it out, humbly praying[3] (*vowing and begging*) all the Holy Ones by their mysterious influences to cause his journey and his return to be without damage.

At the birth of the Master of the Law his mother had dreamt that she saw him going to the West clothed in a white robe—on which she said: "You are my son,

[1] *Saptadaśa bhûmi Sâstra.*

[2] *Yôgâchârya bhûmi Sâstra.*

[3] Much comment has been made on the use of the word "praying" in connection with these translations. It is said that Buddhists do not pray. The Chinese, however, admits of no other rendering than that in the text, which denotes both "aspiration" and "supplication."

where then are you going?" In reply he said, "I am going to seek for the Law." This was the first indication, then, of his foreign travels.

In the third year and the eighth month of the period Chêng Kwan (630 A.D.), he was prepared to make a start. Desiring some happy omen, he dreamt at night that he saw in the middle of the great sea the Mount Sumeru, perfected with the four precious substances—its appearance supremely bright and majestic. He thought he purposed to scale the Mount, but the boisterous waves arose aloft and swelled mightily. Moreover, there was neither ship nor raft; nevertheless, he had no shadow of fear, but with fixed purpose he entered (*the waves*). Suddenly he saw a lotus of stone burst as it were exultingly from the deep;[1] trying to put his foot on it, it retired; whilst he paused to behold it, it followed his feet and then disappeared;—in a moment he found himself at the foot of the Mount, but he could not climb its craggy and scarped sides: as he tried to leap upwards with all his strength, there arose in a moment a mighty whirlwind which raised him aloft to the summit of the Mount. Looking around him on the four sides from the top he beheld nought but an uninterrupted horizon; ravished with joy he awoke.

On this he forthwith started on his journey. He was then twenty-six years of age. At this time there was a Tsin-Chow priest called Hiau-Ta who lived in the capital and studied the Nirvâna Sûtra. His study being finished he was returning to his home—they both went together therefore so far as Tsin-Chow. Having stopped there one night, he met with an associate from Lan-Chow; going on with him he came to Lan-Chow and stopped there one night. Here he met with some mounted men who were returning to Liang-Chow, after escorting an officer. Going with them, he came to that place, and

[1] This passage is very obscure.

stopped there a month and some days. The priests and laymen invited him to explain the Nirvâna Sûtra and the Shi-lun, and the Pan-jo-king.[1] The Master of the Law accordingly opened out the meaning of these works. Now Liang-Chow is the place of rendezvous for people dwelling to the West of the River: moreover merchants belonging to the borders of Si-Fan (*Tibet*) and countries to the left of the T'sung-Ling Mountains, all come and go to this place without hindrance.

On the day of opening the Religious Conference, these men all came together to the place and offered jewels and precious things, as they bowed down and uttered the praises of the Master. And on their return to their several countries they loudly applauded the Master of the Law to their Rulers, saying that he was about to go westwards to seek the Law in the country of the Brahmans.

In consequence of this throughout the kingdoms of the West all persons were prepared with joyful heart to entertain him on his arrival, with magnificence.

The day of the Conference being ended, they offered him in charity abundant gifts, gold and silver money, and white horses without number. The Master of the Law, accepting one half, caused the lamps of the different convents to be lit, and as for the rest of the money he distributed it among the various religious establishments. At this time the administration of the country was newly arranged, and the frontiers did not extend far. There were severe restrictions placed on the people, who were forbidden to go abroad into foreign parts. Just then the governor of Liang-Chow was called Li-ta-liang. Obedient to the Royal mandate he strictly adhered to the rules of prohibition. And now there came a man who addressed Liang thus:—"There is a priest here from Chang'an who is intending to go to the western regions—I do not know his plans." Liang, full of anxiety, called

[1] For the Sanscrit equivalents of these and other titles, *vide* Index to the *Records of the Western World*.

the Master of the Law to his presence and asked him the object of his arrival. The Master replied, "I wish to go to the West to seek for the Law." Liang hearing this, urged him to return to the capital.

There was then at Liang-chow a Master of the Law called Hwui-wei, the most renowned of all priests of the region West of the River, for his spiritual perception and vast abilities. He greatly admired the profound reasoning of the Master of the Law, and hearing of his intention to go in search of the Law, he was very greatly rejoiced. Secretly sending two of his disciples, one called Hwui-lin, the other Taou-ching, he bade them conduct the Master in secret towards the West.

From this time he dare not be seen in public—during the daytime he hid himself, at night he went on.

In process of time he came to Kwa-chow; the governor To-Kiu having heard of his coming was greatly pleased, and provided him with all necessary provisions in plenty.

The Master of the Law inquiring as to the Western roads, he was told in reply that north from this point fifty *li* or more there was the river Hu-lu,[1] the lower part of which is wide, the upper course narrow. Its stream is very impetuous and suddenly becomes deep, so that no boat can pass over it. On the upper part is fixed the Yuh-mên barrier, so that one must pass by this; thus it is the key to the Western frontiers. North-west beyond the barrier there are five signal towers in which officers, charged to watch, dwell—they are one hundred *li* apart. In the space between them there is neither water nor herb. Beyond the five towers stretches the desert called Mo-Kia-Yen, on the frontiers of the kingdom of I-gu.

On hearing these particulars he was filled with anxiety and distress. His horse was dead, and he did not know what steps to take; he remained there a month

[1] *Records*, i. p. 17, n. 31.

or so, sad and silent. Before his departure there came certain spies from Liang-chow, who said: "There is a priest called Hiuen-Tsiang who is purposing to enter on the Si-Fan territory. All the governors of provinces and districts are ordered to detain him." The Governor of the Province, Li-chang, was a man of a religious turn (a man of religion and faith), and he suspected in his heart that the Master of the Law was (*the person named*); accordingly he secretly brought the mandate and showing it to Hiuen-Tsiang he said: "Is not the Master the person here named?" The Master of the Law hesitated and made no reply; on which Chang said: "The Master ought to speak the truth, and your disciple will make some plan for you to escape." The Master of the Law then replied truthfully. Chang, hearing it, was filled with admiration and surprise: and then he said, "Since the Master is indeed capable of such a project, I will for his sake destroy the document;" and forthwith he tore it up before him. "And now, Sir," he said, "you must depart in all haste."

From this time his anxieties and fears greatly increased. Of the two novices who accompanied him, one, called Taou-ching, returned at once to Tun-hwang; the other, called Hwui-Lin, alone remained, but because the Master knew that he had not strength for so distant a journey he let him also return. He now procured a horse by exchange; his only sorrow was that he had no guide to accompany him. On this he proceeded to the temple where he was staying, and bowing before the image of Maitrêya he fervently prayed that he would find him a guide who would lead him past the barrier.

That night there was a foreign priest in the temple who had a dream. His name was Dharma, and in his dream he saw the Master sitting on a lotus flower and going towards the West. Dharma was lost in surprise, and on the morrow he told his dream to the Master of the Law, whose heart was rejoiced thereat, taking it as a sign of his being able to go. He answered Dharma, however, thus: "Dreams are vain and deceptive: what need is there to examine into this matter?" Again he entered the Sacred precinct and worshipped in prayer.

And now suddenly a foreign person came into the temple to worship Buddha, after doing which he saluted the Master of the Law by turning round him three times. The Master then asked him his family and personal name, on which he said, "My family name is Shi, my personal name is Pan-to (Bandha ?)." The foreigner then asked to be allowed to take on him the five-Rules,[1] and having done so he was greatly rejoiced, and asked permission to come back; after a little while he returned with cakes and fruit. The Master of the Law observing his intelligence and strong build, and also his respectful manner, accordingly spoke to him about his purpose to go westwards. The foreigner readily acquiesced, and said he would conduct the Master beyond the five signal towers. The Master of the Law was filled with joy, and gave him some clothes and other property to exchange for a horse, and appointed a time of meeting.

On the morrow at sundown he proceeded towards the bush, where shortly afterwards the foreigner with an old greybeard, likewise a foreign person, riding on a lean horse of a red colour, came to meet him. The Master of the Law was not easy in his mind; on which the young foreigner said: "This venerable greybeard is intimately acquainted with the Western roads, and has gone to and come back from I-gu more than thirty times: I have therefore brought him to go with you, hoping it may give you assurance." Then the senior man said: "The Western roads are difficult and bad; sand-streams stretch far and wide; evil sprites and hot winds, when they come, cannot be avoided: numbers of men travelling together, although so many, are misled and lost; how much rather you, sir, going alone! how can you accom-

[1] That is, of a lay disciple.

plish such a journey? I pray you, weigh the thing with yourself well, and do not trifle with your life."

The Master replied: "This poor priest (*i.e., Hiuen-Tsiang*) aims to reach the Western world to search after the great Law—if he does not in the end reach the land of the Brahmans—there is no return to the Eastward, it matters not if he dies in the mid-route."

The foreign greybeard then said: "If, sir, you will go you must ride this horse of mine: he has gone to and fro to I-gu some fifteen times. He is strong and knows the road; your horse, sir, is a small one and not suitable for the journey."

The Master of the Law then recalled to himself the following circumstance: when he was at Chang'an forming his purpose of visiting the Western world, one day there was a diviner named Ho-wang-ta, who by reciting spells and prognosticating, could tell a great deal about the matters in which one was engaged. The Master of the Law requested him to prognosticate about his journey. *Ta* said, "Sir! you may go; the appearance of your person as you go is that of one riding an old red horse, thin and skinny; the saddle is varnished, and in front it is bound with iron."

Now having observed that the horse which the old foreigner was riding was lean and of a red colour, and that the varnished saddle was bound with iron, agreeing with the words of the diviner, he made up his mind that this was the fulfilment of the augury, and accordingly he exchanged his horse. The old greybeard was much rejoiced thereat, and making his respectful obeisance, they separated.

And now having packed his baggage, he went on through the night with the young foreigner. In the third watch they came to the river, and saw the guard-house called the Yuh-Mên a good way off. At ten *li* from the barrier the upper stream is not more than ten feet wide; on each side there is a scrub composed of the

Wu-tung tree; the foreigner, cutting down some wood, made a bridge and spread over it branches, filling it up with sand. Thus they led over the horses and went on.

The Master of the Law having crossed the river was filled with joy. Being fatigued, he dismounted and sought some repose. The foreign guide also, separated about fifty paces or so from the Master, spread his mat on the ground and so they both slept. After a while the guide took his knife in his hand, and rising up, approached towards the Master of the Law; when about ten paces off, he turned round. Not knowing what his intention was, and being in doubt about the matter, the Master rose from his mat and repeated some Scripture, and called on *Kwan-yin* Bôdhisattva. The foreigner having seen this went back, and slept.

At the first dawn of day the Master called to him and bade him fetch water. Having washed and taken some little food, he purposed to go onwards. The guide said: "Your disciple is leading you forward on a way full of danger and very remote; there is no water or grass; only beyond the fifth tower[1] there is water. It will be necessary to go there at night-time and get the water and pass on. But if at any one place we are perceived, we are dead men! Is it not better to return and be at rest?" The Master of the Law having positively refused to return, they both went forward.[2] (Now the guide), with his knife drawn and his bow strung, begged the Master to go on in front; but the Master of the Law would not consent to the proposal. The foreigner going by himself, after a few *li* stopped and said: "Your disciple can go no further—he has great family concerns to attend to, and he is not willing to transgress the laws of his country." The Master of the Law, knowing his purpose, let him go back.

[1] So Julien translates it; but I think the meaning is, that water could only be found in the neighbourhood (*under*) the *five* watch towers.

[2] The expression denotes that the guide kept looking up and down.

The young foreigner replied: "It is impossible for the Master to carry out his plan: how can you avoid being seized and brought back?"

The Master of the Law answered: "Though they cause my body to be cut up as small as the very dust, I will never return; and I here take an oath to this."

So the matter rested; he gave the young man his horse[1] as a mark of his obligation to him, and so they parted.

And now, alone and deserted, he traversed the sandy waste; his only means of observing the way being the heaps of bones and the horse-dung, and so on; thus slowly and cautiously advancing, he suddenly saw a body of troops, amounting to several hundreds, covering the sandy plain; sometimes they advanced and sometimes they halted. The soldiers were clad in fur and felt. And now the appearance of camels and horses, and the glittering of standards and lances met his view; then suddenly fresh forms and figures changing into a thousand shapes appeared, sometimes at an immense distance and then close at hand, and then they dissolved into nothing.

The Master of the Law when he first beheld the sight thought they were robbers, but when he saw them come near and vanish, he knew that they were the hallucinations of demons.[2] Again, he heard in the void sounds of voices crying out: "Do not fear! do not fear!"[3] On this he composed himself, and having pushed on eighty *li* or so, he saw the first watch-tower. Fearing lest the lookouts should see him, he concealed himself in a hollow of sand until night; then going on west of the tower, he saw the water; and going down, he drank and washed his hands. Then as he was filling his water-vessel with water an arrow whistled past

[1] That is, probably, the horse on which the young man rode, see p. 15.

[2] For a similar account, *vide* Rawlinson. *Ancient Monarchies*, iii. 49.

[3] The account of the illusions witnessed in these deserts, would suggest the connection of the Chinese symbols *Mo-kia* with the word *Maga*. [*Mo-kia-yen*, however, is the Chinese form of the (Takla) Makân desert.]

him and just grazed his knee, and in a moment another arrow. Knowing then that he was discovered, he cried with a loud voice: "I am a priest come from the capital· do not shoot me!" Then he led his horse towards the tower, whilst the men on guard opening the gate, came out; after looking at him they saw that he was indeed a priest, and so they entered in together to see the commander of the guard-house, whose name was Wang-siang. Wang, having ordered the fire to be well lit up for the purpose of inspecting the Master, said: "This is no priest of our country of Ho-si,[1] he is indeed one from the capital:" then he asked him about his object in travelling.

The Master of the Law replied: "Captain! have you not heard men of Liang-chow talk about a priest named Hiuen-Tsiang, who was about to proceed to the country of the Brahmans to seek for the Law?" He answered: "I have heard that Hiuen-Tsiang has returned already to the East. Why have you come here?" The Master of the Law then took him to his horse, and showed him various places on which were written his name and familiar title. On this the other was convinced. He then said: "Sir, the western road is dangerous and long, you cannot succeed in your plan. But I have no fault to find with you. I myself am a man of Tun-hwang and I will conduct you there. There is a Master of the Law there called Chang-kiau, he reveres men of virtue (*sages*) and honours the priesthood: he will be rejoiced to see you: I ask your consent to this."

The Master of the Law replied: "My birthplace is Lo-yang; from a child I have been zealous for religion; in both capitals all those engaged in the study of the Law, in Wu and Shuh the most eminent priests without exception, have come to me for instruction; for their sakes I have explained and discussed and preached on religion; and I may boldly say that I am the leading

[1] That is, of Tangut.

authority of the time. If I wished for further renown and encouragement, should I seek a patron at Tun-hwang? But being afflicted because I found the sacred books of the religion of Buddha were not always in agreement, and were imperfect, forgetful of my own comfort and disregarding all dangers, I have sworn to go to the West to seek for the Law bequeathed to the world. But you, my patron, instead of rousing me to effort in my undertaking, would exhort me rather to turn back and give it up. How then can you profess to have in common with myself a distaste for the follies of life, and wish with me to plant the seed, leading to Nirvâna? But if you must needs detain me here—let me be punished with death! Hiuen-Tsiang will never return one step to the East, nor give up his first intention!"

Siang, hearing these words, filled with emotion, said: "I am indeed fortunate in having met with you! How can I but rejoice? But now, sir, you are fatigued and worn; take some sleep before the day dawns. I will then myself conduct you, and show you the proper route." He then spread out a mat for him to rest upon.

When the morning came, the Master of the Law having taken some food, Siang sent a man to fill his water-vessel, and providing him with some cakes made of flour, he himself conducted him for ten *li* or so, and then he said:—"From this point, sir, the road goes straight on to the fourth watch-tower; the man there is a good-hearted person; moreover, he is a near relation of mine. His family name is Wang, his private name is Pi-lung. When you come to see him you can say that I have sent you to him." Then, with tearful salutations, they parted.

Having gone on till night he came to the fourth watch-tower, and fearing lest he should be detained (*the danger of detention*), he purposed to get some water quietly, and to go on. Coming to the water, and scarcely there, there came an arrow flying towards him; turning round he called out as before, and went forward to the tower. Then the men coming down, he entered the building. The officer of the tower having spoken to him, he answered:—"I purpose going to India, and my way is in this direction. Wang-siang, the officer of the first tower, has commissioned me to meet you." Hearing this he was much pleased, and detained him for the night; moreover, he gave him a great leather bottle for water, and fodder for his horse. Then conducting him by his side he said:—"You had better not, sir, go towards the fifth tower, for the men there are rude and violent, and some mishap may befall you. About 100 *li* from this is the Ye-ma spring, where you can replenish your supply of water."

Having gone on from this he forthwith entered on the *Mo-kia-Yen* desert, which is about 800 *li* in extent. The old name for it is Sha-ho.[1] There are no birds overhead, and no beasts below; there is neither water nor herb to be found. On occasions, according to the sun's shadow, he would, with the utmost devotion, invoke the name of Kwan-shai-yin Bôdhisattva, and also (recite) the Pan-jo-sin Sûtra (*Prajña-pâramîta-hṛidaya Sûtra*).

At first when the Master of the Law was dwelling in Shuh he saw a diseased man whose body was covered with ulcers, his garments tattered and filthy. Pitying the man he took him to his convent, and gave him clothing and food; the sick man, moved by a feeling of deep gratitude, gave to the Master of the Law this little Sûtra-book, and on this account he was in the habit of reciting it continually. Arriving at the *Sha-ho* as he passed through it, he encountered all sorts of demon shapes and strange goblins, which seemed to surround him behind and before. Although he invoked the name of Kwan-Yin, he could not drive them all away; but

[1] That is, the Sandy desert (*Sand-river*).

when he recited this Sûtra,[1] at the sound of the words they all disappeared in a moment. Whenever he was in danger, it was to this alone that he trusted for his safety and deliverance.

After going a hundred *li* or so, he lost his way, and searching for the fountain called *Ye-ma* he could not find it, to get water from. Then when he was going to drink from the pipe of his water-vessel, because of its weight it slipped from his hands, and the water was wasted; thus, a supply enough for 1000 *li* was lost in a moment.[2] Then again, because of the winding character of the road, he did not know which way to follow it. At length, purposing to return eastward to the fourth watch-tower, after going ten *li*, he thought thus within himself, "I made a vow at the first that if I did not succeed in reaching India I would never return a step to the East; what then am I now doing here? It is better to die in the attempt to go to the West, than to live by returning to the East." Then turning his bridle he invoked *Kwan-Yin*, and proceeded in a north-west direction.

At this time (*as he looked*) in the four directions, the view was boundless; there were no traces either of man or horse, and in the night the demons and goblins raised fire-lights as many as the stars; in the day-time the driving wind blew the sand before it as in the season of rain. But notwithstanding all this his heart was unaffected by fear; but he suffered from want of water, and was so parched with thirst that he could no longer go forward. Thus for four nights and five days not a drop of water had he to wet his throat or mouth; his stomach was racked with a burning heat, and he was well-nigh thoroughly exhausted. And now not being able to advance he lay down to rest on the sands, invoking

[1] This Sûtra is regarded by the Chinese as a *Mantra*, or *charm*, to the present day. One of my native teachers (when I was in China), although he professed to despise Buddhism, used to repeat it from memory.

[2] *Yih-chia* = in a trice.

Kwan-Yin without intermission, although worn out with sufferings. And as he addressed the Bôdhisattva, he said:—"Hiuen-Tsiang in adventuring this journey does not seek for riches or worldly profit, he desires not to acquire fame, but only for the sake of the highest religious truth does his heart long to find the true Law. I know that the Bôdhisattva lovingly regards all living creatures to deliver them from misery! Will not mine, bitter as they are, come to his knowledge!"

Thus he spake, (*praying*) with earnest heart and without cessation the while, till the middle of the fifth night, when suddenly a cool wind fanned (*touched*) his body, cold and refreshing as a bath of icy water. His eyes forthwith recovered their power of sight and his horse had strength to get up. His body being thus refreshed, he lay still and fell asleep for a little while. Whilst he slept thus he had a dream, and in his sleep he thought he saw a mighty spiritual being, several *chang* [1] in height, holding in his hand a halberd used for signalling, who spake thus 'Why are you still sleeping and not pressing on with all your might?"

The Master of the Law, rousing himself from slumber, pushed on for ten *li*, when his horse suddenly started off another way and could not be brought back or turned. Having gone some *li* in the new direction, he saw all at once several acres of green grass; getting off his horse, he let him graze; when leaving the grass, purposing to resume his journey, about ten paces off he came to a pool of water, sweet, and bright as a mirror; dismounting again, he drank without stint, and so his body and vital powers were restored once more, and both man and horse obtained refreshment and ease. Now we may conclude that this water and grass were not natural supplies, but undoubtedly were produced through the loving pity of Bôdhisattva, and it is a proof of his guileless character and spiritual power.[2]

[1] A *chang* is = 141 English inches.

[2] This passage is apparently parenthetical, and is not translated by Julien.

Having bivouacked near the grass and fountain of water for a day, on the day following he filled his water-vessel and cut some grass, and proceeded onward. After two days more they got out of the desert and arrived at I-gu. The myriads of dangers and difficulties through which he passed cannot be recounted in detail. Having arrived at I-gu, he stopped in a temple where there were three Chinese priests; one was an old man whose vestment was without any girdle, and whose feet were bare. Coming forth, he embraced the Master of the Law, with many cries and piteous exclamations which he could not restrain; but at length he said, "How could I have hoped at this time, ever to have seen again a man of my own country?" The Master of the Law likewise, as he saw him, was moved to tears.

The foreign priests outside, and the foreign kings also, came to pay their respects to him (*i.e. Hiuen-Tsiang*). The king invited him to his own house and provided him with abundance of entertainment.

At this time the king of Kau-chang, Khio-wen-t'ai, had previously sent some messengers to I-gu, and on this day as they were about to return they met the Master of the Law. Accordingly when they had got back they told the king (*of his arrival*). The king hearing it, immediately sent messengers to order the king of I-gu to send the Master of the Law to him. Moreover the king selected several tens of superior horses and sent his officers and chief ministers to escort him to his presence. After the usual delay of ten days, the king's messengers came and explained the king's plan, and then they earnestly besought him to comply with the arrangement. The Master of the Law had purposed in his mind to take (*the road leading*) past the Mausoleum (*Feou-tu*, Stûpa) of the Khan, but now, notwithstanding his respectful refusal of the king of Kau-chang's request, he could not escape from it—and so was obliged to go. Crossing the southern desert, after six days they came to the borders of Kau-chang, to the town of Pih-li. And now, the sun just set, the Master of the Law wished to stop in this town, but the magistrates and the messengers said, "The royal city is near—we beg you to advance—there are several relays of horses in front." The Master of the Law left his old red horse which he had ridden hitherto behind, to be sent on afterwards, and then in the middle of the night they reached the royal city. The officer of the guard at the gate having informed the king, he commanded the gate to be opened.

When the Master of the Law entered the city, the king, surrounded by his attendants in front and rear, bearing lighted torches, came forth in person to meet him. The Master of the Law having entered the inner hall, took his seat beneath a precious canopy in a pavilion of two stages. After salutation the king said in a most agreeable manner, "From the time that I knew of your honour's name, my happiness has prevented me from sleeping or eating; after calculating the distance of the road, I was sure you would arrive to-night, and therefore my wife and children with myself have taken no sleep, but reading the Sacred Books, have awaited your arrival with respect."

A moment after, the queen, with several tens of servant-women, came in to pay her respects.

And now as the day-dawn came on, he said: "After a fatiguing journey I have a wish to sleep." The king hereupon retired to his palace and left several eunuchs to wait on him during the night.

Then in the morning before the Master of the Law had arisen, the king in person, with the queen also, and her followers, waiting below, came to the door to salute him: after which the king said: "Your disciple (*i.e. the king*) cannot but think how wonderful it is that you by yourself alone should have been able to surmount the difficulties and dangers of the road in coming hither." And in saying these words he could not refrain from tears and exclamations of wonder. After this he ordered food to be provided according to the rules of religion. Moreover, by the side of the palace there was an oratory to which the king himself conducted the Master of the Law and installed him there. Moreover, he commissioned certain eunuchs to wait on him and guard him.

In this convent there was a certain Master of the Law called Tün who formerly studied at Chang'an and was well versed in the details of religion. The king, who highly esteemed him, commissioned him to go visit the Master of the Law. After a short interview he left, on which the king again ordered a Master of the Law called Kwo-tong-wang, about eighty years of age, to take up his residence with the Master of the Law, with a view to persuade him to remain where he was and not to go to the Western regions. The Master of the Law was unwilling to assent, and after ten days' delay he wished to be allowed to go on his way. The king said: "I have already commissioned the Master Tong to confer with you and request you to remain here. What, sir, is your intention?"

The Master replied, "To request me to remain here is surely an act of goodness on the part of the king, but truly my heart cannot consent."

The king replied: "When I travelled in the great country (*i.e. China*) with my teacher during the Sui emperors' time, I visited in succession the Eastern and Western capitals, and the country between Yen-tai and Fen-tsin and I saw many renowned priests, but my heart felt no affection for them: but from the time I heard the name of the Master of the Law my body and soul have been filled with joy, my hands have played and my feet have danced. Let me persuade you, sir, to remain with me here. I will provide for your wants to the end of my life, and I will undertake that all the people of my realm shall become your disciples, if, as I hope, you on your part will instruct them. The priests and thei followers, although not numerous, still amount to several thousands. I will cause them to take the Sacred book in hand (*which you select*) and to attend with the rest to your instructions. I pray you accede to my desire and earnest request, and do not think of going on your journey to the West."

The Master, in declining the invitation, said: "How can I, a poor and solitary priest, sufficiently acknowledge the king's generosity. But I undertook this journey not with a view to receive religious offerings. Grieved at the imperfect knowledge of religion in my native land, and the poorness and defective condition of the Sacred Texts, and being myself agitated by doubts as to the truth, I determined to go and find out the truth for myself. Hence at the risk of my life I have set out for the West, to inquire after interpretations not yet known. My purpose is that the sweet dew of the expanded law[1] shall not only water Kapila, but that the mysterious words may also spread through the regions of the East. The thought of finding my way through the mountains and my earnest desire to seek a friend of illustrious ability, this has, day by day, strengthened my purpose; why then would you cause me to stop midway! I pray your majesty to change your mind, and do not overpower me with an excessive friendship."

The king replied, "I am moved by an overpowering affection towards you; and the Master of the Law must stop here and receive my religious offerings. The Ts'ung Ling Mountains may fall down, but my purpose cannot change. Be assured of my sincerity and do not doubt my real affection."

The Master of the Law answered: "What need is there of so many words to prove the deep regard the

[1] *Fang-teng;* an expression (omitted by Julien) commonly used for the Vaipulya class of Sûtras. It points to the "breadth and width" (*squared-equally*) of this class of book. Cf. the Sc. *Vipula.*

king has for me? But Hiuen-Tsiang has come to the West for the sake of the Law, and as he has not yet obtained his object he cannot halt in the middle of his enterprise. Wherefore I respectfully request to be excused, and that your majesty would put yourself in my place. Moreover, your august majesty in days gone by has prepared an excellent field of merit, and so has become a ruler of men. Not only are you the preserver and sustainer of your subjects, but you are also the protector of the doctrine of Buddha. It is only reasonable therefore that you should support and disseminate (*the principles of religion*). How then is it that you are now opposing that end?"

The king replied: "Never would I venture to place obstacles in the way of the diffusion of Religion; but because my realm has no teacher and guide, I would therefore detain the Master of the Law, in order that he may convert the ignorant and foolish."

But the Master of the Law continued to excuse himself and would not consent (*to remain*).

Then the king, colouring with anger and stretching out his hand beyond the sleeve, said, in loud words and a menacing manner: "I have a different way of deciding this question, sir! If, sir, you still think you can go when you like, I will detain you here by force and send you back to your own country. I commend you to think over this; it will be better for you to obey."

The Master answered: "Hiuen-Tsiang has come here for the sake of the great Law, indeed! and now I have met with one who opposes me—but you have only power over my body, your majesty cannot touch my will or my spirit."

And now he could speak no more on account of his frequent sighs, but the king remained unmoved; still he caused an additional supply of necessary provisions, and each day he pressed on him food provided from the king's own store.

The Master of the Law, seeing that he would be detained by force in opposition to his original design, declared with an oath that he would eat nothing, in order to affect the king's heart. So he sat in a grave posture, and during three days he neither ate nor drank; on the fourth day the king seeing that the Master was becoming fainter and fainter, overcome with shame and sorrow, he bowed down to the ground before him and said: "The Master of the Law has free permission to go to the West! I pray you take a slight morning meal!"

The Master of the Law still fearing his insincerity, required him to repeat his words with his hand pointing to the sun. The king answered: "If it needs be so, let us both go into the presence of Buddha, and bind ourselves mutually together!" Accordingly they went both together into the sacred precinct and paid adoration to Buddha. With them was the royal mother, and the Empress Chang. So regarding the Master of the Law as a brother, he gave him free permission to go and seek for the Law. "But," he added, "when you return I request you to stop in this kingdom for three years to receive my offerings; and if in future ages you arrive at the condition of a Buddha, grant that I, like Prasênajita or Bimbasâra râjas, may be permitted to protect and patronise you!"

Then he invited him to remain one month and to expound the Sûtra called Jin-wang-pan-jo,[1] in order that during the interval the king might prepare travelling garments for the Master. The Master giving his full consent, the empress was greatly rejoiced and desired to be connected with the Master in close relationship during successive ages.

[1] Cf. *Nanjio's Catalogue*, No. 17.

Then the Master consented to eat · (*from this we can see*) the firmness of his will and determination.

And now on a day following the king prepared a large pavilion for the purpose of beginning the religious conferences; the pavilion could seat three hundred persons or so; the empress sat on the right of the king; the masters and chief nobles, all took different seats, to attend the preaching.

Every day at the time of preaching, the king himself conducted the Master, preceding him with a brazier containing incense. When ascending the pulpit the king, humbly bowing, placed his foot-stool and begged him to mount and be seated. Day by day this was done. After the sermon he begged the Master of the Law to arrange for four Śrâmaneras to wait upon him and to make thirty priests' vestments; and considering that the western regions are very cold, he had various articles of clothing made suitable for such a climate, such as face-coverings, gloves, leather boots, and so on. Moreover he gave him a hundred gold ounces, and three myriads of silver pieces, with five hundred rolls of satin and taffeta, enough for the outward and home journey of the Master during twenty years. He gave him also thirty horses and twenty-four servants (*hand-helps*). Moreover he commissioned Hun-Sin, one of the imperial censors belonging to his court, to conduct him to the Khan Yeh-hu.[1] Again he composed twenty-four official documents to be presented at Kiu-chi and twenty-four different countries; each letter had a large roll of satin, accompanying it as a credential. Lastly, he loaded two conveyances with five hundred pieces of satin and taffeta, and fruit of luscious taste, as a present for the Khan Yeh-hu. Accompanying this present was a letter to the following purport: "The Master of the Law, a friend

[1] Julien has *Che-hu*, and probably he is right. It appears to me that this is not so much a personal name, as a titular rank.

of your humble servant, desires to search for the Law in the country of the Brahmans: I beseech the Khan to be kind to him, as he has ever been kind to me, his humble servant." He requested also that he would require the rulers of the different countries of the West to conduct the Master through their territories and provide relays of horses.

The Master of the Law, seeing that the king sent the novices, and these letters, and the silks and satins, &c., with him, was overpowered by a sense of his extraordinary liberality, and made the following grateful oration to him, saying:—

"Hiuen-Tsiang has heard that whoever would traverse the deep expanse of ocean or river must use boat and oar—so those who would rescue (*guide*) the body of living creatures engulphed (*in ignorance*), must avail themselves of the holy words (*of Buddha*). Now for this cause Tathâgata, exercising his great love as of one towards an only son, was born on this much-polluted earth, reflecting in himself the wisdom of the three enlightenments (*vidyâs*), and, as the sun, illuminating the darkness. The cloud of his love hovered over the summit of the heavens of the universe; and the rain of the law watered the borders of the three thousand worlds (*the Chiliocosm*). After procuring advantage and quiet, he quitted the world for the state of true peace—and his bequeathed doctrine has spread Eastwards for six hundred years past. His illustrious doctrine stretched through the country of Hu and Lo, and has shone as a radiant star in Tsin and Liang.

"In agreement with the mysterious character of this doctrine the world has progressed in its higher destiny; only distant people coming to interpret the doctrine (the *sounds* of his doctrine) are not in agreement. The time of the Holy One is remote from us: and so the sense of his doctrine is differently expounded: but as the taste of the fruit of different trees of the same kind is the same, so the principles of the schools as they now exist are not different. The contentions of the North and South have indeed for many hundred years agitated our land with doubts, and no able master has been found able to dispel them.

"Hiuen-Tsiang owing to his former deserts was privileged at an early date to adopt the religious life, and till he had completed about twenty years, received instruction from his masters. The famous sages and eminent friends were all carefully consulted and questioned by him. The principles of the Great and Little Vehicle were each briefly investigated by him.

"His hand never ceased to examine the different Sacred Books, but notwithstanding all his pains he was never free from doubts, until, wearied with his perplexities, he longed to wend his way to the monastery of the Jêtavana, and to bend his steps to the Vulture Peak, that he might there pay his adoration and be satisfied as to his difficulties. But at the same time he knew that the heavens could not be measured with an inch-tube, nor the ocean be sounded by a cock's feather.

"But he could not give up the purpose which humbly inspired him with resolution, and so making preparation he set out on his way, and through much painful travel arrived at I-gu.

"I respectfully desire that your majesty, possessed of the harmonising influences of heaven and earth, and inspired by the soothing power of the two principles,[1] may exercise your authority with advantage to all your subjects. Your renown stretches to the East as far as China, to the West the hundred tribes of uncivilised people, the lands of Leou-lan and of the Yue-ti, the districts of Kiu-sse and Long-wang, all acknowledge your profound virtues, and are obliged to you for your condescending qualities, and in addition, your respect

[1] That is, as it would seem, the two principles that pervade Nature; the *yang* and *yin*.

for learned men and your love for erudition, exhibit themselves in your loving attention to their advantage.

"Having learned of my arrival, your majesty has been graciously pleased to order me escorts, and provisions for my entertainment. Since I came your goodness has continually increased and you have allowed me to discourse publicly on religious subjects. You have moreover condescended to allow me the title of 'brother,' and have entrusted me with letters of recommendation to the Princes of twenty and more kingdoms of the West; you have invited them to show me consideration and kindness, and ordered them to provide me with necessary escort and provisions in proceeding from one district to another. Excited by pity for the wants of a poor pilgrim who is finding his way to Western countries, and on account of the rigours of the climate which will affect him on his journey, you have ordered four novices to accompany him, and you have provided for his use religious vestments, padded caps, boots, and other articles of clothing.

"Lastly, you have added gifts of silks and taffetas, and a large quantity of money, gold and silver, to provide for his wants during twenty years in coming and going. I am overpowered by a sense of my obligation, and know not how to return sufficient thanks. The waters of the united Rivers [1] do not equal in amount your royal gifts; the Tsu'ng-ling mountains are small and light compared with the abundance of your benefits.

"What anxious fear can I now have in facing the passage of the ice-bound glaciers? [2]—no anxiety will afflict me lest I should be too late to pay my reverence at the spots where stand "the heavenly ladder" (at Kapatha), and "the tree of wisdom" (at Gâyâ). By acceding to my wishes you have placed me under this obligation, and to your kind offices all is due.

"After questioning the different masters and receiving

[1] Julien gives "the Yellow River;" which may be right.

[2] Julien translates "of the Hiuen-tu." But the text has *ling k'i*, referring probably to the Muzart Pass.

from their mouths the explanation of the true doctrine, I shall return to my own country and there translate the books I have obtained. Thus shall be spread abroad a knowledge of unknown doctrines; I shall unravel the tangle of error and destroy the misleading influences of false teaching; I shall repair the deficiencies of the bequeathed doctrine of Buddha, and fix the aim of the mysterious teaching (*of the schools*).

"Perchance by these meritorious works I may in some degree repay your large beneficence—but considering the greatness of the task before me (*the distance of the road*), I can delay no further; to-morrow I must take leave of your majesty, and this causes me much pain.

"I can only, in consideration of your majesty's goodness, offer the tribute of my sincere gratitude."

The king, in reply, said: "You have, respected Master, allowed me to regard you as a brother, and therefore you have the right to share with me the wealth of my kingdom. Why then offer me so many thanks?"

On the day of his departure the king, with the religious community and the great ministers and people, escorted him to without the city on his way to the West; then the king and the people embraced him with tears, and their cries and groans resounded on every side.

After this the king ordered the queen and the rest to return home, but he and his suite, with the chief of the religious community, accompanied the pilgrim for several scores of *li*.

The princes and chiefs of the other kingdoms did so likewise, paying him the utmost respect.

After this he journeyed westward, and after passing through the towns of *Wu-pwan* and *To-tsin*, he entered the country of O-ki-ni (Yenki).[1]

[1] Probably equivalent to *Yanghi*, as in *Yanghi-Hissar*. We here take up the Pilgrim's route as detailed in the *Si-yu-ki*.

BOOK II.

Commencing with O-ki-ni, and ending with Kie-jo-kio-she (Kanauj).

FROM this, going westward, he came to the kingdom of O-ki-ni;[1] here is the fountain of A-fu[2] the Master. The fountain is situated to the south of the road on a sandy hillock. The hillock is several *chang* in height, and the water comes from the hill half way up.

The tradition says: There was formerly a band of merchantmen, several hundred in number, who found their supply of water exhausted on their mid-journey. Arriving at this point exhausted and worn out, they knew not what to do. At this time there was a priest in their company, who had brought no provisions for the journey, but relied on the alms of the rest for his support. The others considering the case, said: "This priest serves Buddha: on this account we, as a company, give him our offerings. Although he has travelled ten thousand *li*, he has had no provision of his own—and now, whilst we are full of anxiety, he is unmoved by any care: we ought to ask him about it."

The priest, in reply to their question, said: "You, sirs, who are anxious to get a supply of water, ought each one of you to adore Buddha, and receive the three Refuges and take on you the five moral obligations. Then I will, for your sakes, ascend yonder hill and cause a supply of water to proceed from it."

The entire company, having arrived at such a con-

[1] Cf. *Records of the Western World*, vol. i. p. 17 *ss.*

[2] Possibly connected with the Sc. *Ap* or *Apsu.*

dition of distress, agreed to his order, and received the rules of moral obligation; after which the priest instructed them thus: "After I have gone up the hill you must cry out 'A-fu-sse! cause water to flow down for our use! enough to sustain us.'" With these words he left them. After a little while the company called out and requested, as he had instructed them. In a moment the water began to descend in supplies sufficient for their necessity.

The whole congregation were filled with joy and gratitude; but as the Master did not return they went in a body up the hill to see what had happened, and found that he was dead (*become extinct*). And now having wept and lamented, they burnt his body according to the rules of the Western world; on the place where they found him they collected stones and made a tower, which still exists. Moreover, the water has not ceased to flow, but, according to the number of the travellers who pass by this place, it flows down for their use, in small or large supply. If there is no one there, the fountain dries up (*is a mere secretion*).

The Master of the Law, with the rest, passed the night near the fountain. At sunrise he went on and crossed the "Silver Mountain." This mountain is very high and extensive. It is from this place that the silver is dug which supplies the Western countries with their silver currency.

On the west of the mountain he encountered a band of robbers; after giving them what they demanded, they departed.

After a little they came to the place of the site of the royal city, and passed the night by the side of a stream. At this time some foreign merchants in their company, to the number of several tens, coveting an early sale of their merchandise, privately went forward in the middle of the night. Scarcely had they gone ten *li* when they met a band of robbers who murdered every one of them. And so, when the Master of the Law and the others came to the place, they found their dead bodies there, but all their riches gone; they passed on, deeply affected with the sight, and shortly afterwards they saw the royal city before them.

The king of O-ki-ni (*with his ministers*) coming forth to meet (*the Master of the Law*), conducted him, and invited him to enter (*the Palace*) as his guest. This country formerly was subjected to attacks from brigands belonging to Kau-chang, and as there was still ill feeling (*between the two countries, the king*) was not willing to provide an escort.[1]

The Master of the Law, stopping one night, went forwards and crossed a great river. To the west he traversed a level valley, and after going several hundred *li* he arrived at the borders of the kingdom of K'iu-chi [*formerly written Kwi-tzu, but incorrectly*]. As he approached the capital, the king, accompanied by his ministers and a celebrated priest called Mo-cha-kiu-to (*Mokshagupta*, or *Mokshakûta*) came forth to meet him; other priests, to the number of several thousands, had remained at the eastern gate of the city, outside which they had erected a wide floating pavilion (*pointed like a tent*), and having brought the images (*of Buddha*) in procession, with sounds of music, had placed them there.

The Master of the Law having arrived, the priests rising to meet him, addressed him in affectionate language, and then each one returned to his seat. They then caused a priest to offer to the Master of the Law a bouquet of flowers freshly gathered. The Master of the Law having accepted it, advanced before the image of Buddha, scattering the flowers and offering worship. After this Mokshagupta took his seat beside him. The two being seated, the priests again formed a procession

[1] As Julien remarks, we must remember that Hiuen-Tsiang was accompanied by an escort from Kau-chang.

with flowers (*in their hands*), after which they offered grape juice as they passed. Having thus accepted flowers and grape juice in the first temple, he next received the same in the other temples, and thus going the round, the day began to decline, and the priests and their attendants gradually dispersed.

There were several decades of men belonging to Kau-chang who had become monks in K'iu-chi; they dwelt apart in one particular temple; this temple was to the south-east of the city. As the Master of the Law came from their native country, they were the first to invite him to stop the night with them. Because he accepted this invitation the king and the priests returned each to his own abode. The next day the king invited him to pass over to his palace to receive every kind of religious offerings and the three pure aliments.[1] The Master of the Law would not accept them, at which the king was very vexed; the Master of the Law replied, "This is the license granted by the 'gradual' system of the Law; but the Great Vehicle in which Hiuen-Tsiang has been instructed, does not admit of it. I will accept the other reserved food."

Having finished his repast, he proceeded in a north-west direction from the city to the temple called 'O-she li-ni[2] where the priest Mokshagupta resided. Gupta by his rare ability and intelligence had acquired the respect of all the different schools of religion. He had travelled in India for twenty years and more, learning (*the Sacred Books*). Although he had gone through all the Sûtras, yet he excelled in the knowledge of the Shing-ming (*Śábdavidyá Sûtra*). The king and the people of the kingdom were all affected by the utmost respect for him, and had named him Tuh-po (*without equal*). When he saw the Master of the Law come to his abode, he received

[1] For the "three pure aliments," and the "gradual system," *vide Jul.* ii. 2 *n.*

[2] *Vide Records, &c.*, vol. i., p. 22 *n.*

him with the politeness due to a guest, not knowing as yet his advanced acquaintance with religion.

Addressing the Master of the Law, he said: "In this land we have the Tsa-sin,[1] the Kiu-she,[2] the Pi-sha,[3] and other Sûtras; you can gain sufficient knowledge by studying these here, without troubling yourself to voyage to the West, encountering all sorts of dangers."

The Master of the Law replied: "And have you here the Yoga-Śâstra or not?"

He answered: "What need ask about such an heretical book as that? The true disciple of Buddha does not study such a work!"

The Master of the Law was at first filled with reverence for the person (of *Mokshagupta*), but hearing this reply he regarded him as dirt, and answering, said: "In our country too we have long had the Vibhâshâ and Kôsha; but I have been sorry to observe their logic superficial and their language weak: they do not speak of the highest perfection.[4] On this account I have come so far as this, desiring to be instructed in the Yoga Sâstra belonging to the Great Vehicle. And the Yôga, what is it but the revelation of Maitrêya, the Bôdhisattva next to become Buddha (lit., *the last personal Bodhisattva*), and to call such a book heretical, how is it you are not afraid of the bottomless pit?"

The other replied: "You have not yet understood the Vibhâshâ and the other Sûtras, how can you say they do not contain the deep principles of religion?"

The Master replied: "Do you, sir, at present understand them?" He answered, "I have a complete knowledge of them."

The Master then cited the beginning of the Kôsha, and asked him to continue. Forthwith he began to blunder, and as he came at last to a dead stop, he

[1] Samyuktâbhidarma.
[2] The Kosha.
[3] The Vibhâshâ.

[4] The "highest perfection" inculcated by the *Yoga* system of Buddhism, is, *union* with the supreme object of worship.

changed colour, and said with perturbation: "You may question me on some other portion of the work."

Then he referred to another passage, but neither could he recite this, but said: "The *Sâstra* has no such passage as the one you name." Now at this time the king's uncle, called Chi-Yueh, had become a monk and was well acquainted with Sûtras and Sâstras; he was on this occasion seated by the side (*of Hiuen-Tsiang*). Forthwith, he testified (*to the correctness of the quotation*), in these words: "This passage is really taken from the *Sâstra;*" and then, taking the original, he read it out.

Mokshagupta on this was exceedingly abashed and said: "I am getting old and forgetful."

He was questioned also regarding the other Sûtras, but could give no correct explanation.

And now, as the snow-passes of Mount Ling were not yet open, the Master could not advance, but was obliged to remain, for sixty days or so, detained by this circumstance. On going out to observe the condition of the roads, if they happened to meet together and speak (*i.e. the Master and Mokshagupta*), he did not sit down, but spoke either standing, or as if anxious to pass on. And in a private way he addressed the people and said: "This monk of China is not an easy man to discuss with; if he goes to India the younger class of disciples will be unwilling to present themselves (*i.e. for discussion or examination*).

So much was the Master feared by him and admired.

The day of his departure having come, the king gave him servants and camels and horses, and attended by monks and laymen belonging to the capital, he accompanied him for a good distance.

Going west from this two days' journey, he encountered about 2000 Turkish (*Tuh-Kiuch*) robbers on horseback;

they were in the act of dividing among themselves the booty they had got from a caravan, and when they could not agree they began to fight among themselves and so were dispersed.

Then going forward 600 *li* they crossed a small desert and arrived at the kingdom of Poh-luh-kia[1] [*formerly called Kih-meh*], and stopped there one night. Then proceeding north-west and going 300 *li*, they crossed a desert and came to the Ling[2] Mountain, which forms the northern angle of the T'sung Ling range. This mountain is steep and dangerous, and reaches to the clouds (*heaven*). From the creation the perpetual snow which has collected here in piles, has been changed into glaciers which melt neither in winter nor summer; the hard-frozen and cold sheets of water rise mingling with the clouds; looking at them the eye is blinded with the glare, so that it cannot long gaze at them. The icy peaks fall down sometimes and lie athwart the road, some of them a hundred feet high, and others several tens of feet wide. On this account the extreme difficulty of climbing over the first, and the danger of crossing the others. Moreover the wind, and the snow driven in confused masses, make it difficult to escape an icy coldness of body though wrapped in heavy folds of fur-bound garments. When desirous of food or sleep there is no dry place to be found for a halt; the only way is to hang the pot for cooking, and to spread the mat on the ice for sleeping.

After seven days they began to get out of the mountain; twelve or fourteen of the company were starved and frozen to death, whilst the number of the oxen and horses that perished was still greater.

After leaving the mountains they arrived at the lake called Tsing.[3] The circuit of this lake is 1400 or 1500 *li*, longer from east to west, narrower from north to south. Looking at the watery expanse, the wind sud-

[1] Bâlukâ.—*Records, &c.*, i. 24. [2] *Op. cit.* i. 25 *n.*
[3] *Vide* "Records," p. 25, *n.* 80.

denly arising swells the waves to a height of several *chang*.

Following the borders of the sea for about 500 *li* in a north-west direction, the Master came to the city of Su-yeh.[1] Here he encountered the Khan of the Turks called Yeh-hu, who was then engaged on a hunting expedition. The horses of these barbarous people are very fine; the Khan's person was covered with a robe of green satin, and his hair was loose, only it was bound round with a silken band some ten feet in length, which was twisted round his head and fell down behind. He was surrounded by about 200 officers, who were all clothed in brocade stuff, with their hair braided. On the right and left he was attended by independent troops all clothed in furs and fine spun hair garments; they carried lances and bows and standards, and were mounted on camels and horses. The eye could not estimate their numbers.

When they saw each other, the Khan, full of joy, said: "Stay here for a while; after two or three days I will come back." He then directed one of his chief officers, Ta-mo-chi, to conduct him towards a large tent and to arrange things for his comfort. After three days in this residence the Khan returned, and taking the Master of the Law by the hand he conducted him within.

The tent of the Khan is a large pavilion adorned with golden flower ornaments which blind the eye with their glitter. All the officers (*Ta kwan*) had spread out in front long mats, in two rows, on which they sat; they were clad in shining garments of embroidered silk. The body-guard of the Khan stood behind them. Regarding these circumstances of state, although he was but the ruler of a wandering horde, yet there was a certain dignified arrangement about his surroundings.

The Master of the Law proceeding towards the tent, when about thirty paces from it, the Khan came forth

[1] Or "*shé*."

and conducted him with reverent condescension within, speaking to him through an interpreter: they then entered and were seated.

The Turks worship Fire: they do not use wooden seats, because wood contains fire, and so even in worship they never seat themselves, but only spread padded mats on the ground and so go through with it. But for the sake of the Master of the Law they brought an iron warming-pan covered with a thick padding, and requested him to be seated thereon. A short time afterwards they introduced the Chinese mission and the legates from Kau-chang with their letters of introduction and presents. The Khan examined for himself the one and the other and was much pleased thereat; he then ordered the envoys to be seated, and caused wine to be offered to them with the sound of music.

The Khan with his ministers drank to the envoys, whilst he caused the juice of the grape[1] to be offered to the Master of the Law. After this they drank one with the other, challenging one another in succession, filling their cups and emptying them in succession, ever more and more animated, during all which time the sounds of all kind of music (*Kin, Mae, Li, &c.*)[2] resounded in confused clang. And although the character of the music was the common sort of the barbarians, yet it was nevertheless very diverting both to the ear and the eye, pleasing the thoughts and the mind.

In a little while there were other articles of food brought forward, such as boiled quarters of mutton and veal, which were heaped up before the guests; but for the Master of the Law they prepared distinct entertainment, consisting of the pure articles of food such as rice-cakes, cream, sugar-candy, honey-sticks (barley-sugar?), raisins, &c.

[1] *Pu-t'au*, cf. the Greek βότρυς (*Kingsmill*).

[2] Music of the North, South, East, and West (*Julien in loc*).

When the feast was over they sent round the grape-wine again, and then asked the Master of the Law to expound (*declare*) the doctrines of religion. Then he, with a view to admonish them, spoke upon the subject of the ten precepts (*Dasaśilaṁ*), love of preserving life, and the Pâramitas, and works that lead to final deliverance.

Raising his hands, he (*the King*) humbly prostrated himself to the ground, and joyously accepted the teaching of the Master.

And now having remained there several days, the Khan exhorted him to stop altogether, saying: "Sir; you have no need to go to India (*In-tu-kia-kwo*);[1] that country is very hot, the tenth month there, is as warm as our fifth month: as I regard your appearance I am afraid you will succumb under the climate. The men there are naked-blacks, without any sense of decorum, and not fit to look at!"

The Master replied: "Notwithstanding all this I desire to go and gaze on the sacred traces, and earnestly to search for the law."

The Khan then ordered inquiry to be made in his army for any one who could speak the Chinese language and that of other countries. So they found a young man who had lived for many years at Chang'an, and thoroughly understood the Chinese language.

He was appointed, under the title of Mo-to-ta-kwan, to prepare letters of commendation for the different countries and to accompany the Master to the kingdom of Kapiśa. Moreover, the Khan gave to Hiuen-Tsiang a complete set of vestments in red satin, and fifty pieces of silk; and then with his officers in person he conducted him a distance of ten *li*, or so.

From this, going west 400 *li* or so, he arrived at Ping-yu.[2] This is also called "The Thousand Springs."

[1] I would call attention to this unusual form for *India*, and compare the *Sindhuka* king, named in the "Friendly Letter" of Nagârjuna.

[2] Myn-bulak (*Bingheul*) *vide Records, &c.*, i. 27 *n.*

The district is several hundred *li* square. There are a multitude of pools and springs here, and also trees wonderful for their luxuriant verdure and height. The cool refreshing moisture makes this a fit place for the Khan, when he would avoid the heat of summer.

From Ping-yu, advancing westward 150 *li*, we come to the town of Ta-lo-sse (*Taras*). Again going south-west 200 *li*, we come to the town of Peh-shwui; again going south-west 200 *li*, we come to Kong-yu city; again going south 50 *li*, we come to the kingdom of Nu-chih-kien; again going west 200 *li*, we come to the kingdom of Che-shi. [*This means "The stone country," Ch. Ed.*] This country, on the west, borders on the river Yeh-yeh (or, *She-She*). Again going west 1000 *li* or so, we come to the kingdom of Su-tu-li-sse-na. To the east this kingdom borders on the Yeh-yeh river. This river comes from the northern plateau of the Ts'ung-Ling Mountains and flows to the north-west. Again going north-west, we enter on a great desert without water or grass. We advance guided by observing the bones left on the way. After 500 *li* or so we arrive at the country of Sa-mo-kien. [*This means "The happy country."*] [1] The king and people do not believe in the law of Buddha, but their religion consists in sacrificing to fire. There are here two religious foundations, but no priests dwell in them. If stranger-priests seek shelter therein, the barbarians follow them with burning fire and will not permit them to remain there.

The Master of the Law on his first arrival was treated disdainfully by the king, but after the first night's rest, he discoursed for the king's sake on the destiny (*cause and consequence*) of men and Devas: he lauded the meritorious qualities of Buddha: he set forth, by way of exhortation, the character of religious merit. The king was rejoiced, and requested permission to take the moral precepts as a disciple, and from that time showed him

[1] For the places named in this section, *vide Records, &c.*, i. p. 27 *ss.*

the highest respect. The two young disciples went to the temple to worship, on which the barbarians again pursued them with burning fire—the two Śrâmaṇêras going back told the king of it. The king hearing it ordered them to arrest the fire-carriers; having done so, he assembled the people and ordered the hands of the culprits to be cut off. The Master of the Law, wishing to exhort them to a virtuous life, would not consent to their bodies being mutilated and so saved them. The king having beaten them severely, expelled them from the city.

From this circumstance the higher and lower sort of people regarded him respectfully, and as a body sought to be instructed in the faith. Accordingly, having summoned a large assembly, he received many of them into the priesthood and established them in the convents. It was thus that he transformed their badly disposed (*heretical*) hearts, and corrected their evil customs. And so it was wherever he went.

Again going about 300 *li* to the west, he arrived at K'iuh-shwang-ni-kia.[1] Again going west 200 *li* or so, we come[2] to the kingdom of Ho-Han [*i.e.* "*The easternrest country*," *Ch. Ed.*]. Again going west 400 *li*, we come to the country of Pu-ho.[3] [This means "*The middlerest country*," *Ch. Ed.*] Again going west 100[4] *li* or so, we come to the Fa-ti[5] country. [This means "*The westernrest country*," *Ch. Ed.*] Again going west 500 *li*, we come to the Kingdom of Ho-li-sih-mi-kia (*Khwârazm*). This country on the East borders on the Po-tsu river (*the Oxus*). Again going south-west 300 *li* or so, we come to the country of Kie-shwang-na (*Kesh*). Again going south-west 200 *li*, we enter the mountains. The moun-

[1] Kashania.

[2] The Pilgrim did not visit these countries himself, but wrote from hearsay.—*Vide Records*, i. 34 *n.*

[3] Bokhâra.

[4] The *Si-yu-ki* gives 400 *li*.

[5] The *Fa-ti* or *Vati* country probably represents the country of the Yue-ti (*Vati*).

tain road is deep and dangerous, scarcely wide enough in some places for men to pass, and, moreover, without herbage or water; going 300 *li* or so through the mountains, we enter the Iron Gates. Here the perpendicular precipices, like walls on either side, afford but a narrow passage. The stone contains much iron, which is dug out. Attached to the wall on either side there is a folding-gate, with many cast-iron bells suspended above it; hence the name: this is the barrier against the advance of the Turks. Passing through the Iron Gates we arrive at the country of Tu-ho-lo [*formerly by mistake written To-fo-lo, Ch. Ed.*] From this, having gone several hundred *li*, we cross the Oxus, and arrive at the Kingdom of Hwo (*Kunduz*). This was the residence of the eldest son of the Khan Yeh-hu[1] called Ta-tu-sheh [Sheh *is an official title, Ch. Ed.*] It was he who had married the sister of the king of Kau-chang.

Moreover, the king of Kau-chang had sent letters to this place in recommendation of the Master of the Law; on his arrival, the princess *Hö-kia-tun*[2] was dead, and *Ta-tu-sheh* was sick. When he heard that the Master of the Law had come from Kau-chang with letters for himself and his wife, he was overpowered with grief thereat, and calling the Master, said: "Your humble servant at view of you has received sight! Would that you could remain here a little while, and rest. If I should recover my health, I will personally conduct you to the country of the Brahmans."

At this time, moreover, there was a Brahman priest who had come to recite certain charms—which gradually had the effect of removing (*the sickness of the prince*). Afterwards he (*i.e. the Prince*), married the younger sister of the Princess Ho-kia-tun. She, at the suggestion of her nephew (*the son of her sister who was dead*), prepared a poison and killed her husband. The Sheh being dead, the princess of Kau-chang having only a little child, the nephew who

[1] Or, *She-hu.*

[2] The princess *Kho* (*Julien in loc.*)

had the title Télé violently seized the government and became Sheh, after which he married his step-mother.

As the funeral ceremony (*of the late prince*) was being celebrated, Hiuen-Tsiang was detained for more than a month.

There was then a Śramaṇa called Ta-mo-sang-kia (*Dharmasiñha*), residing in this country. He had travelled for instruction to India; beyond the T'sung-ling Mountains on the western side they called him Fa-tsiang (*i.e. Artizan of the Law*, or *law-maker*). The priests of Su-leh (*Kashgar*) and Yu-tin (*Khotan*) dare not discuss with him. The Master of the Law (*Hiuen-Tsiang*), wishing to know his profound or shallow knowledge, sent messengers to him, to ask how many Sûtras or Śâstras he was able to explain. The disciples who were surrounding him, when they heard the message were piqued—whilst Dharmasiñha answered with a smile: "I can explain any of them you like." The Master of the Law, knowing that he did not understand the Great Vehicle, turned his questions to the Vibhâshâ and other Sûtras belonging to the "Little Vehicle." These questions, not easy to solve, made him allow his inferiority. The disciples were filled with shame. From this time whenever they met, the Śramaṇa was full of expressions of pleasure, and ceased not to praise the Master, acknowledging that he was by no means his equal.

At this time, the new Sheh having been established in his government, the Master of the Law asked him for official envoys to conduct him, and for post-horses (*U-lo: Ulak—Jul.*), as he desired to go south towards the country of the Brahmans. The Sheh, after consideration, said: "Your disciple among his possessions has the country of Fo-ho-lo (*Baktra*), bordering northwards on the Oxus; men call the capital city the *little Râjagriha*—so many are the sacred traces therein. I beg, sir, you will spend some time in paying reverence there (*to these sacred spots*), and afterwards take up your carriage and go southward."

At this time there were in this place many tens of priests of Baktra, who had come to express sympathy with the new Sheh on the death of his predecessor;[1] when the Master of the Law met them, he expressed his intention, and to this they replied: "You ought to go with us at once—the road is open now, but if you delay here longer the change of place will be difficult." The Master of the Law on these words forthwith took leave of the Sheh, and taking up his carriage, departed with those priests. Having arrived at this place (*i.e. Balkh*), observing the city and its suburbs, he noticed the apparently barren character of the city and its neighbourhood, but yet, in truth, it was most excellent land.

There were about a hundred Saṅghâramas and three thousand priests, or so, all belonging to the "*Little Vehicle.*"[2]

Outside the city on the south-west quarter there is the Navasaṅghârâma, which is remarkable for its imposing structure and unusual ornaments. Inside the Saṅghârâma, in the hall of Buddha, there is the water-pot of Buddha, able to contain about two pecks. There is also here a tooth of Buddha, about one inch long, and eight or nine-tenths in breadth, of a yellow-white colour; this relic always irradiates a bright miraculous light.

There is also here the sweeping brush of Buddha, made of Kaśa grass; it is about three feet long, and perhaps seven inches round; the handle is ornamented with various precious substances. These three things are brought out every feast day, and the priests and laymen draw near to worship them. The most faithful, behold a spiritual radiancy proceeding from them.

[1] Whom the *Sheh* had caused to be poisoned.

[2] This seems to show that Buddhism had reached Balkh at an early date.

To the north of the Sañghârâma there is a Stûpa about 200 feet high. To the south-west of the Sañghârâma there is a Vihâra, of an old date. All the priests who have attained to the four degrees of holiness (*the fruition of the four paths*) during successive ages, dwelling here, after their Nirvâna, have had erected to their memory towers, the foundations of which, to the number of several hundreds, are close together in this vicinity. Fifty *li* to the north-west of the capital (*the great city*), we come to the town of Ti-wei; forty *li* to the north of this town there is the town of Po-li. There are two Stûpas in this town, three *chang* in height: in former days when Buddha first arrived at Supreme Enlightenment he accepted some honey and meal at the hands of two merchants, who were in that place; when they had heard from him the fine moral precepts and the ten rules (*sikshâpadas*), they asked to be allowed to present their religious offerings. Tathâgata gave to them, for the purpose, some pieces of his nails and portions of his hair, and ordered them to construct a tower, and furnished them with a model. The two merchantmen,[1] taking (*the relics*), returned to their own country (or, *when about to return to their own country*), and built these two sacred (*spiritual*) towers.[2] About seventy *li* to the west of the city there is a Stûpa more than two *chang* high; they were built in the days of Kâśyapa Buddha long ago.

In the *New Sañghârâma* there was (*a priest*) of the kingdom of Tcheka who had studied the three Piṭakas belonging to the Little Vehicle; his name was Prajñâkara. Hearing that there were many sacred traces of religion in the country of Fo-ho-lo (*Baktra*), he had therefore come to worship and reverence them. This man was of singular wisdom and learning, so that as a youth he was

[1] The Chinese is *Chang-ché*, which corresponds to the Sc. *Shrêshtin* and the Pali *Seṭṭhi*.—*Vide Records*, i. 47, n. 150.

[2] Whatever the historical truth of this record may be, it points at any rate to the belief that even in the days of Buddha, merchants from Baktria had regular commerce with India.

distinguished by his great sagacity. He had thoroughly sounded the nine collections,[1] and mastered the four Âgamas. The fame of his exposition of the principles of the faith had spread throughout India. He was perfectly acquainted with the Abhidharma of the Little Vehicle, the Kosha of Kâtyâyana, the Shaṭpadâbhidharma and other works.

Hearing that the Master of the Law had come from a distance to search for religious books, he was exceedingly glad to meet him. The Master of the Law, in the course of his statement respecting his doubts and difficulties about the Kosha and Vibhâshâ and other books, asked him for some explanations, and was answered in each case with extreme clearness. He remained here a month and studied the Vibhâshâ Śâstra. In this Saṅghârâma, moreover, there were two other (*priests*) versed in the Tripiṭaka according to the Little Vehicle; their names were Ta-mo-pi-li (*Dharmapriya*) and Ta-mo-ki-li (*Dharmakara*); they were exceedingly honoured by the others. Seeing the sacred features of the Master of the Law and the marks of intelligence which distinguished him, they paid him marked respect.

There were at this time to the south-west of Baktra the countries named Jui-mo-to (*Jumadha*) and Hu-shi-kien (*Juzgâna*).[2] Their kings, hearing that the Master of the Law had come from a distant country, both sent their chief ministers to salute him, and to request him to pass through their countries and receive religious offerings; but he declined to go. The messengers having returned and again come back several times, in consequence of his continual refusals, at last he complied with the request. The kings, being overjoyed, offered him gold and precious stones, and abundance of drink and food; the Master of the Law declined all such gifts, and returned.

[1] That is, the nine Aṅgas or divisions of the Sacred Books of Buddhism. *Vide* Burnouf, *Introduction*, p. 51, ss.

[2] For these places, *vide Records, &c.*, vol. i., p. 48.

Going south from Balkh in company with Prajñâkara, the Master of the Law, they entered the kingdom of Kie-chi (*Gaz*).

To the south-east of this kingdom they entered the great Snowy Mountains, and going 600 *li* and more they left the boundaries of the Tu-ho-lo (*Tukhára*) country, and entered the kingdom of Fan-yen-na (*Bâmiyân*). This country from east to west is about 2000 *li* in extent. It is situated in the middle of the Snowy Mountains; the muddy roads and dangers of the passes and tracks are double those of the frozen desert. The pelting hail and snowstorms go on perpetually intermingled; then, the winding and crooked passes that are met with; then, in the level parts, the mud stretching for several *changs;* so that what Sung-yu says about the dangers of the western region, (viz., *of Sz'chuen and the Wu-shan*),[1] "the storeyed ice-like mountains, and the flying snow for a thousand *li*," is applicable to this district also.

Alas! if it were not that I had determined to seek the incomparable Law for the sake of all that lives, much rather would I have pleaded that this body of mine, left by my parents, should have gone on its (*last*) journey (*i.e. that I should have died*). And so Wang-tsun,[2] when he had accomplished the embankments of Kiu-che, himself said: "I am but a loyal servant of Han." The Master of the Law having surmounted the precipices of the Snowy Mountains in search for the sacred Law, is also able to be named "a true son of Tathâgata."

It was thus he gradually arrived at Bâmiyân, the chief town of which possesses something like ten religious foundations, with several thousand priests; these belong to the Little Vehicle, according to the Lôkôttara Vâdinah school.

[1] *Vide Mayers*, Manual, &c., *sub.* 873.
[2] Probably the character *Tsun* is for *To.* Mayers, 822.

The king of Bâmiyân went forth to escort him, and invited him within his palace to receive his religious offerings: after a day or two he went forth to make his observations.

There were there two priests belonging to the Mahâsaṅghika school, whose names were Âryadâsa and Âryasêna, both of them deeply versed in the Law. When they met the Master of the Law they were full of admiration, that so remote a country as China should possess such a distinguished priest. They conducted him from place to place to pay his reverence, or to inspect, and did not cease in their attention and services to him.

North-east of the capital, on the declivity of a hill, there is a standing stone figure[1] about 150 feet high. To the east of the figure there is a Saṅghârâma, to the east of which is a standing figure of Śakya, made of calamine stone,[2] in height one hundred feet. Within the Saṅghârâma there is a figure of Buddha represented as when he was asleep on entering Nirvâna, about 1000 feet in length. All these figures are of an imposing character and extremely good (*execution*).

Going south-east from this, 200 *li* or so, crossing the great Snowy Mountains, we come to a small valley[3] where there is a Saṇghârâma, in which there is a tooth of Buddha, and also a tooth of a Pratyêka Buddha, who lived at the beginning of the present Kalpa. This tooth is five inches long, and four inches broad, or a little less. Moreover, there is the tooth of a Chakravarttin monarch (*king of the golden wheel*), three inches long, and two inches broad. Moreover, there is the iron pot (*pâtra*), which Shang-no-kia-fo-sha (*Śâṇakavâsa*) carried, able to hold eight or nine pints, and also his Saṅghâti robe, of a bright red colour. This man, during five hundred births

[1] But the text does not say "of Buddha," as Julien translates *Vie*, p. 69.

[2] Or, *covered with brass plates*.

[3] The Chinese is *ch'uen* (a stream), which has here, and also in Fa-hien, cap. xvi. *ad finem*, the sense of a valley or gorge.

in the world, had always been born with this robe on him, but afterwards (*when he was ordained*) changed it (or, *it changed*) into a Kashâya garment; the story is a long one, as may be read in the other narrative[1] (*i.e.* the *Si-yu-ki*).

Thus passed fifteen days, and then, leaving Bâmiyân, on the second day he encountered a snowstorm, which caused him to miss his road. Coming to a small sand hillock, he met some hunters, who showed him the way. Crossing the Black Ridge,[2] he arrived at the borders of Kapiśa.

This kingdom is about 4000 *li* in circuit. On the north it is bounded (*backed*) by the Snowy Mountains. The king is selected from the Kshattriya caste. He is a clever, shrewd man, and has brought under his control some ten kingdoms.

When (*Hiuen-Tsiang*) was about to arrive at the capital, the king and all the priests went forth from the city to escort him.

There are some hundred or so religious foundations, the residents in which had sharp words together, each convent wishing to induce the Master to stop there.

There was a temple belonging to the Little Vehicle, which was named *Sha-lo-kia*.[3] The story goes that the temple was built some time ago, when the son of the Han Emperor was held as an hostage. The priests of this temple said: "Our temple was originally founded by a son of the Han Emperor, and now, as you come from that country, you ought first to stop with us."

The Master of the Law seeing them thus, was deeply impressed; and as his companion, Hwui-Sing (*i.e. Prajñâkara,* see p. 50), Master of the Law, belonged to this school of the Little Vehicle, to which these priests were attached, he did not desire to live in a temple belonging to the Great Vehicle; accordingly they went to stop at the temple made for the hostage.

[1] *Vide Records*, vol. i., p. 53.

[2] (Siâh Kôh), or Kôh Baba.

[3] For some remarks on this name, *vide Records*, i. p. 57, n. 203.

Moreover, at this time there was treasured here (*by the hostage*), under the foot of the image of the Great-Spirit King,[1] on the south side of the eastern gate of the Hall of Buddha, a countless quantity of jewels and gems, as a means for the after repairs of the building. The priests, in gratitude for such favours, had in various places painted on the walls the figure of the hostage prince. At the time of the conclusion of the Rest, (*i.e. the Rest during the Rains*), this congregation holds an assembly for preaching and reciting the Scriptures, as a means for planting (or, *perpetuating his*) religious merit;[2] this custom has been handed down from generation to generation, and is still observed.

Recently there was a wicked king who, fired by a covetous disposition, desired to carry off the priests' treasure. Accordingly he sent men to dig underneath the foot of the Spirit-King. Then the earth greatly quaked, and the figure of the parrot which was on the top of his head, seeing them digging, flapped his wings, and screamed violently. The king and his troops were all seized with terror and fell to the earth; after this, they returned home.

There is in the temple a Stûpa. The *tee* (*encircling rings*) of this building having tumbled down, the priests wished to take the treasure and to repair it. On making the attempt, the earth again trembled and roared, so that no one dared to go near.

When the Master of the Law arrived, the whole assembly came together, and, as a body, requested the Master of the Law (*to assist them*), setting forth and relating the previous circumstances.

The Master of the Law and the others then proceeded to the place of the Spirit (that is, *the place of the statue*

[1] That is, *Vaiśravaṇa*: *vide Records*, b. i., n. 207.

[2] Julien's translation is too diffuse. There is no mention of "the hostage" in the text, and the symbol *fuh* relates to "religious merit." It would seem, however, that the *religious service* was designed to perpetuate the memory of the hostage.

of the Spirit-King), and burning incense, he said: "The royal hostage formerly concealed here these precious things, purposing them for the meritorious object of building (*i.e. repairing the building*); now then the time has arrived for opening the treasure (*charity*) and using it. We pray you to penetrate the truth of our purpose, and for a while restrain the power (*virtue*) of your august presence, and permit this proceeding.

"I, Hiuen-Tsiang, will personally superintend (*the work of excavation*), and will measure accurately the weight, and dispense to the master of the Work, justly, what is necessary for the execution of the repairs, and will permit no useless waste. Only we beseech the spiritual power of the god to condescend to search out the truth (*of our intentions*)."

Having said these words, he ordered the men to dig into the ground; they did so calmly and without molestation. At the depth of seven or eight feet, they came to a great copper vessel, which contained several hundred catties of gold, and several scores of pearls. The great congregation were filled with joy, and without exception paid their services to the Master of the Law. The Master of the Law kept the Rain-Rest in this temple.

The king of this country thinks little of the polite arts, he entirely trusts to (*the teaching of*) the Great Vehicle. As he was fond of the sight of religious conferences and discussions, he asked the Master of the Law and Prajñâkara (*Doctor*) of the three Piṭakas, to a religious assembly to be held in a Temple of the Great Vehicle. In that Temple there was (a Doctor) of the three Piṭakas called Manôjñaghosha (*Mo-nu-jo-kiu-sha*), and also a Sa-po-to, A-li-ye-fa-mo (*i.e. Aryavarma of the Sarvâstivâdin school*), and also a priest of the Mi-sha-seh school (*Mahîsâsaka*), named Ku-na-po-to (*Gunabhadra*); these priests were reputed the chief in that convent. Their acquirements, however, were not universal, but confined to one or other points in the

Great or Little (*Vehicle*), as the case might be, and although clear on that point, yet narrowed in its extent (*length*). But the Master of the Law had thoroughly examined the teaching of all the schools, and answered the questions put to him by all comers, according to the several systems of doctrine: so that all present were constrained to acknowledge his superiority.

Thus for five days (*the discussion continued*), then the assembly dispersed.

The king, being overjoyed, gave to the Master of the Law, as a distinct present, five pieces of embroidered silk; and to the others, different offerings.

The Rain-Retreat being ended in the Sha-lo-kia convent, Prajñâkara returned (*to Balkh*), in obedience to the request of the king of Tukhâra. The Master of the Law having separated from him proceeded eastward, and having advanced some 600 *li*, passing the Black Ridge, he entered the borders of India, and came to the country of Lan-po (*Lamghân*).

This country is about 1000 *li* in circuit. There are ten Sañghârâmas, the priests are all devoted to the Great Vehicle. Having stopped three days, he proceeded southward, and came to a little hill on which was a Stûpa. This is where Buddha stopped in former days when he came here from the south, in consequence of which, men, in after days, built this Stûpa from a feeling of affectionate respect. All places to the north of this are called Mi-li-ku (*i.e. frontier lands*) [*Mleččha lands*]. Tathâgata, when he desired to instruct and convert (*these people*), in so doing, used to pass through the air in coming and going, and would not tread on the earth, as the earth trembled and shook under his footsteps.

From this, going south twenty *li* or so, and descending the mountain ridge,[1] after crossing a river, he came to the country of Na-kie-lo-ho (*Nagarahâra*). Two *li* to the

[1] But there is nothing said about "*the black*" ridge, as Julien translates.

south-east of the capital of the country is a Stûpa 300 feet or so in height; it was built by Aśôka râja. It was here Śâkya Bôdhisattva, in the second Asañkhya of years (*from the present time*), met Jen-tang-Fo (*Dipañkara Buddha*). He spread his deer-skin robe and unloosed his hair, to preserve (*the Buddha*) from the mud, and in consequence received a predictive assurance (*that he would become a Buddha*). Although there have passed Kalpa destructions (*since that period*), the traces of this event remain intact. The Dêvas here scatter all sorts of flowers and continually pay their religious services.

The Master of the Law when he arrived at this spot, paid his devotions and religiously circumambulated the building.

There was then, by the side of the Stûpa, an old priest who explained for the Master's sake the origin of the building.

The Master's question was this: "The period of the Bôdhisattva's service in spreading his hair was in the second Asânkhya of years, but since this period to the present time an innumerable number of Kalpas have elapsed. In the course of these Kalpas the universe has been repeatedly perfected and destroyed. As when the destruction by fire has taken place, even Mount Sumeru has been reduced to ashes, how is it that this religious monument (or, *these sacred traces*), cannot be destroyed?"

In reply, he said: "At the time of the dissolution of the universe this monument also is destroyed; but at the period of restoration, this old vestige is also restored to its original condition. So, just as Mount Sumeru is restored, after its destruction, to its former condition, why should this sacred relic alone not reappear? This comparison can admit of no question." Such was the celebrated reply.

About ten *li* to the south-west is a Stûpa; this is the place where Buddha (*i.e.* when he was Dipañkara) bought the flowers.[1]

[1] For the story of Dipañkara purchasing the flowers, *vide Records*, i. 92, 93.

Again, to the south-east, after crossing a sandy peak, we come to the town of Buddha's skull bone.[1] In this town is a double-storeyed tower and in the upper storey is a small Stûpa, made of the seven precious substances, which contains the bone of the top of the head of Tathâgata. This bone is one foot and two inches round. The marks of the hair orifices are quite distinct. The colour of the bone is a yellowish white; it is enclosed in a jewelled box. If any one wishes to know the indications of his guilt or his religious merit, he mixes some powdered incense into a paste, which he spreads upon a piece of silken stuff, and then presses it on the top of the bone: according to the resulting indications the good fortune or ill fortune of the man, is determined.

The Master of the Law, in taking an impression, obtained the figure of the Bôdhi tree: of the two Śrâmanêras who also took impressions, the first obtained a figure of Buddha, the other a figure of a lotus. The Brahman who guarded the bone was overjoyed as he turned to the Master, with his fingers interlaced (*rounded like a ball*), and then scattering flowers before him, said: "That indication which the Master has obtained is extremely rare, and is a sure sign of your having a portion of true wisdom (*Bôdhi*)."

There is also here a tower of the skull bone shaped like a lotus leaf.

Also the eyeball of Buddha, as large as an Âmra fruit, and so bright that its rays dart forth from the box to some distance outside.

Again, there is the Saṅghâti robe of Buddha, made of a very fine silky cotton stuff.

Again, there is the staff of Buddha, the rings whereof are made of tin, and the haft of sandalwood. All these the Master of the Law adored with reverence; after which, in consequence of this opportunity of paying his

[1] Hiḍḍa.

heartfelt respect, he presented (*at the different shrines*), fifty gold pieces, one thousand silver pieces, four silken banners, two pieces of brocaded (*satin*), and two sets of religious vestments: then having scattered flowers, and again prostrated himself in worship, he went forth.

And now he heard that to the south-west of the city of Dipaṅkara, about twenty *li* or so, there was the cave where dwelt the Nâgarâja Gopâla. Tathâgata in former days having tamed this Nâga, left to him as a bequest his shadow to remain in the cavern. The Master of the Law wished to go there to worship; but he was told that the roads were deserted and dangerous, and moreover that they were frequented by robbers, and that for the last two or three years those who had gone for the purpose of seeing (*the shadow*) had not succeeded in their purpose, and so there were few now who went.

And now, when the Master wished to go to pay his adoration to this relic, the envoys sent with him by the king of Kapiśa, earnestly longing to return, besought him not to delay any longer nor think of going to the cave.

The Master of the Law replied: "The shadow of the true body of Tathâgata, during a hundred thousand kalpas can with difficulty be met with: how much rather, then, having come so far as this, should I not go to worship it? As for you, advance on your journey slowly, and I will rejoin you after a little while."

On this he went alone, and arriving at the town of Dipaṅkara, he entered a monastery, and inquired some particulars as to the road, but found no one who would go with him as a guide. After a while he met with a little boy who said: "The farm-house of the convent is not far from the place, I will guide you so far." The Master then went with the boy and arrived at the farm-house, where he passed the night. He then found an old man who knew the place, and so with him as a guide they set out together. After going a few *li* they were met by five robbers who came upon them sword in hand. The Master of the Law immediately removed his loose cloak, so as to let his religious vestments appear. The robbers said: "Where is the Master going?" In reply he said: "I am wishful to worship the shadow of Buddha." The robbers said: "Have you not heard that this road is infested with brigands?" He answered: "Robbers are human beings. I am now going to adore Buddha; though the road be filled with savage beasts, I have no fear; how much less should I fear you, who are my human benefactors (or, *protectors*)?"

The robbers were touched to the heart by these words and allowed him to go to perform his act of worship, and so they arrived at the cave.

The cave lies to the eastward of a stony water-course; the door through the wall (*of the cave*) faces the west. Looking into the cave all is wrapped in gloom and no object visible. The old man spoke to the Master thus: "You must enter and pass straight on to the eastern wall; when you touch that, stop, and then go backwards fifty paces and no more; then face the eastern wall and look; the shadow is in that place." The Master of the Law entered (*the cave*) and paced forward, it may be fifty strides,[1] and touched the eastern wall, and then according to the directions he went backwards and stood still. Then animated by the most sincere desire, he paid his worship with a hundred and more prostrations: but he saw nothing. He reproached himself for his shortcomings, and with lamentable cries, he expressed his deep sorrow. Then again with his utmost heart he paid his worship and recited the *Shing-kwan* and other sûtras, he also repeated the gâthas of the Buddhas, making one prostration after each verse of praise. After about one hundred prostrations, he saw on the eastern wall a great light about the size of a Pâtra[2] (*in circuit*); which disappeared in a moment. Sorrowful and yet rejoicing he

[1] According to this, if he came back fifty paces, he must have stood at the entrance of the cave.

[2] Alms-dish, or bowl.

again paid his adorations, and then there appeared a great light round as a basin, which again as quickly disappeared. Then, filled with additional ardour and desire, he vowed within himself that if he did not see the shadow of the Lord of the world, that he would never leave the place. Then he performed two hundred more acts of worship, and then, whilst the whole cave was brightened up with light, the shadow of Tathâgata of a shining white colour appeared on the wall, as when the opening clouds suddenly reveal the golden Mount and its excellent indications. Bright were the divine lineaments of his face, and as the Master gazed in awe and holy reverence, he knew not how to compare the spectacle; the body of Buddha and his kashâya robe were of a yellowish red colour, and from his knees upward the distinguishing marks of his person were exceedingly glorious; but below, the lotus throne on which he sat was slightly obscured. On the left and right of the shadow and somewhat behind, were visible the shadows of Bôdhisattvas and the holy priests surrounding them.

Having gazed on the vision, he summoned six men, from some distance outside the gate, to get some fire, and bring it in for burning incense. But as soon as the fire was brought in, the shadow of Buddha disappeared. Then he quickly ordered them to put the fire out, and, on his earnest request, the shadow again appeared.

Among the six men, five of the number were able to see the shadow, but one of them could see nothing.

Thus the appearance lasted for the short space of half a mealtime, during which having uttered his praises in worship and scattered flowers and incense, the light then suddenly disappeared.[1]

Having left the cave, the Brahman, who had been his guide, was filled with joy as he extolled the miracle; moreover he said: "If it had not been for the sincere

[1] The entire story of the "Shadow" seems to indicate the use of a lantern and slide as a pious fraud. Had such contrivances already been introduced into India from Persia?

faith and prayers of the Master, this could not have happened." Outside the door of the cave there are many sacred traces [*as detailed in the other narrative*].

As they were returning together those five brigands, laying aside their arms, received the moral precepts and departed.

After this the Master rejoined his companions, and passing over the mountains in a south-easterly direction, after 500 *li* or so, they came to the country of Gandhâra.

This kingdom on the eastern side borders on the Sin-tu river; the capital is called *Po-lu-sha-po-lo*.[1] In this country many sages and saints from old days composed Śâstras, as for instance Na-lo-yen-ti'en (*Nârayâna Deva*), Wu-cho-Pu-sa (*Asañgha Bodhisattva*), Shi-tsin-pu-sa (*Vasubandhu Bodhisattva*), Fa-k'iu (*Dharmatrâta*), Ju-i (*Manôrhita*), Hi-tsun-che (*the venerable Parsvika*), and others, all of whom came from this kingdom.

To the north-east of the capital there is erected a precious tower of the Pâtra of Buddha.

This pâtra afterwards removed itself through various countries, and at present is found in the country of Po-lai-na-se (*Banâras*).

Eight or nine *li* to the south-east beyond the capital is a Pi-po-lo tree, about 100 feet high. The four past Buddhas have all sat underneath this tree, and now there are the figures of these four Tathâgatas placed here. The 996 Buddhas yet to come will also sit here.

By the side of this tree there is a Stûpa; this was built by Kanishka-râja; it is 400 feet high, the foundation part is a *li* and a half in circuit, and 150 feet high. Above the Stûpa is raised a series of imperishable (*diamond*) wheels (or, *metal rings*), twenty-five in number. In the Stûpa there are śarîras (*relics*) of Buddha to the amount of ten pecks (*one hoh*).

[1] Purushapura (Peshâwar).

A hundred paces or so to the south-west of the great Stûpa there is a figure, carved out of white stone, eighteen feet high; it stands with its face to the north. Very many spiritual portents (*are exhibited here*). Frequently there are persons who see the statue at night going round the great Stûpa.

A hundred *li* or so to the north-east of the Sanghârâma of Kanishka, we cross a great river and come to the town of Po-sih-kie-lo-fa-ti (*Pushkalâvati*). To the east of the town there is a Stûpa built by Asôka-râja. Here the four past Buddhas have preached the Law.

Four or five *li* to the north of the town is a Sanghârâma, within which is a Stûpa, about 200 feet high, erected by Asôka râja; it was here that Sâkya Buddha when formerly living (*acting*) as a Bôdhisattva, delighted in performing deeds of charity. For a thousand births he was born as king of this country, and here, during these births, he plucked out his eyes (*and gave them in charity*). Of all these acts there are innumerable holy traces.

The Master of the Law visited these sacred spots in succession, and offered worship.

When he came to a great Tower, or to a great Sanghârâma, he always gave away a portion of the gold and silver and silks and religious vestments which he had received as a charitable donation from the king of Kau-Chang. Having delayed long enough to show the sincerity of his faith in making these offerings, he departed.

From this place he arrived at the town of *U-to-kia-han-cha* (*Uṭakhanḍa*).

Travelling northwards from this town and passing over mountains and valleys, after going 600 *li* or so, he entered the country of *U-ćhang-na* (*Udyâna*).

On either side of the river *Su-po-sa-tu* (Subhavâstu) there were formerly 1400 Sanghârâmas, with some 18,000 priests; but now all is desert and depopulated.[1]

[1] In Sung-yun's time (A.D. 520) the country was in a high state of prosperity. It was probably devastated by Mihirakula.

The priests who observe the Rules and follow the traditions of religion, belong to five schools, viz., the Dharmaguptas, the Mahîśâsakas, the Kâśyapiyas, the Sarvâstivâdas, and the Mahâsaṅghikas.

The king mostly lives in the town of *Mung-kie-li* (*Mungali*),[1] which is well populated and prosperous. To the east of the town four or five *li*, is a great stûpa celebrated for its miraculous capabilities. This is the place where formerly Buddha (*was born*) as Kshânti Rĭshi, and for the sake of Kalirâja allowed his body to be cut in pieces.[2]

To the north-east of the town 250 *li*, entering on a great mountain region, we come to the fountain of the Nâga A-po-lo-lo (*Apalâla*), which in fact is the upper source of the river Suvâstu. It flows to the south-west.

This land is very cold. Even during spring and summer there are frequent frosts, morning and evening, and flying snow-storms, with pelting rain and snow fancifully commingled, reflecting the five colours like confused flowers.

Thirty *li* or so south-west of the Nâga fountain on the north side of the river on the top of a large flat stone, there is a trace of Buddha's foot. This trace appears long or short, according to the merit or prayers of the men who inspect it.

In former days when Buddha subdued the nâga Apalâla, he came to this spot and left this trace as a fortunate indication.

Following down the stream thirty *li* or so, we come to the washing-garment stone of Tathâgata (*i.e. the stone on which he washed his robe*). The marks of the flowery tracery of the Kashâya garment are plainly seen.

To the south of the town 400 *li* or so, we come to Mount Hi-lo. Here Tathâgata in former days, hearing a half-gâtha, in gratitude to the Yaksha, threw his body

[1] Probably the same as Mankalai, Lat. 34° 50′ N., Long. 71° 50′ E., marked on the Indian Survey Map No. 4.

[2] Julien's translation is here in error, *vide*, p. 86.

down (from a tree) for his use.[1] [*A gâtha consists of forty-two words. Ch. Ed.* The *Si-yu-ki says thirty-two.*]

Fifty *li* to the west of the town of Mungali, after crossing a great river,[2] we came to a stûpa called Lu-hi-ta-ka (*Rôhitaka, i.e., red*); it is about ten *chang* high (100 feet), and was built by Asôka-râja. Here Tathâgata in former days being born as Maitribala râja, cut his body with a knife in charity to five Yakshas.

To the north-east of the city thirty *li* or so, we come to a stone stûpa called "The Miraculous" (*Adbhûta*). It is about thirty feet high. It was here that Buddha in olden days preached the law on behalf of Devas and men. After leaving the spot, this stûpa rose out of the earth of its own accord.

To the west of the stûpa, after crossing a great river and going three or four *li*, we come to a Vihâra, in which is a figure of Avalôkiteśvara Bodhisattva, which is possessed of exceedingly august spiritual qualities.

To the north-east of the city, it is said that there are men, who, passing across mountains and valleys, following up (*the river*) in a contrary direction, along many mountain roads full of mud and dangerous defiles—sometimes passing across by iron chains and sometimes over flying bridges—going thus a thousand *li* or so,—come to the valley of Ta-li-lo (*Dâril*) identical with the site of the old capital of U-chang-na (*Udyâna*).[3]

In this valley (*ch'uen*) is a large Sanghârâma, by the side of which is a carved wooden statue of Maitreya Bôdhisattva, of a golden colour and very majestic in appearance. It is about 100 feet in height, and was made by the Arhat Madhyântika. By his power of divine locomotion he enabled an artist to ascend to the Tuśita heaven, and caused him to observe personally the characteristic marks

[1] *Records.* Vol. i. p. 124.

[2] Viz. the *Kumar* River.

[3] In this passage the introduction of the phrase "*there are men, &c.*" is probably an error. The symbol for "a thousand," is also imperfect.

(*of Maitreya's body*). After going there three times, the meritorious work was finished.

Going south from the town of *U-to-kia-han cha*, we cross the Sin-tu river, which is here three or four *li* in width. Its stream is extremely clear and rapid. Poisonous dragons and evil sprites dwell beneath this river in great numbers. Those who cross this river carrying with them rare gems of India, or celebrated flowers, or Sárîras, the boat (*in which they embark*) is suddenly overwhelmed by the waves.

Crossing the river we come to the country of *Ta-ch'a-shi-lo* (Takshaśilâ). To the north of this town, about twelve or thirteen *li*, there is a stûpa which was built by King Aśôka. It constantly emits a sacred light from its surface.

In olden times when Tathâgata was practising the duties of a Bôdhisattva, he cut off his head in this place. He was then king of a great country, and his name was Chandraprabha. By so doing he aimed to acquire the supreme wisdom of Bôdhi, and this he did through a thousand births.

By the side of the stûpa is a Sanghârâma; in old days Ku-mo-lo-to (Kumâralabdha) a master of the Sâutrântika school, composed in this place various śâstras.

From this, going about 700 *li* in a south-easterly direction, we pass through the kingdom of Săng-ho-po-lo (Siṅhapura).

After leaving the northern borders of Takshasîla, and crossing the Sindhu river about 200 *li* to the south-east, we go through a great rocky pass (*gate*). This is the spot where in olden time the Mahâsattva as a Prince Royal, gave up his body to feed the seven cubs of the starving *Wu-t'u* (*tiger cat*, cf. *Ôtu*).[1]

The land here was originally dyed with the blood of

[1] *Vide Records*, i. 146.

the Royal Prince, and now it remains of the same colour; and the shrubs and trees partake of this hue.

Again going from this in a south-easterly direction 500 *li* or so across the mountains, we come to the country of Wu-la-shi (Uraśa). Still going to the south-east, climbing precipitous passes and crossing iron bridges for 1000 *li* or so, we arrive at the country of Kaśmîr.

The capital of this country on the west borders on the Great River. There are 100 religious foundations in it, and about 5000 priests. Moreover, there are four stûpas of wonderful height and great magnificence: these were built by Aśôka-râja. Each of them has about one measure of the śarîras of Tathâgata.

When the Master of the Law first arrived at the borders (*of this kingdom*), he entered it by the stone gates, the western entrance of the kingdom. The king sent his mother and younger brother with chariots and horses to escort him. Having entered the stone gates, he visited successively the Sanghârâmas and offered his adorations; then coming to a temple he passed the night there. The name of the temple was U-sse-kia-lo (*Hushkara*).[1]

That night the priests saw a vision in their sleep; a divine being said to them: "This stranger-priest is come from Mahâ-China; he wishes to study the sacred books, and to adore the sacred traces in India."

The Masters said in humble reply: "We have not yet heard of this man."

"This man who has come (*from afar*) to seek after the Law," he added, "is surrounded by numberless good spirits, who follow him everywhere. Such a man is now in your midst—resting for the night. The merit which attaches to attention paid to distant visitors is very great. You ought now therefore to be diligently reciting the Scriptures, and exciting in him a spirit of praise. Why, then, are ye idle in these duties and plunged in sleep?"

[1] So restored by Julien, *in loc.*

The priests hearing these words awoke, and moving about, or sitting in meditation, recited the Scriptures, till morning—and then coming together they related the incident of the vision one to another, and applied themselves more earnestly to their devotions.

Thus they continued for several days, after which the Master gradually approached the capital; when distant from about it one *li* he reached the preaching-hall (*Dharmasâla*). Then the king, with his assembled ministers and all the priests belonging to the capital, advanced to the preaching-hall, and escorted him onwards, being altogether something like a thousand men, with standards and parasols, with incense and flowers filling the roads. When they met (*the Master*) they all performed a humble salutation and spread before him countless flowers as religious offerings. This done, he was invited to mount a large elephant—and thus escorted, he approached the capital.

They stopped at the *Che-ye-in-to-lo* convent (*Jayendra*). On the morrow the king besought him to enter his palace and receive his religious offerings; he also ordered several tens of the most distinguished priests (*to attend on this occasion*). The repast ended, the king invited them to open the conference, and requested the Master to discuss difficult (*parts of the doctrine*).

Observing his readiness (*joy*), and finding that having come from far, fired by a desire to learn, he had no original texts from whence to read—(*the king*) gave him twenty men to copy the Sacred Books and Sâstras; moreover, he ordered five men to wait on him and obey his orders, and to furnish him, free of expense, with whatever things he required.

The chief of the priests of that establishment was a man of high moral character. He observed with the greatest strictness the religious rules and ordinances. He was possessed of the highest intelligence, and acquainted with all the points of a true disciple. His talents were eminent; his spiritual powers exalted; and his disposition affectionate. Thus he was pleased to invite the illustrious stranger and to honour him as a guest. The Master of the Law likewise with all his heart respectfully questioned him, and night and day begged him ceaselessly to explain and give into his keeping the various Śâstras.

That eminent man was about seventy years of age—his natural forces were somewhat abated—but having had the fortune to meet with a vessel of divine power (*i.e. Hiuen-Tsiang*) he used his utmost efforts to rouse himself (*to the task of explication*). Before noon he explained the *Kosha* śâstra. After noon he explained the *Niyâya-anusârâ* śâstra—after the first watch of the night he explained the *Hêtuvidyâ* śâstra. On these occasions all the learned men within the borders (*of the kingdom*), without exception, flocked together (*to hear the discourse*). The Master of the Law, following the words of his teacher, grasped thoroughly the entire subject—he penetrated all the obscure passages and their sacred mysteries, completely.

So that eminent man was immeasurably overjoyed and spake to the body of priests in these words, "This priest of China possesses wonderful (*vast and immeasurable*) strength of wisdom. In all this congregation there is none to surpass him. By his wisdom and his virtue he is competent to join in succession to the fame of the brother of Vasubandhu (*i.e. Asañgha Bodhisattva*). What a subject for regret, indeed! that belonging to a distant land he cannot at once form a part in the bequeathed fragrance of the saints and sages!"

Then there was in the congregation certain priests versed in the doctrine of the Great Vehicle—viz., *Pi-shu-to-sang-ho* (Visuddhasiṃha), *Chin-na-fan-tu* (Jinabandhu); and of the Sarvâstavâdin school, the following: *Su-kia-mi-to-lo* (Sugatamitra), *Po-su-mi-to-lo* (Vasumitra); and of the school of the Mahâsañghikas, the following: *Su-li-ye-ti-po* (Sûryadeva), *Chin-na-ta-lo-to* (Jinatrâta).

This country from remote times was distinguished for learning, and these priests were all of high religious merit and conspicuous virtue, as well as of marked talent, and power of clear exposition of doctrine; and though the other priests (*i.e. of other nations*) were in their own way distinguished, yet they could not be compared with these—so different were they from the ordinary class.

When they first encountered the Master of the Law, because he was filled with enthusiasm for the great Masters, they did not cease to propose difficult questions, to catch him. The Master of the Law, with clear sight and unembarrassed language, answered them with no hesitation.

From this time forth the sages were abashed in his presence.

This country was formerly a Nâga's lake. Fifty years after the Nirvâna of Buddha, Madhyântika, a disciple of Ânanda, converted the dragon-king. Quitting his lake he founded 500 Sañghârâmas, and invited sages and saints to come and dwell there, and receive the religious offerings of the Nâgas.

After this, Kanishka, king of Gandhâra, in the four hundredth year from the Nirvâna of Tathâgata, at the request of Parśvika, convoked an assembly of saintly men, who were conversant with the esoteric doctrine of the three Piṭakas, and had investigated the exoteric doctrine of the five vidyâs.[1]

Thus 499 men came together, and these, with the venerable Vasumitra, composed 500. The saints and sages then assembled, and recited connectedly the three piṭakas.

First they composed, in ten myriad stanzas, the *Upadêsha-sâstra*, to explain the Sûtra piṭaka.

[1] The text is here defective.

Next in ten myriad stanzas they composed the *Vinaya-vibâshâ-sâstra*, to explain the Vinaya.

Next they composed, in ten myriad verses, the *Abhidhama-Vibâshâ-sâstra*.

Altogether they composed thirty myriad of verses consisting of ninety-six myriad words.

The king ordered these Śâstras to be engraved on sheets of copper, which he enclosed in a stone chest, sealed and inscribed. Then he built a great stûpa and placed the chest within it, commanding the Yaksha spirits to protect and defend it.

The increased light thrown on the very mysterious doctrines of religion, is the result (*force*) of this (*conduct*).

Thus having halted here, first and last, for two years, and having studied the Sûtras and Śâstras, and paid reverence to the sacred traces, the Master took his leave.

Proceeding in a south-westerly direction, he crossed mountains and streams, and going 700 *li*, he came to the kingdom of Pun-nu-tso (*Punach*).

Thence going east 400 *li* or so, he came to Ho-lo-she-pu-lo (*Râjapuri*).

From this, going south-east down the mountains and crossing the river, after 700[1] *li* or so, he came to the kingdom of Tseh-kia (*Ṭakka*).

From Lan-po (*Lamghan*) till arriving in this territory, the common people (being residents in a frontier country of a wild character), differ to some degree in their manners, clothing, and language, from India, having the customs of outlying and scattered districts.

Going from the country of Râjapuri, after two days they crossed the Chandrabhâga[2] river, and came to the town of Che-ye-pu-lo (*Jayapura*), where they lodged for the night in a temple belonging to the heretics. This

[1] Julien has, by mistake, 200 *li*.

[2] The Chenâb.

temple was outside the western gate of the town, and at this time contained about twenty disciples.[1] The day after the morrow, they reached the town of Che-kia-lo (*Sákala*). In this town is a Sanghârâma with about a hundred priests. In the old days Vasubandhu Bodhisattva here composed the treatise *Shing-i-tai-lun.*[2] By the side of the convent is a stûpa, about 200 feet high. This is the spot where in former times the four Buddhas preached the law. They bequeathed traces of their footsteps as they walked to and fro which are still visible.

Leaving this place he arrived at a great forest of *Po-lo-che* trees (Palâśas), just to the eastward of the town of Na-lo-săng-ho (*Nárasiṁha*). In the forest he encountered a band of fifty robbers. These men, having taken the clothes and goods of the Master of the Law and his companions, without leaving anything, then pursued them, sword in hand, till they reached a dried-up marsh, ready to slay them all. This marsh was covered with a tangled mass of prickly, matted creepers. The Master of the Law and the Śrâmaneras who accompanied him, looking eagerly through the interstices of the wood, saw on the southern side of the marsh a water-course wide and deep enough to contain several men. Having privately told the Master of this, he and they together passed through it, and coming out on the south-east side, they ran as quickly as they could for two or three *li*, when they met a Brahman at work ploughing the land.

When they told this man about the robbers he was very much frightened, and immediately unyoked his oxen, and went with the Master to the village. Here he assembled the people by blowing the conch and beating of drums. When he had got about eighty men, each taking what weapon he could, they went in haste to the place where the robbers were. The robbers seeing the crowd of men, quickly dispersed and entered the forest.

[1] The original is ambiguous: it may refer to the number of the company with whom Hiuen-Tsiang travelled. [2] *Cf.* No. 1193, Nanj. B.'s *Cat*

The Master of the Law forthwith went towards the marsh and liberated the men who were bound; and all the people charitably divided their garments among them and conducted them to the village to pass the night.

And now whilst the men were weeping and lamenting, the Master of the Law alone was smiling merrily (*without sorrow*). On this his companions asked him, and said: "The robbers have thoroughly despoiled us of our travelling robes and goods; and we have only just escaped with our lives. Being beggared thus, our difficulties and dangers are at their extremest point. When we reflect and think of the circumstances that occurred in the forest, we cannot but experience the greatest sorrow. How is it that the Master alone does not share in our sorrow, but is able to keep a smile on his face?"

Answering, he said: "The greatest gift which living creatures possess, is life. If life is safe, what need we care about the rest? So in the current books of my country it is said: 'The great treasure of heaven and earth is life;[1] whilst life lasts, so long let the great treasure be prized!' A few garments and a few goods, why care for these so much?"

From these remarks his companions understood fully that as the turbulent waves of a river do not disturb its pure water beneath, so was he.

On the morrow he arrived at the eastern frontiers of the kingdom of Tcheka (*Ṭakka*) and entered a great city.[2]

On the west of the city on the north side of the road, there is a great forest of *An-lo* (Âmra) trees; in this forest dwelt a Brâhmaṇ of 700 years (*sic*),[3] who in appearance was but about thirty years old. His form and complexion were perfect (*of the first class*). His understanding was of a divine character: his reasoning powers, superabundant. He had thoroughly investigated the *chung*

[1] Cf. *St. Matth.* vi. 25.
[2] Probably *Lahore.*
[3] Probably for 170.

and *pih* śâstras (the *Prâṇyamula* and the *Śataśâstra*); he was eminent in the study of the Vedas, and other books. He had two followers, each of whom was aged 100 years or more. When he had an interview with the Master of the Law he was overjoyed in affording him hospitality; and when he heard of the adventure with the robbers he sent one of his servants to tell the people of the town, who were Buddhists, to prepare food for the Master of the Law. In this town there were several thousand dwellings; a few of the people were believers in Buddha, but most of them were heretics (*sacrificing heretics*).

Whilst in the country of Kaśmir, the renown of the Master of the Law had been noised abroad, and the neighbouring countries all knew of it: the messenger, therefore, from the Brâhmaṇ, came to the neighbouring city, and announced as follows: "The priest from China has come to our neighbourhood, and robbers have spoiled him of his clothes and effects: now then let all who hear me understand that this is an opportunity for adding to the amount of their religious merit."

In consequence of this address of the messenger, all hostile religious feeling was laid aside, and some 300 persons of distinction, having heard the circumstances, came together and brought a length of cotton stuff and provisions for eating and drinking, which they respectfully presented to him, placing them before him with extreme humility and reverence.

The Master of the Law, after repeating certain forms of prayer (*incantations*), further proceeded to declare the doctrine of rewards and punishments, as a consequence of present conduct. In consequence of this the men arrived at a knowledge of truth and gave up their erroneous doctrine and returned to right reason. Thus with joyous words and light heart they held their intercourse with the Master and returned.

The aged (*Brahman*) was overjoyed at this wonderful event. Meanwhile the Master divided the cotton stuff among the different persons of the company, each person receiving several pieces for making garments, and when there was still some left, he presented five pieces (*to the Brahman*) in addition.

Here he remained for one month studying the Sûtras, the *Peh-lun* (Śata-śâstra), the *Kwang-peh-lun* (Śata-śâstra vâipulyam). The author of this work (*i.e. Dêva Bôdhisattva*) was a disciple of Nâgârjuna, who himself having received the doctrines of his master, expounded them with clearness.

From this place going 500 *li* to the east, he arrived at the kingdom of *Chi-na-po-tai* (Chînapati), and took up his quarters in the convent called *Tu-she-sa-na* (?). Here there was a renowned priest named Pi-ni-to-poh-la-pó (*Vinitaprabha*). He was of a good reputation and had mastered the three piṭakas. He had himself composed a commentary on the Pañchaskhanda Śâstra, and on the Vidyâmâtrasiddhi-Trîdaśaśâstra.

On this account the Master remained there fourteen months. He studied the Abhidharma Śâstra, the Abhidharma-prakarana-sâsana-Śâstra, the Nyâyadvâra-târaka Śâstra, and others.

To the south-east of the capital, after going 50 *li* or so, we arrive at the Tâmasavana Saṅghârâma; in this convent there are some 300 priests, who belong to the Sarvâstivâdina school.

The thousand Buddhas of the Bhadra Kalpa, are to assemble in this place with both men and Devas, to preach the law to them.

In the 300th year after the Nirvâna of Śâkya Tathâgata, there lived a master of Śâstras called Kâtyâyana who composed in this place the Jnâna-prasthâna Śâstra.

From this, going north-east 140 or 150 *li*, we come to the kingdom of Jâlandhara.[1] On entering this country the pilgrim went to the Nagaradhana convent, where

[1] *Vide Records*, i. 170.

there was an eminent priest called Chandravarma, who was thoroughly acquainted with the Tripiṭaka.

On this account he rested here four months, studying the *Prakaraṇa-pâda-vibâshâ-Sâstra*.

From this, going north-east after traversing precipitous mountain passes and going 700 *li* or so, he arrived at the kingdom of Kulûta.

From Kulûta, going about 700 *li* south across a mountain range and over a river, we arrive at the kingdom of She-to-tu-lu (*Śatadru*).

Going south-west from this kingdom about 800 *li*, we come to the kingdom of Po-li-ye-ta-lo (*Pâryâtra*).

From this, going east about 500 *li*, we come to the kingdom of Mo-t'u-lo (Mathurâ).

There are Stûpas containing relics of the bodies of Sâkya Tathâgata and his holy disciples still existing in this place: to wit, of Sâriputra, of Maudgalyâyana, of Purnamâitreyânîputra, of Upâli, of Ânanda, of Râhula, and of Mañjus'ri.

Every year, on religious festival days, priests and disciples assemble at these several stûpas, according to their school, and offer religious worship and offerings.

The followers of the Abhidharma offer to Sâriputra; the Quietists (*those who practice meditation*) offer to Maudgalyâyana; the students of the Sûtras offer to Purnamâitreyânîputra; the followers of the Vinaya offer to Upâli; the Bhikshunis offer to Ananda; the Srâmaṇeras offer to Râhula; the followers of the Great Vehicle offer to the Bôdhisattvas.

Five or six *li* to the east of the city there is a mountain Saṅghârâma which was founded by the venerable Upagupta: there are herein relics of his nails and hair.

In a precipice to the north of the Saṅghârâma there is a stone house about twenty feet high and thirty feet wide. Within this cave there are heaped up a number of bamboo splints, about four inches long. The venerable Upagupta,[1] when he preached the law and led a husband and wife to the attainment of the fruit of Arhatship, for each one so converted deposited in this cave one bamboo slip: but as to others (*not so related*) although they attained the fruit, he did not record their conversion.

Going north-east from this about 500 *li*, we come to Sa-ta-ni-shi-fa-lo (*Sthânêśvara*). Still going east about 400 *li* we come to Lu-le-na (*Srughna ?*).[2]

On the east this kingdom borders on the river Ganges, on the north it abuts on a great mountain (*range*), through its centre flows the river Yamunâ (*Jumnâ*).

Going about 800 *li* to the east of this river we come to the source of the river Ganges. This head-stream is about three or four *li* in width; it flows south-east, and where it enters the sea it is about ten *li* in width. Its waters are sweet and soft to the taste, and the stream carries with it sands of extreme fineness. The ordinary books of the country speak of it as the "blessed River;" those who bathe in it are cleansed from sin; those who drink its waters, or even rinse their mouth therefrom, escape from all dangers and calamities, and when they die forthwith are born in heaven, and enjoy happiness.

So the common folk, men and women, are always congregating on the banks of the river. But this is merely the heretical belief of the district, and is not true. In after times, when Dêva Bôdhisattva showed them the right meaning of all this, then the erroneous belief began to disappear.

There was a renowned priest in this kingdom named Jayagupta, who had well studied the Tripiṭaka. The Master of the Law therefore remained here one winter

[1] Upagupta, so celebrated in the Northern Legends, is unknown in the Pâli Records. This shows the radical character of the separation of the Buddhist community after the Council of Vâiśâli.

[2] As M. Julien observes, we must substitute *Su-lu-kin-na* for the symbols given in the text: *vide Records*, i. 186.

and half the spring season, and heard him explain the Vibhâshâ according to the school of the Saûtrântikas.

After this he crossed to the eastern bank of the river and came to the kingdom of Matipura.

The king of this country is of the caste of Sûdras. There are some ten Sanghârâmas and about eight hundred priests here. They study the Little Vehicle, according to the school of the Sarvâstivâdins. To the south of the capital four or five *li*, there is a little Sanghârâma with about fifty priests in it; it was here that Guṇaprabha of old composed the *Pin-chin*[1] and other Śâstras, amounting to about one hundred in all. This doctor was originally a native of Parvata, and was a student of the Great Vehicle, but afterwards he became attached to the Little Vehicle.

At this time the Arhat Dêvasêna had visited the Tushita heaven. Then Guṇaprabha wished to see Maitrêya to dispel some doubts, which hindered his religious progress. He therefore asked Dêvasêna to transport him by his spiritual power to the courts of that heaven; having looked upon Maitrêya he saluted him without prostrating himself: "I am a religious mendicant (*he thought*) in full orders; Maitrêya occupies this heaven like a layman; it is not becoming that I should prostrate myself in worship before him."

And so he came and went three times, but rendered him no homage. He was puffed up by self-conceit and got no explanation of his doubts.[2]

Three or four *li* to the south of the Sanghârâma of Guṇaprabha, there is a Sanghârâma with about two hundred priests, who also study the Little Vehicle. It was here the Doctor of Śâstras called Saṅghabhadra ended the years of his life. This doctor was originally a native of Kaśmir. He was a man of distinguished learning and great talents. He thoroughly understood the Vibhâshâ of the Sarvâstivâdin school.

1 *Vide Records*, vol. i. p. 191, n.
2 *Vide* the whole of this story, *Records*, i. 192

At this time Vasubandhu Bôdhisattva had also disnguished himself for his profound learning. He had already composed the Abhidharma-Kosha-Śâstra to confute the professors of the Vibhâshâ. His deep reasoning and ornate style were the admiration of all Western students. The very spirits and demons also studied and followed his teaching.

From the time of Saṅghabhadra's appearance (*as an author*), his mind had become full of impatient desire.

After twelve years of extended reflection he composed the Kôsha-karikâ-śâstra, in 25,000 ślôkas, and eighty myriad words. Having finished it, he longed for an interview with Vasubandhu, to settle the truth or falsehood of his points. But he died without attaining this object. Afterwards Vasubandhu saw the treatise, and loudly praised its wise comments, and said: "The force of the thoughts herein contained is not inferior to that of the followers of the Vibhâshâ school. Nevertheless, as its leading principles are entirely in agreement with my own, let it be named the Nyâyânusâra Śâstra;" accordingly it was so done, in agreement with this opinion.

After Saṅghabhadra's death they erected to his memory a stûpa in an Âmra grove, that still remains; by the side of this grove there is a stûpa which contains the relics of Vimalamitra, a Doctor of Śâstras. This doctor was a native of the country of Kaśmir; he belonged to the school of the Sarvâstavâdins, and had travelled through the five Indias, and was deeply versed in the Tripiṭakas.

Being about to return to his own country, as he passed on his way by the stûpa of Saṅghabhadra, he was deeply affected to think that the undertaking of this doctor had not been matured and published before his death; and so, moved by the thought, he took an oath that he would himself compose such treatises as would overcome the principles of the Great Vehicle, and put out the name of

Vasubandhu; and so he thought to perpetuate for ever the fame of the Doctor (Saṅghabhadra).

After having said this, his intellect became confused, his bowels and tongue protruded, and his blood burst forth over all his body.[1] Then perceiving that the origin of his sufferings was from his perverse views, he tore up his writings and with deep contrition exhorted his disciples never to abuse the principles of the Great Vehicle, and so saying, he died. Where he died the earth opened and there is a great ditch.

In this kingdom there was an eminent priest called Mitrasêna, ninety years of age. He was a disciple of Guṇaprabha and deeply versed in the Tripiṭakas. The Master of the Law stopped with him half the spring and the summer following, studying the Tattvasạtya śâstra, the Abhidharma-jnāna-prasthâna-śâstra, and others.

Proceeding northward from this 300 *li* or so, we come to the country of *Po-lo-hi-mo-pu-lo* (Brâhmapura); again south-east of this, going 400 *li* or so, we come to the kingdom of *Hi-chi-ta-lo* (Ahikshêtra).

Again, going south 200 *li* or so, we cross the Ganges, and then going south-west we arrive at the country of *Pi-lo-na*[2]*-na* (Vîrasana).

Again, going east 200 *li* or so, we come to the country of *Kie-pi-tha* (Kapitha).

About twenty *li* to the east of the city there is a Saṅghârâma, within the court of which there are three ladders composed of the precious substances;[3] they are placed (*side by side*) in a direction from south to north and face the east. It was down one of these that Buddha of old descended from the Taryastriṁshas heaven, and returned to Jambudvîpa after preaching for the sake of his queen-mother Mâya.[4] The middle ladder is of gold,

[1] *Records*, i. 197.

[2] *Na* for *shan*. *Records*, i. 201.

[3] Literally, "three precious ladders."

[4] In Legge's translation of *Fâ-hien*, p. 43 n. 2, the author speaks of Mâya being re-born in the Tuśita heaven, adopting an error of Eitel's, which he had corrected.

the one on the left of crystal, the one on the right of silver. Tathâgata, leaving the Saddharma Hall,[1] accompanied by the congregation of Dêvas, descended by the middle ladder; Mahâbrâhma, with a white chowrie in his hand, descended by the silver ladder on the right; whilst on the left Śakradeva, with a precious parasol, came down by the crystal ladder.[2]

At this time a 100,000 dêvas and the great Bôdhisattvas followed him in his descent.

Several centuries ago these ladders existed in their integrity; but at the present time they have disappeared (*been swallowed up*). Kings who came afterwards, from a principle of affection and respect, have reconstructed the foundations of these ladders with stone and brick, ornamented with various gems, to a height of about seventy feet, and over this they have erected a Vihâra, in which is placed a figure of Buddha in stone.[3] On the right and left of this statue are the figures of Brâhma and Śakra, very glorious in appearance and just as in the original. At the side is a stone pillar in height seventy feet, placed there by Aśôka-râja.

Near this is a stone foundation (*raised path*) fifty paces or so in length, and seven feet high; this is the spot where Buddha formerly paced to and fro.

From this, going north-west 200 *li*, we come to Kie-jo-kio-she-kwŏ (*Kanauj*).

This kingdom is four thousand *li* in circuit; the capital borders on the Ganges on the West; it is about twenty *li* in length, and five or six *li* across.

There are about 100 Sanghârâmas and 10,000 priests.

[1] That is, the preaching hall of Śâkra.

[2] *Vide Records*, i. 203.

[3] Julien translates, "in the middle of which is placed," &c. This is correct enough, and shows that the symbol *tang* in *Fâ-hien* (*cap.* 17), referring to this story, ought to be translated "facing" or "opposite to" the middle ladder, &c.

The priests study the Great and Small Vehicle promiscuously.

The king is a Bais Rajput.[1] His name is Harshavardhana; his father's name was Prakaravardhana;[2] his senior brother was called Râjyavardhana. Harshavardhana, the present king, is virtuous and patriotic; all people celebrate his praises in songs.

At the time (*when Râjyavardhana was on the throne*) the king of Karṇa-survarṇa, in Eastern India, whose name was Śasañka-râja, hating the superior military talents of this king, made a plot and murdered him.

Then the great minister Bhaṇi[3] and the subordinate officers, afflicted to see the people without a ruler, agreed to place on the throne his younger brother Śilâditya.[4] His royal appearance and demeanour were recognised, in conjunction with his vast military talents. His qualifications moved heaven and earth; his sense of justice was admired by Dêvas and men. He was soon able to avenge the injuries received by his brother, and to make himself master of India. His renown was spread abroad everywhere, and all his subjects reverenced his virtues. The empire having gained rest, then the people were at peace. On this he put an end to warlike expeditions, and began to store up in the magazines, the lances and swords. He gave himself up to religious duties; he prohibited the slaughter of any living creature. He himself set the example, and ordered all his people to abstain from flesh meat, and he founded Sanghârâmas wherever there were sacred traces of religion.

Yearly during three or seven days (or, perhaps, *during three seven-days*, i.e. *three weeks*) he provided food for the whole body of priests.

Every fifth year he convoked a grand assembly of deliverance (*Mahâ-môksha-parishad*), and distributed the

[1] *Vide Records*, i. 209, n. 12.

[2] For Prabhâkaravarddhana.

[3] *Vide Records*, i. 210, n. 18. He is also called Bhaṇḍi (Max Müller's *India*, p. 288).

[4] That is, Silâditya Harshavardhana.

stores of his treasuries in charity. To describe all his conduct, would be but to tell again the deeds of Sudâna.[1]

To the north-west of the city is a Stûpa about 200 feet high.

Six or seven *li* to the south-east, south of the river Ganges, is a Stûpa also about 200 feet high. Both were built by Aśôka-râja, in places where Buddha had formerly preached the law.

When the Master entered the kingdom he went to the temple called Bhadra-Vihâra. He stopped there three months, and under the direction of Viryasêna, a doctor of the three Piṭakas, he read the Vibhâshâ of Buddhadâsa, which is called *Varmavibhasha-vyâkaraṇa.*[2]

[1] That is, Prince Visvântara, the hero of the Wessantara Jâtaka. He must be distinguished from Sudatta, *i.e.* Anâthapiṇḍika. This is plain from a comparison with *Sung-Yun's* account (*Records*, I xcviii.) Julien's note therefore (*in loc.*) is in error.

[2] I see no other way of translating this passage. Julien seems to have had a different text. The sentence in my original is, "*Yueh* (*i.e.*, *viz.*) *chan-pi-po-sha-ki.*" Instead of *yueh*, Julien's text seems to have had *Shing*. Concerning the Vibhâshâ composed by Buddhadâsa, *vide Records*, i. 230.

BOOK III.

From Ayôdhyâ to Hiranyaparvata.

FROM this, going 600 *li* or so to the south-east and crossing the Ganges, on the south of the river we come to the kingdom of *'O-yu-to* (Ayôdhyâ). There are here about one hundred temples with several thousand priests, who study both the Small and the Great Vehicle.

In the capital city is an old Sanghârâma. Here the Bodhisattva Vasubandhu composed his treatises on the Great and Little Vehicle, and preached for the good of the community.

North-west of the city four or five *li*, and by the side of the river Ganges, is a great Sanghârâma, in which is a Stûpa about 200 feet high. This was built by Aśôka râja on the spot where Buddha in old days delivered the Law for three months.

By the side of this Stûpa is a spot where the four Buddhas of the past age walked for exercise.

To the south-west of the city five or six *li*, is an old Sanghârâma; this is the place where Asañgha Bôdhisattva explained the Law. The Bôdhisattva, during the night, ascended to the Tuśíta heaven, and received from Mâitreya Bôdhisattva the Yôga-śâstra, the Alaṁkâra-Mahâyâna-śâstra, and the Madhyânta-vibhañgha-śâstra. The next day he descended from the heaven, and declared the Law for the sake of the community.

Asañgha, who is also called Wu-cho, was a man of Gandhâra. He was born in the middle of the thousand years following the Nirvâna of Buddha,[1] and became a

[1] That is, the middle of "the period of images," beginning 500 years after the Nirvâna.

disciple in the school of the Mahîsâsakas. Afterwards he joined the school of the Great Vehicle. His brother, Vasubandhu, became a disciple in the school of the Sarvâstivâdins, but afterwards joined the Great Vehicle. Both these brothers were, in point of endowments, vessels full of wisdom and holiness. Asañgha possessed vast ability in composition, and wrote many śâstras, in explanation of, and comment on, the Great Vehicle. He was the principal composer of śâstras in India. For example, he wrote the Mahâyâna-samparigraha-śâstra,[1] the Prakaraṇâryavâchâ-śâstra-kârikâ, the Abhidharma śâstra, the Vidyâmâtra-śâstra, the Kosha-śâstra, and others.

The Master of the Law left the kingdom of Ayôdhyâ, having paid reverence to the sacred traces, and following the course of the river Ganges, proceeded eastward, being on board a vessel with about eighty other fellow-passengers. He wished to reach the kingdom of *'O-ye-mu-khi* (Hayamukha).[2] After going about a hundred *li*, both banks of the river were shrouded by the thick foliage of an Aśôka forest, and amid these trees on either bank were concealed some ten pirate boats. Then these boats, propelled by oars, all at once burst forth into the mid-stream. Some of those in the ship, terrified at the sight, cast themselves into the river, whilst the pirates, taking the ship in tow, brought it to the bank. They then ordered the men to take off their clothes, and searched them in quest of jewels and precious stones.

Now these pirates pay worship to Dûrga, a spirit of heaven, and every year during the autumn, they look out for a man of good form and comely features, whom they kill, and offer his flesh and blood in sacrifice to their divinity, to procure good fortune. Seeing that the Master of the Law was suitable for their purpose, both

[1] B. Nanj. Cat., No. 1202.
[2] *Vide Records*, &c., vol. i. p. 229.

in respect of his distinguished bearing and his bodily strength and appearance, they exchanged joyful glances, and said, "We were letting the season for sacrificing to our god pass by, because we could not find a suitable person for it, but now this Śraman is of noble form and pleasing features—let us kill him as a sacrifice, and we shall gain certain good fortune."

The Master of the Law replied, "If this poor and defiled body of mine is indeed suitable for the purpose of the sacrifice you propose, I, in truth, dare not grudge (*the offering*), but as my intention in coming from a distance was to pay reverence to the image of Bôdhi and the Gṛîdhrakûta Mountain, and to inquire as to the character of the Sacred Books and the Law (or, *the Law of the Sacred Books*), and as this purpose has not yet been accomplished, if you, my noble benefactors (*dânapatis*) kill this body of mine, I fear it will bring you misfortune (*instead of good fortune*)."

Moreover, his fellow-passengers all, with one voice, asked them to spare him, and some even prayed to be allowed to die in his stead; but the pirates would not consent.

Then the captain of the gang despatched some men with water to arrange the ground, and to erect in the midst of the flowering grove an altar besmeared with mud. He then commanded two of the company to take their drawn knives and to bind the Master of the Law upon the altar. And now, when they were about to use their knives for the purpose of sacrificing him, the Master of the Law showed no sign of fear in his face, insomuch that all the pirates were moved to astonishment.

When he saw there was no escape, however, he spoke to the pirates and begged them to allow him a little time and not to crowd round him painfully—but "let me," he said, "with a joyous mind, take my departure."

Then the Master of the Law, with an undivided mind

bent on the courts of Tuśita heaven, thought on the Bôdhisattva Mâitrêya, and earnestly prayed to be born in that place, that he might pay reverence and his religious offerings (*to the Bôdhisattva*), and receive from him the Yogâchariya-bhûmi-śâstra, and listen to the sound of the excellent Law. Then having perfected himself throughout in wisdom, "let me return (*he prayed*) and be born here below, that I may instruct and convert these men, and cause them to practise themselves in doing good and to give up their evil deeds, and thus by diffusing, far and wide, the benefits of religion, to give rest to all the world."

Then the Master of the Law, paying worship to the Buddhas of the ten regions, collected his mind into perfect composure, and sitting still, fixed his thoughts on Mâitrêya without any interruption. Thus he seemed in his innermost thoughts as if he rose up above Mount Sumeru and successively ascending one, two, three heavens, he gazed upon the courts of Tuśita, the place of Mâitrêya, with its excellently precious adornments (*galleries*) and the multitude of devas surrounding him on every side. At this time his body and soul were ravished with joy, he knew nothing of the altar on which he was, he had no recollection of the robbers. And now, whilst his fellow passengers gave way to cries and tears, suddenly a black tempest (*typhoon*) arose from the four quarters of heaven, smiting down the trees; clouds of sand flew on every side; and the lashing waves of the river tossed the boats to and fro. The robbers and their company, greatly terrified, asked the companions of the Master, "Whence comes this Śraman?—what is his name and title?" and so on. They, answering, said: "He comes from the country of China—he is the renowned person who is in search of the Law; if you, my masters, kill him, your guilt will be immeasurable; look now and see the winds and waves—these are but indications of the anger of the spirits of heaven: haste then to repent!"

The pirates then, filled with fear, urged each other to repentance and confession of their fault; then with bowed heads they made profound obeisance (or, *they embraced the religion of Buddha*). And now one of the robbers accidentally touching the Master of the Law with his hand (or, *touching the hand of the Master of the Law*), he opened his eyes and said to the robber, "Has the hour come?" The robber answered: "We dare not hurt the Master! we pray you accept our repentance!" The Master then accepted their reverence and confession of faults, and then preached to them about the future punishment in Avîchi[1] of those who gave themselves up to murder, robbery, and impious sacrifices, and other evil deeds. "How would you then risk the woes of the long-during asañkhêya of ages for the sake of this body of yours, which is but in point of time as the lightning flash or the dew of the morning?"

The robbers then bowed their heads and confessed their faults, saying: "We indeed, individually, were perverted by a foolish tone of mind, and led to do what we ought not to do, and to sacrifice (*pay religious rites*) to what we ought not to sacrifice. If we had not met with the Master—whose religious merit has moved even the mysterious powers of heaven—how should we ever have been led to repentance? And now we ask to give up from the present day these evil ways of ours, and we pray the Master to be witness to our sincerity!"

On this they each encouraged one another to deeds of amendment, and collecting their various instruments of robbery together, they cast them into the river, and whatever clothes or private property they had taken, they restored these to their rightful owners, and then they took on themselves the five obligations of a lay-believer.

Then the winds and the floods subsided, and the

[1] The lowest of the Buddhist hells.

pirates were all overcome with joy, and bowed their heads in adoration. His fellow voyagers, moreover, were filled with surprise and admiration more than ever, whilst those present and absent who heard of the event could not help exclaiming with wonder at the occurrence: "If it were not for the power of his high resolve in seeking for the Law, this could not have come to pass!"

From this, going east about 300 *li*, after crossing the Ganges to the north side, we come to *'O-ye-muh-khi* (Hayamukha).

From this, going south-east 700 *li* or so, after crossing to the south side of the Ganges, on the north of the River Jumnâ, we come to the country of Prayâga.

To the south-west of the town, in a grove of Champaka flowers, there is a stûpa built by Aśôka-râja. This is the spot where in old days Buddha overcame the heretic (or, *heretics*). By the side of it is a Sanghârâma. Here Dêva Bôdhisattva composed the enlarged Śata-śâstra and vanquished the heretics of the Little Vehicle. To the east of the capital is the spot where the two rivers join, and to the west of this point is a level plain about fourteen or fifteen *li* in circuit. The ground is perfectly level and straight. From ancient days till now, royal and noble personages endowed with virtue and love, in the distribution of their charitable offerings, have all resorted to this spot for the purpose; and hence the name of the *Field of Great Beneficence* has been given to it. At the present time Śilâditya râja, following this custom, has distributed here the accumulated wealth of five years, during a period of seventy-five days. From the three precious objects (*Buddha, Dharma, Samgha*), down to the poorest orphan, there is no one but has shared in his bounty.

From this, in a south-west direction, we enter a great

forest, in which we frequently encounter evil beasts and wild elephants. After going 500 [1] *li* or so, we arrive at *Kiau-shang-mi* (Kauśâmbî).

There are about ten Saṅghârâmas here, with some 300 priests. Within the city is an old (or, *ruined*) palace (*i.e. palace-precinct*), in which is a large Vihâra about sixty feet high, in which is a sandal-wood figure of Buddha, surmounted by a stone canopy, made by King Udâyana.

In old times Tathâgata dwelt during an entire season of Rest in the Trayâstriṁshas heaven, for the purpose of preaching to his mother. The king, thinking of him with affection, requested Mâudgalyâyana to transport a clever sculptor to this heaven, who might observe the honourable features and figure of Buddha, and on his return might carve from sandal-wood a true likeness of his appearance. When the Lord of the World came down again, this was the figure which arose to meet him.

South of this is a ruined dwelling, the old house of the nobleman [2] Gośira.

Not far south of the city is an old Saughârâma, which was built on the garden-site of this nobleman. In it is a stûpa, about 200 feet high, which was raised by Aśôka-râja.

Again, south-east of this, is a double-storeyed tower, where Vasubandhu composed the Vidyâmâtra-siddhi-śâstra.

Again, to the east, is an Âmra grove, in which are some old foundation stones.[3] This is where Asañgha Bôdhisattva composed the Prakaraṇâryavâchâ - śâstra-kârikâ.[4]

Going about 500 *li* from this, we come to the kingdom

[1] In my translation of the *Si-yu-ki*, p. 234, I have, by mistake, said that Hwui-lih (*i.e.* the present work) states the distance as 50 *li*.

[2] *Chang-ché.*

[3] *Ku-ki.* This expression is constantly used by Hiuen-Tsiang where Fa-hien only uses the symbol *ku*; showing plainly enough that Fa-hien would denote that the buildings he refers to are in ruins. Julien also translates *ku* by *ruins*, Jul. i. 122, l. 11.

[4] N. B., 1202.

of Pi-so-kia (*Viśâkhâ*). It has about twenty Sanghârâmas and some 3000 priests, belonging to the Sammatîya school of the Little Vehicle.

On the left-hand side of the road which goes south-east is a great Sanghârâma. This is where in old days the Arhat Devaśarman composed the Vijñâna-kâya-pâda-śâstra, which affirms the non-existence of "self," or, of (*individual*) man. Here also the Arhat Gôpa composed the śâstra *Shing-Kiau-in-Shih*, which affirmed the existence of "self," and of "(*individual*) man." These views of religious doctrine led to many wrangling treatises.

Here also is the place where Dharmapâla Bôdhisattva during seven days overthrew a hundred writers of *śâstras* belonging to the Little Vehicle. By the side of this spot is the place where Tathâgata during six years preached the Law.

There is a tree here about seventy feet high. Here in former days Buddha, having cleaned his teeth, flung the fragments of the wood on the ground. Immediately they took root, and the umbrageous tree which grew up remains there till now. The followers of heretical views often came to destroy it, but as often as they cut it down it grew up again as flourishing and verdant as at first.

Going north-east from this 500 *li* or so, we arrive at the kingdom of Shi-lo-fu-shi-ti (Śrâvastî). It is about 6000 *li* in circuit and has several hundred Sanghârâmas and several thousand priests,[1] all of whom belong to the Sammatiya school. The capital of this country was where King Prasênajita dwelt when Buddha was alive.

Within the city there are the old ruins (*ku ki*) of the king's palace.

Not far east from this is a stûpa erected on some old foundations; this was the spot where stood a great

[1] This seems to contradict the account found in the Si-yu-ki *Records* (ii. 2), unless the symbol "*sho*" be taken as a verb; the passage would then read, "the Sanghârâmas amount to 100 and the disciples amount to 1000.

preaching hall erected by King Prasênajita for Buddha's use.

Next we see a tower; this was where stood the Vihâra of Prajâpati Bhikshunî, the elder maternal aunt of Buddha.

East of this again is a tower; this marks the spot of the ruined house [1] of Sudatta. By the side of the house is a great stûpa; this is where the Añgulimâlya gave up his evil design (or, *heresy*).

Five or six *li* to the south of the city is the grove of Jeta, the same as "the garden of the Friend of the orphans and desolate." There was formerly a Sanghârâma here, but now it has been overturned and destroyed.

On the right and left side of the eastern gate [2] there have been built stone pillars about seventy feet high. These were placed there by Aśôka râja. All the rooms are completely destroyed except one little stone chamber in which there is a golden figure. This figure was made by King Prasênajita when Buddha in old days ascended to the Trayastriṁshas heaven to preach for his mother's sake. The king's heart being deeply affected, and hearing that King Udâyana had caused a sandal-wood figure to be made, he, on that account, made this one.

Behind the convent, not far, is where the Brahmachâri heretic killed the woman and accused Buddha of the murder.[3]

To the east of the convent about 100 paces is a great chasm; this is where Devadatta went down alive into hell after trying to poison Buddha. To the south of this, again, is a great ditch; this is the place where the Bhikshu Kukâlî went down alive into hell after slandering Buddha. To the south of this, about 800 paces, is the place where

[1] I might perhaps say "ruinous house," but the whole context shows that *ku* has the sense of what we should call dilapidated.

[2] That is, of the "entrance gate" or "principal door;" it is difficult to know what Dr. Legge means in his translation of Fa-hien, when he says, "on each side of the door, when open, there was a stone pillar" (*o. c.*, p. 56). Were the pillars not there when the door was shut?

[3] I have no doubt that the woman Sundarî was killed, and not that she killed another.

the Brahman woman Chañścha went down alive into hell after slandering Buddha. All these chasms are without any visible bottom (*are bottomless pits*).

To the eastward of the Sanghârâma about seventy paces is a Vihâra-Sanghârâma, lofty and large, in which is a sitting figure of Buddha facing the east. This is the place where in old times Buddha disputed with all the heretics.

To the east of this, again, is a Dêva temple equal in size to the Vihâra; when the sun's rays move in the direction of these buildings—the shadow of the Dêva temple does not reach the Vihâra, but the shadow of the Vihâra always enshrouds the temple.

East from this three or four *li*, is a Stûpa; this is the place where Śâriputra discussed with the heretics.

North-west of the capital city sixty *li* or so, is an old (*ruinous*) city. This was the town of the father of Kâśyapa Buddha, who lived during the Bhadra Kalpa when men's lives reached to 20,000 years.

To the south of the city is the place where (*this*) Buddha first saw his father after having arrived at perfect enlightenment.

To the north of the city is a tower. This tower contains the relics of the entire body of Kâśyapa Buddha. All these were founded by Aśôka-râja.

From this, going south-east about 800 *li*, we come to the kingdom of Kapilavastu. This country is about 4000 *li* in circuit; the capital, as well as some 1000 villages, are all waste and ruined. The inner city is fifteen *li* round; it is completely encircled and is exceedingly strong.[1]

Within the city are some old foundations (*ku ki*)[2]

[1] But probably there is a mistake in the text, and it should be "it is built of bricks and is," &c.

[2] In this and all the following cases the ruined condition of the buildings is denoted in Fâ-hien by the symbol "*ku*."

belonging to the chief palace of Suddhôdana râja. Over these ruins a Vihâra has been built in which is a figure of the king.

To the north of this, again, are some old foundations; these belong to the sleeping hall of Queen Mâya. Over this site is built a Vihâra, in which is a figure of the queen. By the side of this is a Vihâra; this is where Sâkya Bôdhisattva descended *as a spirit*,[1] into the womb of his mother. In it is placed a picture of Bôdhisattva descending to be born.

The Sthavira school says that this took place on the 30th day of the month U-tan-lo-'an-sha-cha (*Uttarâshâḍha*), descending as a spirit into his mother's womb on that evening. This would be the 15th day of the fifth month (*with us*). The other schools fix the 23rd day of the month, which would correspond with the 8th day of the fifth month (*with us*).

To the north-east of this is a Stûpa; this is the spot where the Rishi Asita took the horoscope of the prince royal.

On the left and right of the city is the place where the royal prince contended in athletic sports with the Śâkyas.

Again there is the place where the royal prince left the city on horseback (*i.e. when he gave up his secular life*).

And there are the places where he turned back in his chariot, having first seen outside the four gates, the old man, the sick man, the dead man, and the Śraman, who had given up the world from disgust.

[1] Julien translates the passage as though "*shin*" referred to Mâya, and he makes the expression equal to "his divine mother." But this has no authority, and is expressly contradicted in the *Si-yu-ki* (K. vi. fol. 9. a. col. 2 and col. 5), where it is said "the picture of the descent as a spirit" (there being no mention of Mâya) is on the wall of the palace (cf. v. 4. Kiuen I. of the *Buddhacharita*). This leads me to observe that the descent of Buddha as a spirit, does *not* mean that he descended in the *shape of an elephant*, but that he was *riding on an elephant*, but being a *spirit* was invisible. *Vide* the Chinese picture in *Legge's* Fâ-hien, p. 65.

From this, going through a wild forest about 500 *li* east, we come to the country of Râma (Râmagrâma). This country has but few houses or inhabitants.

To the east of the old city is a brick Stûpa about 100 feet high. After the Nirvâna of Tathâgata the old king of this country, having obtained a share of the relics (*Śarîras*), returned home and built this stûpa. It constantly emits rays of glory.

By the side of it is a Nâga tank. The Nâga frequently changes his appearance into that of a man, and as such encircles the tower in the practice of religion (*i.e. turning religiously with his right hand towards the tower*). Wild elephants, with flowers held in their trunks, constantly come to offer their religious offerings.

Close by the side of this Stûpa is a Sanghârâma of which a Śrâmaṇêra is the subdirector (*Karmadâna*).[1] The tradition is this:—There was formerly a Bhikshu who had induced some fellow-disciples to travel afield to pay reverence (*to the sacred spots*). Then they saw the wild elephants, carrying flowers in their trunks, lay them down before this tower. And again they saw them dig up the herbage with their tusks, and in their trunks bring water for sprinkling; the company seeing this were astonished and affected with emotion.

There was one Bhikshu in the company who resolved to give up the great rules of moral obligation, and remain there on the spot to render his religious offerings (*at the shrine*). Speaking to the others, he said: "The wild elephants, beast born as they are, know how to reverence this sacred tower; they gather flowers, and sprinkle water, and sweep! How then can we, belonging to the human race and devotees of Buddha, behold this desert spot and not render our religious assistance!"

So taking leave of his companions he remained there. He constructed a dwelling-place, cleared the land, and

[1] 寺 for 事

planted flowers, and cultivated fruits: he let not a moment pass in idleness, either during winter or summer.

The people of the neighbouring countries, hearing of him, all contributed of their wealth and valuables to construct therewith a Sanghârâma, and they besought this priest to take the direction of the establishment as steward. From this time through successive generations things have been managed according to this old plan.

Going about 100 *li* to the eastward of the Śrâmaṇêra convent through a great forest, we find a Stûpa built by Aśôka-râja. It was here that the prince royal, having passed through the city, and reaching this spot, took off his ornaments and clothes and the hair jewel of his sacred tiara, and gave them to Chandaka. Both here and where he cut off his hair there are commemorative towers.

Having left the forest we come to the kingdom of *Ku-shi-na-k'ie-lo*.[1] This place is altogether desert and waste.

Within the city at the north-east angle is a Stûpa built by Aśôka-râjâ on the site of the old house of Chunda. In the house is a well which was dug when he was about to make his religious offering. The water of this well is still sweet and clear.

Three or four *li* to the north-west of the town we cross the *'O-shi-to-fa-tai* (Ajitavatî) river. Not far from the bank of the river we come to a Śâla grove. This tree resembles the Ho: only its bark is a greenish-blue, and its leaves white, and very shining and lustrous. There are four trees in pairs, of equal height; this is the place where Buddha died.

There is a great Vihâra here, built of bricks, within which is a figure of the Nirvâna of Tathâgata; his head is towards the north, and his appearance is as if he were asleep. By the side of the Vihâra is a Stûpa about 200 feet high, constructed by Asôka râja. There is, moreover,

[1] Kuśinagara, *vide Records*, ii. 31.

a stone column standing here, which records the circumstances of the Nirvâna of Buddha, but does not state the year or the month.

The current tradition relates that Buddha lived in the world eighty years, and that he entered Nirvâna the 15th day of the latter half of the month Vaiśâkha, which corresponds with the 15th day of the second month (*with us*). The school of the Sarvâstivâdins again say that Buddha entered Nirvâna during the second half of the month Kârtika. This would correspond with the 8th day of the ninth month (*with us*).

Some say that 1200 years have passed since the Nirvâna: others, 1500 years: others, more than 900 years, but not yet the full period of 1000 years.[1]

Again, there are towers erected where Tathâgata, sitting up in his golden coffin, preached on behalf of his mother, and stretching out his arms questioned Ânanda, and showed his feet to Kâśyapa; also where they burnt his body with scented wood, and the eight kings divided his bone-relics.

Again, passing 500 *li* or so through a great forest, we come to the kingdom of Pó-lo-ni-sse (*Bânâras*).

This kingdom is about 4000 *li* in circuit. The capital borders, on the west, on the river Ganges, it is about ten *li* in length, and five or six *li* in breadth.

There are about thirty Saṅghârâmas, and 2000 priests who study the teaching of the Sarvâstivâdins, belonging to the Little Vehicle.

Crossing the *Pó-lo-ni-sse* river (Varaṇâ), and going north-east ten *li* or so, we come to the Saṅghârâma of the "Stag-desert." The lofty turrets (*of the convent*) mingle with the clouds, and the long galleries unite at the four corners of the building. There are about 1500 priests here, who study the Little Vehicle according to the Sammatîya school.

Within the great court is a vihâra 100 feet high;

[1] *Records*, ii. 33, *n.* 91.

there are stone steps, and brick niches arranged in regular order round the storeys of the building, in each niche is a gilded figure of Buddha.

Within the great hall (or *house*) is a figure of Buddha in brass (*calamine stone*),[1] of the actual size of Tathâgata's body; he is represented as turning the wheel of the law.

To the south-east of the Vihâra is a stone Stûpa, erected by Aśôka-râja, about 100 feet high; in front of it is a stone column about 70 feet high. This is the place where Buddha first began to preach. By the side of it is the place where Mei-ta-li (*Maitri*) Bôdhisattva received the predictive assurance.

Again to the west is a Stûpa; this is the place where Buddha in former days was born as Prabhâpâla Bôdhisattva [2] in the midst of the Bhadra Kalpa, when men lived to 20,000 years of age. At this time Kâśyapa being Buddha, he received a predictive assurance here.

To the south of this spot is a place where the four Buddhas of the past age walked to and fro. In length this terrace is about 500 feet, and in height seven feet. It is made of a greenish blue stone and bears on its surface the impression of the four Buddhas walking to and fro.

To the west of the Sanghârâma is the washing tank of Tathâgata, and where he cleansed his begging dish and washed his clothes. These tanks are protected by Nâgas, so that no one may defile the water.

By the side of the lake there is a Stûpa where Buddha, whilst he was practising the preparatory life of a Bôdhisattva in the form of a six-tusked white elephant, gave his tusks in charity to a hunter.

Here also is the place where, when he was born as a bird, he joined the company of a monkey and a white elephant, and making a covenant as to their age according to a Nyagrôdha tree, went forth to convert men.

[1] Or, covered with brass plates.

[2] Or, *Jyotipâla* Bodhisattva. See Dr. Mitra's *Nepalese Buddhist Catalogue*, p. 121, &c.

Again there is the spot where Buddha was born as a deer-king; and also where he converted Kauṇḍinya and the others, altogether five men.[1]

From this, following the course of the Ganges for about 300 *li* eastwards, we arrive at the kingdom of Chen-chu (*Ghâzipur*). From this, going north-east and crossing the Ganges, after 140 or 150 *li*, we come to the kingdom of Vâiśâlî.

This kingdom is about 5000 *li* in circuit; the soil is loamy and richly watered; it produces many Âmra and Mocha fruit-trees. The capital town is waste and in ruins; its old foundations are sixty or seventy *li* in circuit; the inhabitants are very few in number.

Five or six *li* to the north-west of the royal precincts is a Saṅghârâma, by the side of which is a stûpa; this is the place where in old times Buddha recited the Vimalakîrtti Sûtra.

Again, three or four *li* to the north-east of this is a stûpa; this is the site of the ruined house of Vimalakîrtti; this house is the scene of many strange spiritual portents.

Not far from this is a house constructed from piled-up stones; this is the place where Vimalakîrtti, when taken with sickness, preached the Law.

By the side of this is the old dwelling of Ratnâkara[2] and of the Lady Âmradârikâ.

Next, about three or four *li* to the north, there is a stûpa; this is where Buddha stopped when about to proceed to the kingdom of Kuśinara to attain Nirvâṇa, surrounded by Devas and men.

To the west, again, is the place where Buddha (turned round) to behold Vâisalî for the very last time.

[1] For the various fables referred to in this section, cf. *Records*, ii. p. 47 and following.

[2] *Vide Records, &c.*, vol. ii. p. 67, n. 70.

Again, to the south, is the place where the Lady Âmradârikâ gave the garden in charity to Buddha.

Again, there is the place where Buddha consented (*to attain*) Nirvâṇa, in accordance with the request of Mâra râja.

Leaving the southern borders of Vâisalî and following the Ganges river for 100 *li* or so, we came to the town of Svêtapura, where the Master obtained the Sûtra called Bôdhisattva-piṭaka.[1]

Again, going south and crossing the Ganges river, we come to the kingdom of Magâdha.[2] This kingdom is about 5000 *li*[3] in circuit. The population is learned and highly virtuous. There are about fifty Sanghârâmas and ten thousand priests, mostly attached to the Great Vehicle.

To the south of the river there is an old town about seventy *li* in circuit. Although it is waste and desolate, the parapets of the walls still remain.

In old days, when men's lives were of immeasurable length, then this town was called Kusumapura;[4] because the king's palace had so many flowers, it was so called. Afterwards, when men's lives dwindled down to a few thousand years, then it was called Pâṭaliputtra-pura, after the Pâṭali tree[5] (*the trumpetflower-tree*).

One hundred years after the Nirvâṇa there was a king called Aśôka, the great grandson of Bimbisârarâja;[6] he transferred his court from Râjagriha to this place. Since then many generations have passed, and now nothing but the old foundations remain, and of several hundred convents only two or three survive.

To the north of the old palace (*precinct*), bordering on the river Ganges, is a little town; this town has about 1000 houses; to the north of the palace there is a stone

[1] This seems to be parenthetical.

[2] *Records*, Book viii.

[3] Julien gives 600 *li* by mistake.

[4] Explained to mean *the city of the palace of fragrant flowers*.

[5] For the story of this tree, *vide Records*, vol. ii. p. 83.

[6] Cf. Dipavaṁsa, vi. 15, 18 (Oldenberg's translation). According to this work (v. 25 and vi. 99) the great grandson of Bimbisâra was Susunâga, who, in the first passage, is described as the father of Asôka, and the latter passage spoken of as Asôka (Kâlâsoka) himself. Cf. *Records*, ii. 85 and 102, n. 41.

pillar several tens of feet high; this is the place where Aśôka made the hell (*place of torture*).

The Master of the Law remained in the little city seven days, and paid worship to the sacred traces.

To the south of the place of torture is a Stûpa; this is one of the 84,000 which the king built by the aid of human artificers. Within it is a measure of the relics of Tathâgata, which ever and again exhibit a divine brilliancy.

Again, there is a Vihâra in which is a stone on which Tathâgata walked: on the stone is an impression of the feet of Buddha: in length a foot and eight inches, in breadth six inches. Under either foot is the sign of the 1000-spoked wheel, and on each of the ten toes is the mark of the *swastika*, with figures of flowers, vases, fishes, &c., all of which sparkle with light. These are the traces left on a great square stone[1] upon which Buddha stood, when, after leaving Vâisalî, he reached this spot, being about to attain Nirvâṇa; he was on the southern side of the river, and addressed Ananda thus, as he stood: "This is the very last time that I shall gaze (*at a distance*) upon the Vajrâsana[2] and Râjagriha," and the traces of his feet on this stone remained.

To the north of the Vihâra is a stone column about thirty feet high; on this pillar is written a record that Aśôka-râja three times gave the whole of Jambudvîpa in charity to Buddha, Dharma and Saṁgha, and three times bought back his inheritance (*i.e. his empire*) with jewels and treasure.

To the south-east of the old city are the ruins of the Kukkutârama[3] convent, which was built by Aśôka

[1] This phrase is omitted by Julien, but it is an important one, as it enables us to identify Pl. xxvi. fig. 1, *Tree and Serpent Worship*, with this scene.

[2] That is, the *diamond-seat*, on which he had reached perfect enlightenment.

[3] Asokârama, Dip., vii. 59.

râja: it was here he convoked the 1000 priests and supplied them with the four kinds of religious offerings.[1]

The Master of the Law paid reverence to all these sacred traces, during seven days, visiting them severally.

Then going south-west six or seven *yôjanas* he came to the Tiladaka[2] convent. In this convent were several tens of priests of the three piṭakas (*i.e. Buddhist priests*), who hearing of the arrival of the Master of the Law came out in a body to meet and escort him.

From this, again, proceeding southwards 100 *li* or so, we come to the Bôdhi tree. The tree is protected by high and very solid brick walls; the wall stretching east and west is long, but narrower from north to south. The principal gate faces the east looking towards the river Ni-len-shan (*Nairañjâna*). The southern gate borders on a great flower-tank. The west a mountain side protects. The north gate leads into the great Saṅghârâma. Within this on every side are the sacred traces of religion, vihâras, stûpas, and so on, all of which kings and great ministers and rich nobles have constructed from a principle of reverence, and for the perpetual memory (*of their religion*).

In the centre of the whole enclosure is the Diamond throne, which was perfected at the beginning of the Bhadra Kalpa, and rose up from the ground when the world was formed. It is the very central point of the universe, and goes down to the golden wheel, from whence it rises upwards to the earth's surface. It is perfected of diamond, and is about 100 paces round. In using the word *diamond* we mean that it is firm and indestructible, and able to resist all things.[3] If it were not for its support the earth could not remain; if the seat were not so strong as diamond, then no part of the world could

[1] *Vide* the Dipavansa, vii. 57, 58, 59. The statement in the Text, agreeing as it does with the Dîpavaṁsa, evidently refers to the third Buddhist council held under Dhammâsoka. Cf. *Records*, ii. p. 95.

[2] *Vide Records*, ii. p. 102 *n.*

[3] ἀφθιτον ἀει.

support one who has entered the samâdhi of *perfect fixedness* (*vajra samâdhi*).

And now, whoever desires to conquer Mâra, and to attain perfect wisdom, must sit here; if it were assayed elsewhere, the earth would overtop itself. Therefore, the 1000 Buddhas of the Bhadra Kalpa have all attained their emanicipation here.

But again, the place of completed wisdom is also called the arena of wisdom (*Bôdhimaṇḍa*). If the world were shaken to its foundations (*overturned*), this place alone would not be moved.

After one or two hundred years from the present time, the merit of the human family becoming less, on coming to the Bôdhi tree, the Vajrâsana will no longer be seen.

After the Nirvâna of Buddha the kings of the different countries agreed to define the limits (*of this sacred enclosure*) towards the north and south[1] from the point of the two images of *Kwan-tsze-tsai* Bôdhisattva, which are seated looking towards the east. According to tradition, when these images of the Bôdhisattva become invisible, then the Law of Buddha will perish. The southern image has already been swallowed up as far as the breast.

The Bôdhi tree is the same as the Pippala tree (*Ficus religiosa*).

Whilst Buddha was in the world the height of the tree was several hundred feet; but as wicked kings have continually cut it down and destroyed it, the tree is now only about fifty feet high. As Buddha, whilst sitting beneath this tree, reached perfect wisdom (*anuttara Bôdhi*), it is therefore called the Bôdhi tree. The bark is of a yellowish white colour, and its leaves of a shining green; it retains its leaves through the autumn and winter; only, when the day of Buddha's Nirvâṇa comes, the leaves all fall off, but when the day has passed, they

[1] The passage evidently refers to the limits of the Bodhimaṇḍa, not to the territories of the kings, as Julien translates.

all grow again. Every year on this day the kings of the countries, the ministers and magistrates, assemble beneath the tree, and pour milk on its roots and light lamps and scatter flowers, then collecting the leaves, they retire.[1]

The Master of the Law when he came to worship the Bôdhi tree and the figure of Tathâgata at the time of his reaching perfect wisdom, made (*afterwards*) by (*the interposition of*) Mâitrêya Bôdhisattva,[2] gazed on these objects with the most sincere devotion, he cast himself down with his face to the ground in worship, and with much grief and many tears in his self-affliction, he sighed, and said: "At the time when Buddha perfected himself in wisdom, I know not in what condition I was, in the troublous whirl of birth and death; but now, in this latter time of image (*worship*), having come to this spot and reflecting on the depth and weight of the body of my evil deeds, I am grieved at heart, and my eyes filled with tears."

At this time there happened to come to the spot, from different quarters, a body of priests who had just broken up from their religious retreat, numbering several thousand men; these persons, when they beheld (? *the Master*) were all moved to pity and sorrow.

For a *yôjana* around this spot the space is full of sacred traces. The Master therefore remained here for eight or nine days to pay his worship at each spot successively.

On the tenth day he went to the Nâlanda temple; the congregation there had selected four of their number, of distinguished position, to go and meet him; journeying in their company about seven *yôjanas* he reached the farm-house[3] belonging to the temple. It was in (*the village, where*) this house (*stands*), that the

[1] Perhaps this is the reason why it is sometimes called the *Pei-to*, *i.e.*, "the leaf tree."

[2] *Vide Records*, vol. ii. p. 120.

[3] So I translate *chwang*.

honourable Maudgalyâyana was born. Halting here for short refreshment, then, with two hundred priests and some thousand lay patrons, who surrounded him as he went, recounting his praises, and carrying standards, umbrellas, flowers and perfumes, he entered Nâlanda.

Having arrived there he was joined by the whole body of the community, who exchanged friendly greetings with the Master, and then placing a special seat by the side of the Sthavira (*presiding priest*), they requested the Master to be seated. The others then also sat down.

After this the Karmadâna [1] was directed to sound the Ghaṇṭa and proclaim: "Whilst the Master of the Law dwells in the convent, all the commodities used by the priests and all the appliances of religion are for his convenience, in common with the rest."

Then selecting twenty men of middle age, skilful in explaining the religious books and of dignified carriage, they deputed them to conduct the Master to the presence of *Ching-fa-tsong* (treasure of the good law). This is the same as Śilabhadra.

The congregation, from the excessive respect they have to him, do not venture to call him by his name, but give him the appellation of *Ching-fa-tsong*.

Whereupon, following the rest, he entered to salute this eminent person. Having seen him, then the chief almoner presented him (*i.e. Śilabadra*) with all things necessary without stint, paying his respects according to the proper ceremonial, approaching him on his knees and kissing his foot, and bowing his head to the ground. The usual greetings and compliments being finished, *Fa-tsong* ordered seats to be brought and spread out, and

[1] In the original *Wei-na*, *i.e. Vena*, "the early riser." He is the sub-director of the Convent. Vena, in the sense of the *rising sun*, or, *the early riser*, is found in the Rig-Veda, *vide Wallis*, "Cosmology of the Rig Veda," p. 35. But Vena has also the sense of the "Knower," and hence the Chinese rendering "*Chi sse*," *he who knows things*, or, *business*. He is, according to Julien, also called *Karmadâna*, which appears to be allied to the Chinese *hing* (karma). The Pâli equivalent in *Bhattuddesako*.

desired the Master of the Law and the rest to be seated. When seated he asked the Master of the Law from what part he came; in reply he said: "I am come from the country of China, desiring to learn from your instruction the principles of the Yoga-Śâstra."

Hearing this, he called for his disciple Buddhabhadra, whilst tears filled his eyes; now Buddhabhadra was the nephew of *Fa-tsong*, and upwards of seventy years of age, thoroughly versed in the Sûtras and Śâstras, and excellent in discourse. *Fa-tsong* addressing him said: "You may recount for the sake of the company present, the history of my sickness and sufferings three years ago."

Buddhabhadra having heard the request sobbed aloud and wept—but then restraining his tears he declared the past history and said: "My master (*Upâdhyâya*) some time ago was painfully afflicted with colic. On each occasion when the attack came on, his hands and feet were cramped with pain, and he would suddenly cry out with agony as if he had been burned with fire, or pierced with a knife; the attack would subside as suddenly as it came on; and this went on for twenty years and more. But three years ago the severity of his suffering was so hard to bear, that he loathed his very life and desired to starve himself to death. In the middle of the night he had a dream in which he saw three Dêvas (*heavenly men*), one of the colour of gold, another of the colour of bright crystal, another as white as silver, their appearance and form commanding, of dignified presence, and clad in light shining garments; approaching the Master they asked him, saying: 'Are you anxious to get free from this body of yours? The Scriptures speak, saying, the body is born to suffering; they do not say we should hate and cast away the body. You in one of your past births were the king of a certain country, and you caused much suffering among living creatures, and now you have this suffering as your recompense. Search out therefore and examine your past faults, and repent of them sincerely; take your affliction quietly and patiently; labour diligently in explaining the Sûtras and Śâstras; you will thus get rid of your pain yourself; but if you loathe your body, there will be no cessation to your sufferings.'

"The Master having heard these words, paid his adorations with the utmost sincerity.

"Then the golden-coloured one, pointing to the one that shone like crystal, said to the Master: 'Dost thou know or not that this one is Avalôkiteśvara Bôdhisattva?' and then pointing to the silver-coloured one he added: 'and this is Mâitreya Bôdhisattva.'

"The Master immediately paid worship to Mâitreya and asked him, saying: 'Your servant Śilabhadra has ever prayed that he may be born in your exalted palace courts, but he knows not whether he will gain his wish or not.' In reply, he said, 'You must widely disseminate the true law, and then you shall be born there.'

"The golden-coloured one said: 'And I am Manjuśri Bôdhisattva. Seeing that you desired to get rid of your life, contrary to your true interest, we are come to exhort you to the contrary; you should rely on our words, and exhibit abroad the true law, the *Yoga sâstra* and the rest, for the benefit of those who have not yet heard it. Your body will thus by degrees become easy and you will suffer no further pain. Do not overlook that there is a priest of the country of China who delights in examining the great Law and is desirous to study with you: you ought to instruct him carefully.'

"Fă-tsong having heard these words worshipped and answered: 'I shall obey, according to your honourable instructions.' Having said this, they disappeared.

"From that time the sufferings of the Master from his disease came to an end."

The company present hearing this history were all filled with wonder at the miraculous event.

The Master of the Law having heard for himself this narrative was unable to control his feelings of sympathy and joy. He again paid his respects and said: "If it be so, as you say, then Hiuen-Tsiang ought with his utmost strength to listen to and practise (*your religious advice*). Would that your reverence, of his great compassion, would receive me for the purpose of instruction."

Then *Fa-tsong* asked him further, "For how many years have you been on your journey?" He answered, "During three years;" and so, as the particulars of his directions, received in his dream, were completely fulfilled, he caused the Master of the Law to rejoice in their relationship as Master and disciple.

After these words he retired and went to the college of Bâlâditya-râja and took up his residence in the dwelling of Buddhabhadra, having four storeys (or, *the fourth storey*), who entertained him for seven days. After this he went to reside in a dwelling to the north of the abode of Dharmapâla Bôdhisattva, where he was provided with every sort of charitable offering. Each day he received 120 Jambiras,[1] 20 *Pin-long-tseu* (pûga, *areca nut*) 20 *tau-k'au* (*nutmegs*), an ounce (*tael*) of Camphor, and a *ching* (peck) of Mahâśâli rice. This rice is as large as the black bean, and when cooked is aromatic and shining, like no other rice at all. It grows only in Mâgadha, and nowhere else. It is offered only to the king or to religious persons of great distinction; and hence the name kung-ta-jin-mai (*i.e. rice offered to the great householder*).

Every month he was presented with three measures of oil, and daily a supply of butter and other things according to his need.

A pure brother (*a Upāsaka*)[2] and a Brahman, relieved

[1] A fruit.

[2] Julien translates *tsing jin* by *Śraman*, but it evidently means a *lay-brother*. Cf. *Fa-hien*, cap. iii. Probably, however, it had better be translated a *Brahmachârî*.

from all religious duties, accompanied him with a riding elephant.

In the Nâlanda convent the abbot entertains a myriad priests after this fashion, for besides the Master of the Law there were men from every quarter; and where in all their wanderings have they met with such courteous treatment as this?

The Nâlanda monastery is the same as the "*charity without intermission*" monastery.[1] The tradition of the old people is this:—To the south of the convent, in the middle of an Âmra garden, is a pool. In this pool is a Nâga called Nâlanda, and the convent built by the side of the pool is therefore called after his name. Again there is a saying that Tathâgata whilst a Bôdhisattva was the king of a great country and built his capital in this place. He was deeply affected towards the orphans and destitute, and, ever moved by this principle, gave away all he had for their good. In memory of this goodness they named the place "*doing charitable acts without intermission.*"

The place was originally the garden of the lord (*Shreshṭin*) Âmra[2] (or, *Amara*). Five hundred merchants bought it for ten lacs of gold pieces, and presented it to Buddha. Here Buddha preached the law for three months, and most of the merchants obtained the fruit of Arhatship, in consequence.

After the Nirvâṇa of Buddha an old king[3] of this country called Śakrâditya, from a principle of loving obedience to Buddha, built this convent.

After his decease his son Buddhagupta-râja seized the throne, and continued the vast undertaking; he built, towards the south, another Sañghârâma.

Then his son[4] (*successor*) Tathâgata-râja built a Sañghârâma to the eastward.

[1] *Records*, 167, *n.*

[2] *Vide* Max Müller's *India*, p. 327.

[3] Or, *a former king*, *vide* p. 112, *infra*, n. 1.

[4] The expression *chi-tsz'* need not mean "his son," but his *direct descendant*. This would reconcile the two accounts in the *Si-yu-ki* and here. *Vide Records*, ii. 168.

Next, his son (or, *direct descendant*) Bâlâditya[1] built a Sañghârâma to the north-east. Afterwards the king, seeing some priests who came from the country of China to receive his religious offerings, was filled with gladness, and he gave up his royal estate and became a recluse.[2]

His son[3] Vajra succeeded and built another Sañghârâma to the north.

After him a king of Mid-India built by the side of this another Sañghârâma.

Thus six kings in connected succession added to these structures.

Moreover, the whole establishment is surrounded by a brick wall, which encloses the entire convent from without. One gate opens into the great college, from which are separated eight other halls, standing in the middle (*of the Sañghârâma*). The richly adorned towers, and the fairy-like turrets, like pointed hill-tops, are congregated together. The observatories seem to be lost in the vapours (*of the morning*), and the upper rooms tower above the clouds.

From the windows one may see how the winds and the clouds (*produce new forms*), and above the soaring eaves the conjunctions of the sun and moon (*may be observed*).

And then we may add how the deep, translucent ponds, bear on their surface the blue lotus, intermingled with the Kie-ni (*Kanaka*)[4] flower, of deep red colour, and at intervals the Âmra groves spread over all, their shade.

All the outside courts, in which are the priests' chambers, are of four stages. The stages have dragon-projections and coloured eaves, the pearl-red pillars, carved and ornamented, the richly adorned balustrades,

[1] Bâlâditya = the *young*, or *rising* sun. May we compare with this *Pallas* (Minerva)?

[2] *Records*, vol. ii. 169.

[3] Here the expression denotes that Vajra was the *son* of Bâlâditya, and this agrees with the *Si-yu-ki*.

[4] *Butea frondosa* (M. Williams' Sc. Dict. *s.v.*)

and the roofs covered with tiles that reflect the light in a thousand shades, these things add to the beauty of the scene.

The Saṅghârâmas of India are counted by myriads, but this is the most remarkable for grandeur and height. The priests, belonging to the convent, or strangers (*residing therein*) always reach to the number of 10,000, who all study the Great Vehicle, and also (*the works belonging to*) the eighteen sects,[1] and not only so, but even ordinary works, such as the Vêdas and other books, the Hetuvidyâ, Śabdavidyâ, the Chikitsâvidyâ, the works on Magic (*Âtharvavêda*), the Saṅkhya; besides these they thoroughly investigate the "*miscellaneous*" works. There are 1000 men who can explain twenty collections of Sûtrâs and Śâstras; 500 who can explain thirty collections, and perhaps ten men, including the Master of the Law, who can explain fifty collections. Śîlabhadra alone has studied and understood the whole number. His eminent virtue and advanced age have caused him to be regarded as the chief member of the community. Within the Temple they arrange every day about 100 pulpits for preaching, and the students attend these discourses without any fail, even for a minute (*an inch shadow on the dial*).

The priests dwelling here, are, as a body, naturally (or, *spontaneously*) dignified and grave, so that during the 700 years since the foundation of the establishment,[2] there has been no single case of guilty rebellion against the rules.

The king of the country respects and honours the priests, and has remitted the revenues of about 100 villages for the endowment of the convent. Two hundred householders in these villages, day by day, contribute

[1] That is, the eighteen schools (*p'u*) of Buddhism.

[2] This seems to throw light on the date of Śakrâditya, if he "after the Nirvâṇa," was the first to found the Nâlanda Convent, and this was 700 years before *Hiuen-Tsiang*, we may suppose he lived about the first century B.C. The expression, therefore, in the *Si-yu-ki*, "not long after" (*Records*, ii. 168), must be taken, *cum grano*, to mean "a good while after."

several hundred piculs[1] of ordinary rice, and several hundred catties[2] in weight of butter and milk. Hence the students here, being so abundantly supplied, do not require to ask for the four requisites.[3] This is the source of the perfection of their studies, to which they have arrived.

The Master of the Law having resided in the Nâlanda Temple for some time, then proceeded towards Râjagrĭha to examine, and pay reverence to, the holy traces there.

The old city of Râjagrĭha is that which is called Kiu-she-kie-la-po-lo (*Kuśâgarapura*). This city is in the centre of Magadha, and in old times many rulers and kings lived in it. This land, moreover, produces some excellent scented grass (*Kuśâ*), and hence the name given to the city. On the four sides it is entirely shut in by lofty and steep mountains, as if they had been cut out (*like a wall*). On the west side the approach is through a narrow passage; but passing in from the north, is a large gate. The land is extended from north to south, and narrow from east to west: it is about 150 *li* in circuit. Within it is another little town, the foundation walls being about thirty *li* round. On every side are forests of the Kanaka tree, which flower all the year round, the petals being of a golden colour.

Outside the north face of the royal precinct there is a stûpa; this is the spot where Devadatta in conjunction with Ajâtaśatru râja let loose the *treasure-protecting* drunken elephant[4] wishing to destroy Buddha.

North-east of this is a stûpa; this is the spot where Śâriputra heard the Bhikshu Aśvajita explain the Law, and in consequence attained the fruit (*of Ârhatship*).[5]

Not far to the north of this is a large and deep ditch;

[1] 1 picul = 133⅓ lbs.

[2] 1 catty = 160 lbs.

[3] Clothes, food, bedding, and medicine.

[4] Called Ratnapâla or Vâsupâla, according to Rockhill (*Life of the Buddha*, p. 93), or Dhanapâla, according to Spence Hardy (*Manual*, p. 321). The scene at Ajanta (Speirs' *Anc. India*, p. 290) has been rightly identified with this episode.

[5] *Vide Records*, ii. 175.

this is the place where Śrîgupta, obeying the words of the heretics, desired to destroy Buddha by fire (*concealed in*) the ditch, and by poisoned food.[1]

Again, to the north-east of the great ditch, in a corner of the mountain city, is a Stûpa; this is the place where the great physician, Jîvaka, built a preaching hall for Buddha. By the side of it is the old house of Jîvaka, still visible.

Going north-east of the palace-city (*i.e. Kuśâgarapura*) fourteen or fifteen *li*, we come to the mountain called *Ki-li-to-lo-kiu-to* (*Gridhrakûta*). This mountain is a connected succession of ridges, the northern peak, rising grandly above the rest, stands up boldly by itself, and is in shape like a vulture; it also has the form of a high tower; hence its name (*Tower*, or *Peak of the Vulture*). The springs are clear, the rocks singular in shape, and the trees covered with rich verdure.

When Tathâgata was in the world he used frequently to live here, and it was here he declared the Fă-hwa (*Saddharma pundarika*), the Ta-pan-jo (*Mahâprajña*), and other sûtras innumerable.

Going through the north gate of the mountain city one *li* or so, we come to the bamboo garden of Kalanda, where there is still a brick house.

Here Buddha in old time often dwelt, and here he laid down the binding rules of the Vinaya. The owner of this garden was called Karanda; he had before given this garden in charity to different heretics, but after he had seen Buddha and heard the deep truths of his Law, he was sorry that he had not given the garden in charity to Tathâgata. The earth-spirit, knowing his thoughts, caused such prodigies to appear as frightened the heretics, and then, with a view to make them go away, he spake as follows: "The lord of the place wishes to give this garden in charity to Buddha: you had better begone

[1] This history of Śrîgupta's plot forms the fifth story in the Jâtal mâlâ-Śâstra.

quickly!" The heretics, concealing their vexation, went away. Then the lord of the place, filled with joy, built a Vihâra, and when he had finished it he went and invoked Buddha to come there and reside; so Buddha accepted the place as a gift.

To the east of the garden is a stûpa, which was built by Ajâtaśatru râja. After the Nirvâṇa of Tathâgata the different kings received a portion of his relics; Ajâtaśatru râja, having got his share, coming back, built a tower for the purpose of paying them religious worship. Aśôka-râja, exciting his heart to religion, desired to build in every place sacred edifices, and so he opened this tower and took the relics; but he let a small portion of them remain, which, even down to the present time, on occasions, emit a brilliant light.

Going south-west from the Bamboo garden five or six *li*, by the side of a mountain, there is another garden, of the same sort, in which is a great house.[1] This is where the honourable Mahâ Kâśyapa with 999 Arhats after the Nirvâṇa of Buddha, collected together the three Piṭakas.

At the time of the collection there were an innumerable number of holy persons assembled together, like clouds. Kâśyapa addressing them, said: "Among those present those may remain who have a personal knowledge of the three vidyâs, and who possess the six supernatural powers, and have completely mastered the entire treasure of the Law of Buddha, without flaw or omission. Of the rest let each return to his place of residence."

There remained, in consequence, 999 men who were Arhats, in the selected place of study.

On this Kâśyapa addressed Ânanda: "You have not yet got rid of all remains (*leaks*, i.e. *human frailties*); do not soil, by your presence, this pure congregation."

Ananda, ashamed, retired. During the night, how-

[1] That is, the Sattapaṇṇi cave. But refer to *Records*, ii. p. 156 n.

ever, by diligent application, he snapped the bonds of the three worlds, and became perfect as an Arhat.

Then returning he came and humbly bowed at the door of the assembly.

Kâśyapa then asked him, saying: "Art thou free from fetters?"

He replied: "Yea!"

Then he added: "If it is so indeed, there is no need to unfasten the door and open it; enter in as thou wilt!"

Ananda then entered in through a small crevice in the door, and saluted the feet of the priesthood.

Then Kâśyapa taking his hand, said: "I was anxious that you should get rid of all imperfections, and obtain the holy fruit, and so excluded you; knowing this, you should have no grudge in your heart."

Ananda said: "If I felt any grudge, how could I be said to be free from fetters?"

On this he saluted him respectfully and sat down.

They then kept the first fifteen days of the Rain-Rest.

Kâśyapa addressing Ananda, said: "Tathâgata always termed you in the congregation a disciple, or listener (*Sêkha*),[1] who thoroughly knew the laws of religion. You may therefore now mount the pulpit, and for the sake of the assembly recite the Sûtra piṭaka, which is the same as all the Sûtras."

On this Ânanda, obeying the mandate, arose, and after bowing down towards the mountain of the Parinirvâṇa of Buddha (*his grave*, or, *the place of his death*), he mounted the pulpit and repeated the Sûtras. The congregation received them at his dictation and wrote them down. Having so recorded them, he (*Kâśyapa*) requested Upâli to recite the Vinaya piṭaka, that is, the whole body of the Moral Rules.

This being done, Kâśyapa himself recited the Abhidharma piṭaka, *i.e.* the collection (*Sûtra*) of the meaning of the Śâstras.

[1] Lotus, p. 296.

During the rest of the three months, having finished the collection of the three piṭakas, and inscribed them on leaf of the Peito (*the palm leaf*), they then distributed them everywhere for use.

Then the holy men said one to another, "Our collection may well be termed 'the result of the goodness, or kindness of Buddha,' for from this alone (*i.e. his goodness*) proceeds what we now have had the privilege of hearing."

From the fact of Kâśyapa being the president among the priests, this collection (or, *assembly*) is called that of the Sthaviras.

Twenty *li* to the west of this place is a Stûpa built by Aśôka-râja; this is the spot where the assembly of the Great Congregation (*Mahâsañghikas*) was held.

The many thousand priests both of those who had reached complete wisdom, and those of inferior condition,[1] who were not admitted to the assembly of Kâśyapa all collected here, and said among themselves: "During Tathâgata's lifetime, we had all one master, but now the Lord is dead, they have excluded us by their vote; why should not we also make a collection of the Dharma piṭaka, in return for the goodness of Buddha?"

So they made another collection of the Sûtra-piṭaka, and the Vinaya-piṭaka, and the Abhidharma-piṭaka, and of the Miscellaneous-piṭaka, and the Dhâranî-piṭaka, five piṭakas in all.

As in this assembly there were both ordinary persons[2] and holy men present; it is called the convocation of the Mahâsañghikas.[3]

North-east of this three or four *li* we come to the town of Râjagriha; the outside walls have been destroyed, within the city there are still lofty (*buildings*).

[1] Sâicha and asaicha, *vide* Lot. *ut supra*.

[2] *Fan fu*, "mixed people.' *Cf.* the Pâli *puthujjana*.

[3] This differs from the usual account which derives the Mahâsaṅgika school from the schism at Vaiśali.

It is about twenty *li* round, and has one gate.

Formerly, when Bimbisâra râja lived in Kuśâgârapura, the population was large and the houses were closely packed. In consequence of this the calamity of fire was of frequent occurrence. So a decree was made that in whatever house a fire next occurred through negligence, that the owner should be expelled and placed in the "cold forest." The "cold forest," in that country, means the evil place where they cast the dead.

Shortly afterwards the royal palace suddenly caught fire and was destroyed; the king said: "I am a ruler of men: if I transgress and do not act in agreement with the law, I cannot repress the lower orders in transgressing."

He then ordered the Prince royal to conduct the government during his absence, and he himself went to reside in the cemetery.

At this time the king of Vaiśâlî hearing that Bimbisâra was living alone in the desert beyond the city, was anxious to summon his troops and to capture him. The outpost guards, finding this out, informed the king, and fortified the place where he was. And because the king first dwelt here, they therefore called the place Râjagriha.[1] This is the new city. Afterwards the King Ajâtaśatru established his authority here in succession to his father—and it remained so, till Aśôka-râja removed the capital to Pâṭaliputra and gave the old town to the Brâhmaṇs: so now in the city, there are only about 1000 families of Brâhmaṇs.

Within the palace-city towards the south-west corner there is a Stûpa: this is the site of the ruinous house of Jyôtishka, the nobleman.[2] By the side of it is the place where Râhula was received as a disciple.

To the north-west of the Nâlanda convent there is a

[1] "The house of the king."

[2] *Chang-che.*

great Vihâra in height about 200 feet, which was built by Balâditya râja. It is highly decorated and of an imposing character. In it there is an image of Buddha the same as the image under the Bôdhi Tree.

To the north-east of the Vihâra is a Stûpa, the site where Buddha formerly preached the law for seven days.

To the north-west again is a place where the four past Buddhas sat down.

To the south of this is the brass-covered Vihâra constructed by Śilâditya râja; the work, though not yet finished, is sufficiently advanced to show that its plan denotes a height of 100 feet and more, when completed.

Again to the east about 200 paces is a copper image of Buddha about eighty feet high, housed over by a pavilion in six stages. This was the work of Pûrṇavarmarâja in old days.[1]

Again going eastward several *li* there is a stûpa which denotes the place where Bimbisâra-râja, with many myriads of people, went to meet and first saw Buddha, who having arrived at supreme wisdom, was directing his way towards the city of Râjagrĭha.

Again going east thirty *li* or so we come to the Indraśilâguha Mountain.

In front of a Saṅghârâma on the eastern cliffs is a stûpa called Haṁsa.

Formerly this Saṅghârâma was given to the doctrine of the Little Vehicle called the "gradual stage," which permits the use of the three pure condiments. On one occasion the steward of the establishment, not having been able to procure the necessary provisions, was standing by the side in great distress, seeing no mode of escape (*at a loss what to do*), when he beheld a flock of wild geese flying past; then he cried out in jest—"To-day the priests are in dire want, my good masters! recognise the opportunity!" Having spoken these words, the

[1] *Vide Records*, ii. 174.

leading goose, on the sound of the appeal, turned and fell down from the clouds on high, and lay his body prostrate. The Bhikshu having seen (*this miracle*), filled with astonishment and fear, spread the news abroad among the fraternity. The priests had nothing to say in reply, on hearing the news; but filled with reverential fear, with many sighs and tears, they talked together and said: "This is a Bôdhisattva! What man among us would dare to taste the flesh?" When Tathâgata established his "gradual method" of instruction, he forbade us to suppose that these early words of his, were intended to be final;[1] he warned us against foolishly supposing there could be no change, and hence this admonition!

From that time and afterwards they adopted the method of the Great Vehicle, and used no more the three pure aliments.

Then they built a "spiritual tower," for the burial of the dead goose, and signified thereby for the good of posterity, their mind in so doing. Such was the origin of this tower.

Thus the Master of the Law having visited the sacred traces all round, and paid his reverence to them, returned to the Nâlanda Monastery, and requested Śîlabhadra, Master of the Law, to explain the Yôga-śâstra, in the presence of many thousand auditors.

The exposition being ended, after a little time there was a Brahman who uttered some piteous cries outside the assembly, and then in turn began to laugh.

Some messengers asked him why he acted so.

In reply he said: "I am a man of Eastern India; formerly I made a vow (*prayer*), in the place where the image of Avalôkitêśvara stands on the Pôtaraka Mountain, that I might become a king.

"Bôdhisattva then appeared for my sake and reproved

[1] This amounts to a declaration of belief in the principle of "religious development."

me, saying: 'Make not such a prayer as this: hereafter, in such a year and month and day, the Master of the Law, Śîlabhadra, for the sake of a priest of China, will explain the Yôga-śâstra; you should go there and listen! from hearing this discourse you will hereafter be able to see Buddha: what good then in being a king?'

"And now," he said, "I have seen the priest of China come, and the Master for his sake expounding the law, in agreement with the old prophecy, and this is why I weep and laugh."

On this account the Master of the Law, Śîlabhadra, requested him to remain there and listen to the explanation of the Sûtras for fifteen months: and after the lectures, he sent a man with the Brahman to Śilâditya râja, who allotted him the revenues of three villages for his sustenance.

The Master of the Law whilst he stopped in the convent, heard the explanation of the Yôga-śâstra, three times: the Nyâyâ-Anusâra-śâstra, once; the *Hin-hiang-tui-fă-ming,* once; the Hetuvidyâ-śâstra and the Śabdavidyâ and the *tsah liang* śâstras, twice; the Prâṅyamûla śâstra-ṭîkâ, and the Śata-śâstra, thrice. The Kosha, Vibhâshâ, and the Shaṭpadâbhidharma śâstras, he had already heard explained in the different parts of Kaśmir; but when he came to this convent he wished to study them again to satisfy some doubts he had: this done, he also devoted himself to the study of the Brâhmaṇ books and the work called Vyâkaraṇa on Indian letters, whose origin is from the most remote date, and whose author is unknown.

At the beginning of each Kalpa, Brahma-râja first declares it, and then transmits it for Devas and men to use. Being thus declared by Brahma-râja, therefore men call it *Fan,* or Brahmâ, writing. The words of this book are very extensive, comprising a hundred myriad ślokas. It is the same as the old commentary calls the Vyâkara(*na*)-śâstra. But this pronunciation is not complete, if correct it would be Vyâkaraṇam, which is another name for "a treatise relating to the record of the science of sounds." It treats at large, in a mnemonic way, on all the laws of language and illustrates them, hence the name.

At the beginning of the Kalpa of perfection (*vaivarta kalpa*) Brahma-râja first declared this book; it then comprised 100 myriad of ślôkas; afterwards, at the beginning of the *Vaivarta-siddha-Kalpa*, that is, the kalpa, or period, of establishment, Ti-shih (*Śakra-raja*) reduced them to ten myriad ślôkas. After this a Brahman of the town Śâlâtura in Gandhâra of North India, whose name was Pâṇini Ṛishi, reduced them to 8000 ślôkas. This is the work at present used in India.

Lately a Brahman of South India, at the request of a king of South India, reduced them further to 2500 ślôkas. This work is widely spread, and used throughout all the frontier provinces, but the well-read scholars of India do not follow it as their guide in practice.

This then is the fundamental treatise relating to sounds and letters of the Western world, their branch-divisions, distinctions and mutual connections.

Again, there is a Vyâkaraṇam work (*mnemonic treatise*) of a short kind having 1000 ślôkas; again, there is one of 300 ślôkas on the roots (*bases*) of letters (*i.e. letter roots* or *bases*); again, there are (*treatises on the*) two separate kinds of letter-groupings, one named Maṇḍaka in 3000 ślôkas, the other called Uṇâdi in 2500 ślôkas. These distinguish letter-groupings from letter-roots. Again, there is the treatise called Ashta-ḍhâtu (*Ḍhâtu vṛitti?*) in 800 ślôkas; in this work there is a brief conjunction of letter-bases and letter-groupings. These are all the Vyâkaraṇa treatises.

In distinguishing active and passive expositions (*i.e.* in expounding the principles of grammar, relating to active and passive verbs) there are these two rules: the first, called Ti-yen-to-shing (*Tiñanta-vâjyam*) having eighteen inflections; the second Su-man-to-shing (*Subanta vâjyam*), having twenty-four inflections; the Tiñanta "sounds" are used in elegant compositions, but seldom in light literature. The twenty-four "sounds" are used in all kinds of composition alike. The eighteen inflections of the Tiñanta "sounds" are of two characters: 1st, Parasmai, 2nd, Âtmane; each of these has nine inflections, and so together there are eighteen. With respect to the nine which come first: we know that in ordinary discourse *everything* has three ways of being viewed, (*i.e. as one thing*, or *two things*, or *many things*); *every other person* has three ways of being considered (*i.e. as one other*, *two other*, or *many other*), and also "oneself" can be considered in three ways (*i.e.* as I *myself*, *two of us*, or *many of us*). Thus every single thing may be regarded in these three ways, as one, two of a class, or many; here then are three (three *persons* and three *numbers*, altogether *nine*). In both (*voices*) the root-word is the same, but the (*final*) sounds are different. So there are two sets of nine.

Now, taking the Parasmai sounds: we may speak of a thing as existing or not existing, in all cases. Supposing then we says a thing exists, there are three ways of putting (*naming*) this fact; we may say "it exists" (*bhavati*) or, "two things exist" (*bhavapa*)[1] or, "they exist" (*bhavanti*). And so, speaking of another, we may say "thou dost exist" (*bhavasi*), or, "you two exist" (*bhavapa*, for, *bhavathah*), or, "you all exist" (*bhavatha*); and so again speaking of oneself we may say "I exist" (*bhavâmi*), or, "we two exist" (*bhavâvah*), or, we all exist (*bhavâmas*).

With regard to the nine case-endings of the Átmane class, they simply take underneath the nine inflections just named the word "vyati," (or, the words *ve, ya, ti*); in other respects they are the same as the above.[2]

[1] For, *Bhavatah*.

[2] This passage is omitted by Julien. He gives, however, a note found in the original, which states that in the four Vedas (*Veda śâstras*) the form *bhavamah* is used, but elsewhere the form is *bhavamas*.

Thus touching these things, we see how a skilful writer in this language is saved from ambiguity, and also how his meaning may be expressed in the most elegant manner.

With respect to the twenty-four inflections of the Subanta "sound (endings)," it is to be observed that every word has altogether eight inflections (*cases*), and that each of these cases or inflections is subject to three conditions as to number, viz., when one, or two, or many, are concerned. Hence arise the twenty-four (*sound-endings*). Then, again, in connection with these twenty-four inflections we have three other terms, viz., the masculine sound ending, the feminine, and the neuter. But regarding the eight inflections, the first exhibits the substance, or basis, of the thing conceived (*nominative*); the second exhibits the deed done (*objective*); the third, the means by which, and the doer (*instrumental*); the fourth, for whom the thing is done (*dative*); the fifth, what causes the thing (*ablative*); the sixth, whose is the thing (*genitive*); the seventh, that which determines (*localises*) the thing (*locative*); the eighth, the calling, or summoning, the thing (*vocative*). Now, for example, let us take the masculine ending, as in the word "man," and go through the eight cases named above.

The word "man" in Indian speech is *Purusha.* The root-word has three inflections, viz., Purushah, Purushâu, Purushâs. The thing done (*object*) has three, Purusham, Purushau, Purushân; the instrument by which the thing is done by the doer has also three inflections—*Purushêṇa*, *Puru*(shâ)*bhyâm*, *Purushâbhih* or *Purushais*; "for whom the thing is done," *Purushâya*, *Purushâbhyâm*, *Purushshêshu*; "the cause from which the thing proceeds," *Purushât*, *Purushâbhyâm*, *Purusheshu*; "whose is the thing," *Purushasya*, *Purushâbhyam*, *Purushânâm*; "the place where," *Purushê*, *Purushayôs*, *Purushânâm*; "the calling case," *Hi Purusha*, *Hi Purushau*, *Hi Purushâh.*

From these one or two examples, other cases may be understood; it would be difficult to make a full statement of particulars.

The Master of the Law thoroughly investigated the language (*words and phrases*), and by talking with those men on the subject of the "pure writings," he advanced excellently in his knowledge. Thus he penetrated, and examined completely, all the collection (*of Buddhist books*), and also studied the sacred books of the Brahmans during five years.

From this place he again went to the country of Hiraṇyaparvata; by the way he came to the Ka-po-tih[1] Saṅghârâma (the Kapôtika convent). Two or three *li* to the south of this is a solitary hill, its steep and rugged sides and lofty peaks, its bushy trees and luxuriant verdure, its fountains of pure and clear water, and its shining flowers exhaling their perfume, have made this spot much renowned; it is covered with sacred buildings, all of which exhibit many and various spiritual prodigies. In the middle of an open space is a Vihâra in which is a sandal-wood figure of the Bôdhisattva Avalôkiteśvara; its appearance is divine and truly worshipful. There are many tens of men who for seven or fourteen days continue without food or drink, putting up their prayers and entreaties (*in the presence of this figure*). Those whose minds are most sincere, forthwith behold the Bôdhisattva with all its characteristic marks, glorious and resplendent, come forth from the sandal-wood figure, and graciously speak with those men concerning the subject of their prayers. There are very many men who have thus beheld the Bôdhisattva, and on this account the worshippers have increased in number.

The persons (*congregation*) that minister in religious

[1] 路 for 德

matters at this shrine, fearing that the crowds who come to worship might pollute the sacred figure, have erected all round it, at a distance of seven paces, a strong wooden balustrade pointed with iron, so that all who come to worship must stand outside the rails. Not being able to come nearer to the image, they cast from the distance the flowers which they bring as offerings; those who succeed in making the flowers rest on the hands of the figure, or hang from its arms, are considered very lucky, and will get their prayers answered. The Master of the Law wishing to go to put up his request, bought every kind of flower, and stringing them into garlands, he went to the place of the image. Having in the greatest sincerity paid his worship and offered his praises—he fell down on his hands and knees towards the image and put up these three vows:—

1st. Would that I, having finished my studies, may return in peace and quiet to my own country without accident: if so, may the flowers alight on the hands of the venerable one!

2nd. Would that, in return for the merit and wisdom I am aiming to acquire, I may be born in the Tuśita courts, and be permitted there to worship Mâitreya Bôdhisattva: if so, may the flowers hang on both the arms of the venerable one!

3rd. The holy writings say that there is a portion of creatures born in the world, who are without "the nature of Buddha." Hiuen-Tsiang in his ignorance knows not what is his case. But if he has the nature of Buddha, and so by preparatory conduct may at last reach perfection as a Buddha, then let the flowers hang suspended from the neck of the venerable one!

Having thus spoken he flung the garlands from the distance, and they each alighted according to his vow.

Having thus accomplished what he sought, he was overpowered with joy, and those who were worshipping by his side, and the guardians of the Vihâra, having seen what had occurred, clapped their hands and stamped their feet, as they said: "It is a miracle! hereafter, if you arrive at Perfect Wisdom, remember the history of this day, and first come to save us."

Going on gradually from this spot he came to the country of Hiraṇya. There are ten monasteries and about 4000 priests in this kingdom; the priests mostly study the Little Vehicle, and belong to the school of the Sarvâstivâdins.

Recently there was a frontier king who deposed the ruler of this country, and bestowed the capital on the priests; in it, moreover, he built two convents, each containing 1000 priests. There are two eminent brothers here, one called Tathâgatagupta, the other Kshântisiṁha, both belonging to the Sarvastivâdin school. Here the Master stopped one year and read the Vibhâshâ and the Nyâya-anusâra, Śâstras, and others.

To the south of the capital is a Stûpa; here Buddha in old days preached for three months for the good of Devas and men. By the side of it are traces where the past Buddhas walked to and fro. On the western borders of this country, south of the river Ganges, is a little solitary hill. Here Buddha in old days rested in retreat for three months, and subdued the Yaksha Vakula.

South-east of the hill, under a steep precipice, is a great rock, on which are traces of Buddha as he sat on it. They are deep in the rock an inch or more, in length 5 feet 2 inches, in breadth 4 feet 1 inch.

There is also a depression in the rock of about an inch where Buddha placed his water-jar. It resembles the eight petals of a flower.

To the south of this country all is waste and forest. There are great elephants there, large in size and of great height.

BOOK IV.

Beginning at Champâ and ending with an Account of the Invitation of the King of Kâmarûpa.

FROM this place, following the southern bank of the Ganges in an eastward direction 300 *li* or so, we come to the kingdom of Champâ. There are here some ten Saṅghârâmas, with about 300 priests, who study (*practise*) the Little Vehicle.

The city walls are of brick, and several *chang* in height. The ditch round the town is deep and large, so that the place is exceedingly strong.

Formerly, at the beginning of the kalpa, men dwelt in caves. Afterwards, a divine maiden coming down, as she walked beside the Ganges, bathed herself therein. The divine influence of the river affecting her person, she bore four sons, between whom she divided the whole of Jambudvipa. They then traced out the limits of their territory and built cities. This was the capital city of one of the sons.

Many tens of *yôjanas* from the southern frontiers of this country, there are great mountain forests, thick and wild, embracing a space of 200 *li* and more. Here are many hundred wild elephants who roam in herds. Hence the elephant army of Hiraṇya and Champâ is very numerous. Every now and again they send elephant masters to go round and catch them. In these countries they keep them for drawing carriages (or, *riding*). Wolves, the rhinoceros, and black leopards[1] are abundant, so men dare not go there.

[1] Such "black leopards" threatened Fa-hien on his ascent of the Gridrakûta hill, near Râjagriha. Fâ-hien indeed calls them *lions*, but we

There is a tradition here of the following kind. Formerly, before Buddha came into the world, there was a certain cowherd tending several hundred heads of cattle. As he drove them, they came into this forest, when a certain ox strayed from the herd by itself alone, and was thus continually away in some unknown place.

Towards evening its custom was to return, and on joining the herd it seemed to be of a radiant colour, very remarkable for its beauty, and its bellowings were different from all the others. The rest of the herd always seemed to be afraid of it, and would not venture to come near it. This happened for several days. The cowherd, astonished at the circumstance, set a private watch, and at the moment when the ox departed on its wander, he followed and watched it. Then he saw it enter a stone door (or, *a hole in a rock*). The man also followed him and entered. After going on about four or five *li* along a valley, suddenly there was a great light, and a forest park appeared, sparkling with brilliancy; the flowers were numerous and varied; the blossoms and fruit were all shining like flame, dazzling the eye, and contrary to anything in ordinary life.

He now saw the ox at a certain place browsing on a herb. The herb was of a yellow colour, and highly scented, and such as the man had never seen in the world. The fruit on the trees were yellow and red, like gold; aromatic, and very large. He plucked one of them, but although his heart had coveted its possession, he had not courage to taste it. After a little while the ox went out, and the man also followed. Scarcely had he got out of the hole in the rock, when in the very passage an evil demon snatched away the fruit and kept it. On this the cowherd consulted a

all know the Chinese idea of "a lion"—to which indeed Sung-Yun refers; there is, however, a *sthа-kála*, or "black lion," referred to by Childers sub. v. *stho.*

great doctor, and described to him the shape of the fruit. The doctor said: "You must not eat it at once, but by the use of some stratagem, having taken one, manage to get out, and bring it to me."

On the second day, again following the ox, he entered, and forthwith plucked one of the fruit, and concealing it in his bosom, proceeded to return. The demon again met him, to take the fruit away. The man then took the fruit and put it in his mouth. The demon forthwith seized him by the throat; but the man managed to swallow the fruit. Directly it had entered his inside, his whole body began to swell enormously. His head indeed was outside the entrance, but the rest of his body was still within the cavern, so that he could not drag it through the hole.

After this his relations began to search for him, and at length, seeing him thus changed in form, they were very much frightened. But on going to him, he was still able to speak a few words about his misfortune. The friends then returned, and bringing a number of other persons with them, they tried by force of main strength to get him out from where he was fixed. But they were not able to move him.

The king of the country hearing of the circumstance, himself went to see the man; and fearing some future calamity, he sent some persons to dig him out; but even so they could not move him.

Months and years having elapsed, the man was gradually changed into stone, but he still kept his human form.

After this, again, there was a king knowing that it was a fairy fruit that caused the change, addressed his ministers and said: "That man's body was changed by virtue of a medicinal herb, then his body must partake of this medicinal quality; and although apparently he is only a stone, nevertheless his substance must contain in it something spiritual and divine. You must send men with axes and chisels to separate some few fragments from the rock and then bring them to me."

The ministers in obedience to the king's orders despatched master workmen to the place and themselves accompanied them. During ten days they worked with chisels and axes, but were not able to get so much as a fragment of the rock. It is still visible.

From this, going eastward 400 *li* or so, we come to the kingdom of *Ki-shu-ho-kie-lo* (Kajûghîra). Here also he examined and reverenced the sacred traces. There are six or seven Sanghârâmas with about 300 priests.

Going east from this and crossing the Ganges, after about 600 *li* we come to *Pu-na-fa-tan-na* (Pundravardhana). Here again he paid reverence to the sacred traces. There are about twelve Sanghârâmas here and 3000 priests, belonging to the Small and Great Vehicle.

Twenty *li* or so to the west of the capital is the *Po-chi-sha* [1] Sanghârâma. The towers and balconies are lofty and grand. There are about 700 priests. By the side of it is a stûpa, built by Aśôka-râja. Here Tathâgata formerly dwelt for three months preaching the Law. The stûpa frequently emits a shining light, moreover there are traces where the four past Buddhas walked up and down.

By the side of it there is a Vihâra, in which is a figure of Avalôkiteśvara Bôdhisattva. Whoever prays here with perfect sincerity, is always answered.

Going south-east from this 900 *li* or so, we come to the country of *Kie-lo-na-su-fa-la-na* (Karṇasuvarṇa).

There are about ten Sanghârâmas here and 300 priests; they study the Little Vehicle belonging to the Sammatîya school.

Besides these there are two Sanghârâmas where they do not use either butter or milk—this is the traditional teaching of Devadatta.[2]

By the side of the capital is the Sanghârâma called

[1] For *po-chi-po*, vidé *Records*, ii. 195, *n.* 23.
[2] *Vide Records*, ii. 201, *n.* 39.

Ki-to-mo-chi (*red mud:* the Si-yu-ki gives *Lo-to-wei-chi*, Raktaviṭi). In old days before this country had heard of the law of Buddha, then a Shaman of South India in his wanderings came here, and having overcome in argument a heretic who wore round his person some copper sheets, on that account the king of the country established this convent.[1]

By the side of it is a stûpa built by Aśôka-râja: here Buddha in old times preached for seven days.

Going from this south-east we come to the country of Samataṭa, whose frontiers border on the great sea. The climate is in consequence soft and agreeable. There are about twenty Sanghârâmas here, with 3000 priests. They affect the teaching of the Sthavira[2] school. The heretics also who worship the spirits of heaven are numerous.

Going not far out of the city is a stûpa built by Aśôka-râja; this is the place where in old times Buddha preached the law in favour of Devas and men for seven days.

Again going from this a short distance is a Sanghârâma in which is a green-jade figure of Buddha, about eight feet high; its characteristic marks are beautiful and imposing. It exhales constantly of itself a delicious perfume, which fills the temple court like that of opening flowers wafted from far. From time to time it emits a heaven-like shining light of the five different colours. Every one seeing or hearing of this wonder, is deeply affected in his religious consciousness.

Going from this north-east along the borders of the sea, across mountains and valleys we come to the country of *Chi-li-t'sa-ta-lo* (Śrîkshetra); still going south-east, in a bay of the sea, is the country of Kâmalâṅkâ (Pegu); east of this is the country of Dvârapati (Sandoway); east of this is the country of Iśânapura; east of this is

[1] *Records*, ii. p. 202.

[2] Not, as Julien says, the *Sarvâstivâdas*.

the country of Mahâchampâ (Siam: also called *Lin-I*); west of this is the country of Yen-mo-lo (*Yamarâja*; but probably a mistake for *Yen-mo-na-chau*, the country of the Yavanas).[1] These six kingdoms are bordered by mountains and the deep sea. Although Hiuen-Tsiang did not enter their territory, he was yet able to gain knowledge of the customs and manners (*of the people*).

Going from this country of Samataṭa in a westerly direction about 900 *li*, we come to the kingdom of Tâmralipti, which lies along a bay of the sea. There are some ten Sanghârâmas here, and a congregation of about 1000 priests.

By the side of the city is a Stûpa, about 200 feet high, which was built by Aśôka-râja; by the side of it are traces where the four past Buddhas walked to and fro.

At this time the Master heard that in the middle of the ocean there was a country called Siṁhala;[2] it was distinguished for its learned doctors belonging to the Sthavira school, and also for those able to explain the *Yoga-śâstra*.

After a voyage of 700 *yojanas*, it was possible to reach that country.

On hearing about this he inquired of a priest of South India, who, in consultation, told him, as follows: "Those who go to the Siṁhala country ought not to go by the sea route, during which they will have to encounter the dangers of bad weather (*winds*), the Yakshas, and rolling waves; you ought rather to go from the south-east point of South India, from which it is a three days' voyage. For although in travelling you may have to scale mountains and pass through valleys, yet you are safe. Moreover, you will thus be able to visit Orissa and other countries, and observe the sacred traces.

[1] *Vide Records, &c.*, ii. p. 200. [2] The *lion-taking country*.—Ch. Ed.

The Master of the Law immediately set out in a south-westerly direction towards Orissa (Uḍa).[1] There are here about 100 Saṅghârâmas, and 10,000 priests or so. They study the Great Vehicle. Moreover, there are heretics who worship the powers of heaven, living in mixed society with the others. There are about ten Stûpas, all of which were built by Aśôka; they exhibit spiritual indications.

The south-eastern frontiers of the country border on the great sea. There is a town called *Chi-li-ta-lo* (Charitra). This is a rendezvous for merchants who embark on the sea, and for others from distant places who travel here and there.

At a distance of 20,000 *li* south,[2] is the country of Siṁhala. Every night when the sky is clear and without clouds, can be seen at a great distance the glittering rays of the precious gem placed on the top of the Stûpa of the tooth of Buddha; its appearance is like that of a shining star in the midst of space.

From this, going south-west and passing through a vast forest about 1200 *li*, we come to the country of *Kong-u-t'o* (Konyôdha, Ganjam ?).

From this, going south-west 1400 or 1500 *li* through a wild forest, we come to the *Kie-ling-kia* country (Kaliṅga). There are about ten Saṅghârâmas here, occupied by some 500 priests, who study the Law according to the Sthavira school. Formerly the population of this country was very dense, but on account of some trouble with a Ṛishi possessed of the five supernatural powers, who being angry, imprecated ruin and destruction on the kingdom, the population, young and old, perished; afterwards, people from other places gradually migrated here, but even now the population is sparse.

Going north-west from this about 1800 *li*, we come to Southern Kôsala. The king is of the Kshattriya

[1] Or, Uḍra: *vide Records.* ii. 204.

[2] Julien gives 2000.

caste. He deeply reverences the law of Buddha, and is well affected towards learning and the arts. There are 100 Saṅghârâmas here, and 10,000 priests. There are a great number of heretics who live intermixed with the population, and also Deva temples.

Not far to the south is an old Saṅghârâma. By the side of it is a Stûpa built by Aśôka râja. In old days Tathâgata exhibited great spiritual changes in this place and overcame the heretics. Afterwards Nâgârjuna Bôdhisattva dwelt here. At that time the king of the country was named Sadvâha *So-to-p'o-ho*; he highly esteemed Nâgârjuna, and abundantly supplied all his wants.

At this time Deva Bôdhisattva came from the country of Siṁhala to seek to discuss on some (*religious*) difficulties. Coming to the door he requested permission to pass through. The gate-keeper announced him; on this Nâgârjuna, knowing his name of old, filled a dish full of water and told a disciple to take it and show it to him.

Deva seeing the water, without speaking, cast a needle into it. The disciple then brought it back.

Nâgârjuna having seen it was full of joy and said: "This water so bright and full is the symbol of my character (*qualities*). That man who has come and thrown a needle into it, has done so to show that he can investigate these to the bottom: if such be the man, I can discuss with him on the dark and mysterious doctrines of religion, and he may hand down the light (*lamp*)." He immediately caused him to be brought in, and having seated him, they entered on mutual conversation, as pleasant and agreeable, as the fish finds the water to be. Then Nâgârjuna said: "I am now old and worn out; does the pure, shining orb of Wisdom reside with you (*i.e. are you able to succeed me as Teacher*)?"

Deva, rising and reverently bowing at the foot of Nâgârjuna, said: "Although your servant is of small ability yet he will venture to hand down your loving instructions."

In this country there was a Brahman who was skilled in explaining the treatise called *In-ming;* the Master of the Law remained here a month and some days and read (with him ?) the *Tsah-liang-lun.*

From this, tending southwards, he passed through a great forest, and going some 900 *li* south-east, he came to the kingdom of Andhra.

By the side of the capital is a large Saṅghârâma with richly ornamented beams, extensive courts, and its whole appearance venerable and majestic. Before it is a stone stûpa several hundred feet high which was constructed by the Arhat Achala.

South-west of the Saṅghârâma, about twenty *li,* is an isolated hill on the top of which is a stone stûpa; here the Bodhisattva Ch'in-na (*Jina?* or was his name *Yuvana jana?*) composed the Śâstra *In-ming* (Hetuvidyâ ?).

Going about 1000 *li* to the south of this we come to the kingdom of Dhanakaṭaka. To the east of the capital resting against a mountain is a Saṅghârâma called Pûrvaśilâ. To the west of the capital resting against a mountain is a Saṅghârâma called Avaraśilâ.[1] A former king of this country founded these for Buddha's sake; he thoroughly investigated the rules and patterns of *Ta-hia*[2] (*for constructing such buildings*). The woods and fountains, flourishing and charming, the spirits of heaven defending and protecting, caused both wise men and holy men, to reside here. In the middle of the 1000 years after Buddha's Nirvâṇa, there were ever laymen and clerics coming here together to keep their religious rest. The

[1] I can only surmise that the expression "resting against a mountain" means, that the Saṅghârama was hewn out of the mountain side: but *vide Records, &c.,* ii. 221 and notes. With respect to the terms *Pûrvaśilâ* and *Avaraśilâ,* as denoting two minor schools of the Mahâsaṅghika sect, *vide* my *Travels of Buddhist Pilgrims,* p. 143, n.

[2] *Ta-Hia* is constantly used by Taou-Sün as equivalent to *North India,* or, that part of *North-west India,* conquered by the Yue-ti. Mr. Kingsmill restores *Ta-hia* to Tocharia; which may be correct, but is vague. I believe the reference to the text is to the Stûpas erected in North-West India, by the Indo-Scythians (so called).

season of rest being past, all who were Arhats would mount into space and depart. After the 1000 years, both laymen and holy men lived together here, but for 100 years or so the Mountain Spirit changing itself (*into various shapes*) has caused great annoyance, and the religious people (*those practising religion*) have all been so alarmed that they no longer come or go. Hence the place is now entirely waste and desert, without either priest or novice.

Not far to the south of the capital is a great stone mountain; this is where the Master of Śâstras Bhâvavivêka rests in the palace of the Asuras awaiting the time when Maitrêya Bôdhisattva shall reach perfect wisdom, and shall then explain some difficulties in his way.

The Master of the Law, whilst in this country, met with two priests, the first named Subhûti, the second Sûrya: both of them eminent for explaining the Tripitaka according to the Mahâsañghika school.

The Master of the Law on this account remained there several months studying the Mûlâbhidharma and other śâstras, according to the Mahâsañghika school.[1] They also studied the various śâstras of the Great Vehicle under the direction of the Master of the Law. And so becoming bound together in mind they all went in company to pay reverence to the sacred traces of their religion.

Going from this about 1000 *li* to the south we come to the kingdom of Chulya.

South-east of the capital is a stûpa built by Aśôka râja. This is the spot where in old days Buddha, when in this district, exhibited great spiritual prodigies and overcame the heretics, preaching the Law for the conversion of Devas and men.

[1] It seems evident that these Sañghârâmas, in the neighbourhood of Amrâvti, were built by the followers of the Mâhâsaṁghika sect, which is distinctly opposed to the Sthavira sect of Ceylon.

To the west of the capital is an old Sanghârâma; this is the place where the Dêva Bôdhisattva discussed with the Arhat Uttara. After the seventh round of questions the Arhat gave no further answer; but by the exercise of his supernatural faculties, he passed into the Tuśita heaven, and there asked Mâitreya Bôdhisattva respecting his difficulties. The Bôdhisattva gave him the explanations required, and then, taking advantage of the occasion, addressed him thus: "That Deva, having a long accumulated store of merit, will, during this Bhadra Kalpa, perfect himself in the highest wisdom. You must not treat him lightly." Having returned to the spot he now undertook to explain the former difficulties. The Deva said: "This is the reasoning of Mâitreya Bôdhisattva and not your own, and your wisdom is derived from him."

The Arhat, filled with confusion, confessed his inferiority, and paying him reverence left the place.

Going south from this through a great forest some 1500 or 1600 *li*, we come to the kingdom of Drâvida; the chief capital of this kingdom is named Kânchîpura; this was the birthplace of Dharmapâla Bôdhisattva. He was the son of a great minister of this kingdom. As a child he exhibited wonderful wisdom. After he had assumed the virile cap, the king, enamoured by his talent, wished to give him a princess of his family in marriage. The Bôdhisattva, who had long disciplined himself to reject sensual pleasures, had no mind to incur the pollutions of love; on the evening preceding the consummation of the marriage, he was overcome with feelings of grief and despondency, and betook himself to an image of Buddha before which he offered up his prayers and besought his protection and deliverance from his present difficulties, and this he did with all his heart.

There was a great king of the spirits who (*in consequence*) transported him by his power several hundred *li* from the city. He deposited him in a mountain convent, in the middle of the hall of Buddha. The priests coming in and seeing him there, agreed together that he was a thief. The Bôdhisattva himself related his adventure, on which his auditors were filled with astonishment and could not but admire his high resolve. He now entered the religious life, and applied himself thereafter with all his powers to the practice of the true Law. In consequence he was able to penetrate the meaning of all the schools, and to exercise himself in the art of religious composition. He drew up the following works: the *Sabdavidyâ-samyukta-śâstra*, in 25,000 ślôkas; a commentary on the *Śataśâstra-vâipulyam;* on the *Vidyâmâtra-siddhi;* and on the *Niyâya-dvâra-târaka-śâstra*—altogether several tens of books: very extended and highly significant of his eminent virtue and great talent. There is, moreover, a personal narrative of his history.

The city of Kânchîpura is situated on the mouth (*bay*) of the southern sea of India, looking towards the kingdom of Simhala, distant from it three days' voyage.

In the interval (before the Master of the Law left this kingdom) the king of Simhala died: the country was at that time suffering from famine and in a state of disorder, there were two eminent priests there called Bôdhimêghêśvara and Abhayadanshṭra.

These two with 300 other priests, coming to India, arrived at Kânchîpura.

The Master of the Law, having obtained an interview with them, asked them as follows: "It is reported that the chief priests of your kingdom are able to explain the Tripiṭaka according to the Sthavira school, and also the Yôga-śâstra. I am anxious to go there and study these books. May I ask why you have come to this place?" In reply, they said: "The king of our country is dead: and the people are suffering from famine, without any resource for help. We heard that Jambudvîpa possessed abundance of food and was at peace and settled. This, too, is the place of Buddha's birth, and full of sacred traces of his presence: for this reason we have come. Moreover, among the members of our school who know the Law there are none who excel ourselves as to age and position; if you have any doubts therefore, let us, according to your will, speak together about these things."

The Master of the Law then gave examples of choice passages of the *Yoga-śâstra*, both long and short sections, but they were not able to explain any of them as Śîlabhadra did.[1]

It is reported that 3000 *li* or so from the frontiers of this kingdom is the country of Malakûta; as it borders on the sea-coast it is exceedingly abundant in different gems.

To the east of its chief town is a stûpa built by Aśôka-râja. This is the spot where in old days Tathâgata preached the Law and exhibited many spiritual changes, for the conversion of an innumerable company of persons.

To the south of this kingdom bordering on the sea is Malayagiri, with its precipices and ravines, towering upwards and lying deep. Here is found the white sandal-scented tree, the Chandanêva tree. This tree is like the white poplar. Its substance being of a cold nature, many kinds of snakes frequent the trees during summer, but in the winter they conceal themselves in the ground. Thus this kind of sandal tree is distinguished.

Again there is the Karpûra scented tree. It is like the pine in its trunk, but leaves different, as also its blossoms and fruit. When the tree is cut down and full of sap, it has no scent, but when it has been cut down and dry, then dividing it through the middle there is found the scented portion, in appearance like mother of pearl and of the colour of congealed snow. This is what is called Dragon-brain scent (*camphor*).

Again, it is reported that on the north-east by the

[1] The *Yoga* system was probably unknown, or slightly known, in Ceylon It was a late development of Buddhism.

border of the sea is a city, and from the city, going south-east 3000 *li* or so, we come to the country of Siṁhala.

The circuit of this country is about 7000 *li*: and its capital about forty *li* round. It is thickly populated and produces an abundance of grain. The people are black, small of stature, and very impulsive: such is their character.

The country was originally called *Po-chu*, having many gems of a rare character. Afterwards there was a woman of South India betrothed to one of a neighbouring kingdom, who on her journey met with a lion-king. The servants and the attendants, filled with fear, were scattered here and there, leaving the woman alone in the palanquin. The lion approaching, bore the woman far away. Entering the deep mountains he gathered fruits and chased the game in order to provide her with food. After a captivity of some years she gave birth to a son and daughter, in appearance like human beings, nevertheless of a hot and violent temper.

The youth having grown up addressed his mother thus, "Of what kind am I?—my father a beast, my mother a human being." The mother then recounted to him the old history, for his information.

The son said, in reply: "Since men and beasts are of two different kinds, why not leave him and keep a mutual guard, one against the other?"

The mother said: "I have no disinclination to do so, only I see no method of escape."

The son then followed his father as he passed over mountains and through valleys, and observed his route; then on another day, taking advantage of his father's absence, he carried off his mother and sister to a neighbouring village. Then arriving at the native country of his mother, he inquired after her male relatives, but found they were all extinct. They then sought refuge in a neighbouring village.

The lion-king returning and not finding his wife and children, filled with fury left the forest angrily roaring, and destroyed many women and men of the villages, as he roamed to and fro.

The people informed the king of these facts, and he collected the four kinds of troops, the most courageous he had, to surround (*the lion*) and kill him with their arrows. The lion having observed this, uttered the most dreadful roars, and frightened both men and horses, so no one dared to attack him.

So many days passed without any result. The king then issued another proclamation promising a hundred thousand gold pieces to any one who could slay the lion.

Then the son spake to his mother thus: "The cold and want we suffer are sad calamities. I will respond to the invitation of the king—what think you?"

The mother said: "It is impossible; for although he is a beast, yet he is your father, and if you should kill him, how can you claim the name of a man?"

The son said: "Unless I follow out my plan he will certainly not go away: and whilst he is pursuing and following us he may enter the village, and then some morning the king will know of our return, and our death will not be long deferred. What then? The lion by his fury is a source of disaster, and it will befall us also. How can it be that for the sake of one, many should suffer loss? I have thought over it again and again; it ought not to be so, I must comply with the request."

So he went out (*to attack the lion*)! The lion when he saw him was subdued in manner, and was full of joy: he cast off all evil designs of slaughter. The son taking a knife cut his throat and rent his belly. Although agonised with suffering the lion still retained his love and deep affection, and bore his pain patiently and never moved till he died.

The king hearing of the lion's death, was rejoiced, but on account of the strangeness of the circumstances, he inquired as to the cause (*of the son's conduct*).

At first he prevaricated, but being hardly pressed, he was betrayed at last into a confession of the truth.

The king hearing it exclaimed: "Psha! who except one born of a beast could have had such a heart? Although I shall not recede from my first promise as to the reward; yet as you have shown yourself to be a man guilty of the crime of a parricide, you may no longer remain in this country."

He then directed the magistrates to give him abundance of gold and precious jewels, and afterwards to drive him into banishment.

Accordingly they equipped two ships, in which they placed a quantity of gold and treasure of all sorts, and provisions. Having conducted them[1] to the mid ocean they then let them drift at the mercy of the tide. The ship containing the young man, after beating about a long while, arrived at Po-chu, where, seeing the abundance of its rare productions, he resolved to stay.

Afterwards merchantmen with their family connections came there in search of jewels, and took up their abode in his neighbourhood. On this he killed the merchants and detained their wives and daughters. Thus the children and grandchildren increased through many generations, and when the population became by degrees very numerous, they elected a ruler and ministers, and because their distant ancestor had captured and slain the lion, they called their country (by its name, *Siṁhala*).

The ship which carried the girl, after beating about at sea, came to the western parts of Persia. Falling into the hands of demons who dwell there, she gave birth to a number of daughters, and this is now the country of the Western women.

But it is also said that Siṁhala is the name of a merchant's son, who by his rare wisdom escaped from the murderous purpose of the Raksha demons, and afterwards,

[1] That is, the brother and sister.

being elected king, came to this Po-chu island and slew the Rakshas, and established his capital in the country. Hence the name, as narrated in the *Si-yu-ki.*[1]

This kingdom in former days was without the law of Buddha. One hundred years after the Nirvâṇa of Tathâgata, the younger brother of Aśôka-râja, Mahêndra by name, giving up and rejecting the pleasures of life, taking with him *four*[2] Śramanas, forthwith travelling here and there through space, came to convert this country. In order to exhibit and exalt the teaching of Buddha, he manifested his miraculous powers. The people of the country, full of faith and admiration, founded a Saṅghârâma. At present there are some hundred such foundations, with 10,000 priests. They follow the teaching of the Great Vehicle, and belong to the school of the Sthaviras. The lay disciples are grave and respectful, following the directions of the moral code with intelligence and zeal, stimulating one another to mutual diligence.

By the side of the king's palace is the Vihâra of Buddha's tooth, several hundred feet high. It is decorated with every kind of precious substance. On the top of it is erected a signal staff, which is surmounted by a great ruby (*Padmarâga jewel*), and fixed to the *tee.*[3] Its brilliant sparkling lights up the heaven, and on a clear and cloudless night it can be seen by those who are even 10,000 *li* distant.

By the side of this is another Vihâra decorated with every kind of gem. Within this building is a golden statue made by a former king of the country, in the tiara of which is a precious gem of incalculable value. In after times there was a man who wished to steal this jewel. The place, however, was so well guarded and watched that he could not get inside. He then excavated

[1] Records, ii. 240. [2] Dipavaṁsa, xii. § 25.
[3] The Khettiya, or graduated spire.

a subterranean passage and so entered the building. When he was just going to take the gem the figure gradually grew higher, so that the robber was not able to reach it. Then as he went away, he said: "Tathâgata, when he practised the discipline of a Bôdhisattva in former days, did not grudge to sacrifice his life for the sake of all flesh, nor did he scruple to give up his country or his (*native*) city—how comes it then that he is now niggard in his gifts? We fear that these reports about him are not true." The image, on this, bent himself down and gave the jewel. The thief having taken it, went forth and proposed to sell it. But the men who saw it and recognised it, seized the robber and brought him to the king. The king demanded how he got the gem. He replied, Buddha himself gave it me—and he related the whole transaction. The king on his part, seeing the head of the image bent downwards, perceived that the event was spiritual and sacred, and so his faith was greatly deepened, and he gave the robber all kinds of gems and precious substances in exchange for the (*stolen*) jewel. Then taking it back he replaced it on the tiara of the image, and there it still is.

At the south-east corner of the country is Laṅkâgiri. Many dêvas and associates of evil spirits dwell here. Tathâgata in old time delivered the Laṅkâvatâra Sûtra on this mountain.

To the south of the country, many thousand *li* across the ocean, is the island called Nârikîra. The men of this island are small of stature, about three feet in height; they have the bodies of men, but with beaks like birds. They have no grain-food, but live on cocoa-nuts.

This country[1] being too remote, and separated by an expanse of sea, the Master was not able to visit it himself, but has related in detail all that he heard from men's mouths.

[1] *i.e.* Siṁhala.

From Drâviḍa he went north-west in company with about seventy priests from Simhala, and visited the sacred traces for the purpose of reverent observation.

After going about 2000 *li*, we come to *Kin-na-po-lo*[1] [*Kongkaṇapura*]. There are about 100 Sanghârâmas here, and 10,000 priests belonging both to the Great and Little Vehicle. The heretics who practise the worship of Dêvas are also very numerous.

By the side of the royal palace precincts is a large Sanghârâma with about 300 resident priests, all of them greatly reverenced for their literary talents. In this Vihâra is a precious head-dress[2] of the Prince Siddhârtha about two feet high; it is preserved in a richly adorned casket. Every religious fast day it is taken out and placed on a high pedestal; those who offer it sincerest reverence, frequently see it lit up with radiance.

In a Sanghârâma by the side of the city is a Vihâra in which is a carved sandal-wood figure of Maîtreya Bôdhisattva, about ten feet high. This, also, frequently glistens with radiance. It is said that twenty million Arhats carved the image.

To the north of the city is a forest of Talas trees, about thirty *li* in circuit. The leaves of this tree are long, and of a shining appearance. The people of these countries use them for writing on,[3] and they are highly valued.

From this, going north-west, we pass through a great forest which is infested with savage animals and desert; after 2400 or 2500 *li*, we come to the kingdom of Mahârâshtra. The people of this country despise death, and highly esteem right conduct.

The king is of the Kshattriya caste. He is fond of military affairs, and boasts of his arms. In this country, therefore, the troops and cavalry are carefully equipped,

[1] For, *Kong-kin-na-po-lo*.

[2] Julien gives "the *statue* of the Prince;" but it is not so in the text.

[3] Hence it is sometimes called the *Pei-to*, *i.e.* the leaf (*patra*) tree.

and the rules of warfare thoroughly understood and observed. Whenever a general is despatched on a warlike expedition, although he is defeated and his army destroyed, he is not himself subjected to bodily punishment, only he has to exchange his soldier's dress for that of a woman, much to his shame and chagrin. So, many times, those men put themselves to death to avoid such disgrace. The king always supports several thousand men of valour, and several hundred savage elephants. When these are drawn up in battle array, then they give them intoxicating spirits to drink, till they are overpowered with it—and then at a given signal, when in this condition, they excite them to rush against (*the enemy*). His foes are thus without fail put to flight. Relying on these advantages, he holds in contempt all the frontier powers that contend with him for the mastery.

Śilâditya râja, boasting of his skill and the invariable success of his generals, filled with confidence himself, marched at the head of his troops to contend with this prince—but he was unable to prevail or subjugate him.[1]

There are about 100 Saṅghârâmas here, and 5000 priests, who belong to the Great and Little Vehicle promiscuously. There are also followers of the heretics who worship the Dêvas, and cover themselves with ashes.

Within and outside the capital there are five Stûpas, all of them several hundred feet (*in height*). These were built by Aśôka-râja, as mementos of the places where the four past Buddhas had walked to and fro.

From this kingdom, going north-west a thousand *li* or so, crossing the river Ni-mo-to (*Narmmadâ*), we come to the kingdom of *Po-lu-kie-chen-po* (Baroche).

From this, going north-west about 2000 *li*, we come

[1] *Vide Records*, vol. ii. p. 256. The Prince's name was Pulakeśi.

to the country of *Mo-la-p'o* (Mâlava).[1] The people of this country in their manner are polished and agreeable. They exceedingly love the fine arts. In all the five Indies, Mâlava on the south-west, and Magadha on the north-east alone have the renown of loving the study of literature, of honouring virtue (or *goodness*), and of polite language and finished conversation.

There are about 100 Saṅghârâmas in this country, with 20,000 priests who study the Small Vehicle and belong to the Sammatîya school. There are also heretics who cover themselves with ashes and worship the host of Dêvas. Tradition says: Sixty years before this there was a king called Śilâditya,[2] of high talent and singular learning. He was humane, affectionate, generous, and sweetly attached to his people. He was from the first supremely reverent to the doctrine of the three precious ones; and from the time he became king to his death no improper word had proceeded from his mouth, nor had his face ever flushed with passion.

His thoughts towards his ministers and his wives were always tender, nor would he even injure a fly or an ant. He caused the water given to his horses and elephants first to be strained and then to be given them, lest he should destroy the life of a water insect. He impressed on the chief people of the kingdom to avoid taking life, and hence the beasts of the desert became attached to men, and the wolves ceased to be injurious. All the occupants within his borders were quiet, and the indications of good fortune daily presented themselves. He constructed temporary residences on the largest and grandest scale, and made figures of the seven Buddhas. He also convoked the assembly called "Môksha (*Mahâparishad*)."

Thus for fifty years he continued on the throne carrying out these most excellent works without cessation;

[1] *Vide Records*, ii. 260.
[2] This was Silâditya of Ujjain, *Records*, i. 108, *n*. 91.

and he thus endeared himself to his people, and his memory is still revered.

Twenty *li* or so to the north-west of the capital by the side of Brâhmaṇapura (*the city of the Brâhmans*) is a deep ditch; this is the place where a great arrogant Brâhman when he abused the Great Vehicle with a view to its destruction, went down alive into hell, as is related in the *Su-yu-ki*.[1]

From this, going north-west 2400 or 2500 *li*, we come to the kingdom of *O-ch'a-li* (Aṭali). This district produces the *Hu-tsian* tree, the leaves of which are like those of the pepper-tree of Sz'chuen. It also produces the *Hiun-lu* (*Tagara* (Jul.)) perfume tree, the leaves of which are like those of the *Thang-li* (*the mountain ash*).

From this, going north-west three days, we come to the kingdom of K'ie Ch'a. About 1000 *li* to the north of this we come to the kingdom of Fa-la-pi (Vallạbhî). There are about 100 Sanghârâmas here, and 6000 priests who study the Little Vehicle, according to the Sammatîya school.

Tathâgata when alive frequently sojourned in this country. Aśôka-râja erected distinguishing mementos in all the places where Buddha stopped. The present king belongs to the Kshattriya caste; he is son-in-law (*nü sai*) of Śilâditya râja of the kingdom of Kanyâkubja; his name is Dhruvabhaṭa.[2] He is of a quick and impulsive nature, and his manners are heavy and dull, but yet he esteems virtue and advances learning. He is faithfully attached to the three treasures, and every year he assembles a great gathering, and for seven days he entertains priests from all countries and bestows on them

[1] *Records*, ii. 264.

[2] This name is explained in the *Si-yu-ki* by the symbols for "ever intelligent" = Dhruvabaṭṭa, but in the Text it is translated "Royal helmet," probably a mistake for "ever helmeted" or "armed" = Dhruvabhaṭa. *Vide Records*, ii. 267, *n.* 73.

food of the best description, choice jewels, bedding and clothes, with varieties of medicaments and other things of different kinds.

From this, going north-west about 700 *li*, we come to the country of Ânandapura.

Again, going 500 *li* or so to the north-west, we come to the kingdom of *La-su-c'ha* (for Su-la-c'ha), (*Surashṭra*).

From this, going north-east 1800 *li*, we come to the country of *Kiu-che-lo* (Gurjjara).

Again, going south-east 2800 *li* or so, we come to the country of *U-che-yen-na* (Ujjayanî). Not far from the capital is a stûpa; this is the spot where Aśôka-râja constructed his (*place of punishment called*) Hell.[1]

From this, going north-east about 1000 *li*, we come to the country of Chi-ki-to.

From this, going north-east 900 *li* or so, we come to the kingdom of Mahêśvarapura.

From this, going back in a westerly direction, we again come to the country of Suratha.

Going hence to the west we come to the kingdom of *O-tin-p'o-chi-lo* (Atyanabakêla). When Tathâgata was alive he repeatedly sojourned in this country, and Aśôka râja has raised stûpas on all the spots he visited (*left sacred traces*), all of which still exist.

From this, going west about 2000 *li*, we come to the country of Lang-kie-lo (*Laṅgala*), which lies near the Great Sea, towards the country of the Western women.

From this, going north-west, we come to the country of Po-la-sse (*Persia*), which is not within the boundaries of India. It is said that this territory abounds in pearls and precious substances, in silken brocades and wool, sheep, horses, and camels. There are two or three Sanghârâmas here, with some hundred disciples, who study the Little Vehicle, according to the school of the

[1] But *cf.* p. 102. The story must have been carried from Magadha into Mâlava.

Sarvâstavâdins. The pâtra of Sâkya Buddha is at present in the royal palace of this country. On the eastern frontier is the city of Ho-mo (*Ormuz*), the north-west borders on the country of Fo-lin.[1] On the south-west, on an island, is the country of the Western women. These women have no male children among them, but the country abounds with precious substances; it is tributary to Fo-lin. The king of Fo-lin every year sends men to cohabit with the women, but whatever male children are born, they do not rear them.

Again, going north-east from the kingdom of Lâṅgala, about 700 *li*, we come to the kingdom of Pi-to-shi-lo (Pitâśilâ). Here is a stûpa, several hundred feet high, which was built by Aśôka-râja. It contains relics which often emit a brilliant light. When Tathâgata was formerly born as a Ṛishi, he was slain here by the cruelty of the king of the country.

From this, going north-east about 300 *li*, we come to the kingdom of O-fan-ch'a (Avaṇḍa). North-east of the capital, in a great forest, are the ruins of a Saṅghârâma. Buddha, when formerly living in this place, permitted the Bhikshus to wear *Kih-fuh-to*[2] (leather boots). There is a stûpa built by Aśôka râja; by the side of it is a vihâra, in which is a standing figure of Buddha, made of blue stone, which frequently emits a brilliant light.

South of this, about 800 paces in a large forest, there is a stûpa, which was built by Aśôka-râja. Tathâgata, in old days, was stopping on this spot, when, the night being cold, he wrapped himself up in three garments, one over the other. When the morning came, he gave permission to the Bhikshus to wear quilted garments.[3]

Going from this eastwards 700 *li* or so, we come to the country of Sin-tu (*Sindh*). This country produces

[1] Probably Ba(*bylon*).
[2] *Records*, ii. 280, *n.* 97.
[3] 納 for 衲.

gold, silver, calamine stone (*t'au shih*), oxen, sheep, camels, red salt, white salt, black salt, &c.

This last kind of salt is used in different places for making medicines. Tathâgata when alive, frequently sojourned in this country; whatever sacred traces of his presence there are, Aśôka-râja has built stûpas on those spots as mementos. There are also here traces of the great Arhat Upagupta, who sojourned here whilst engaged in the conversion of men.

From this, going east 900 *li* or so, crossing the river[1] to its eastern bank, we come to Mu-lo-san-po-lo (Mûlasthânapura or Multân, *Si-yu-ki*, ii. 274). The people sacrifice to the gods and worship *U-fa-tsun* (Âditya ?),[2] that is, the Sun[3]-God. His image is cast out of yellow gold, and adorned with every kind of precious stone. People from all neighbouring countries come here to offer their prayers. The flowery woods, the tanks and ponds, the tastefully arranged tiles, the surrounding steps, all these, when viewed as a pleasurable sight, cannot but inspire feelings of admiration.

From this, going north-east 700 *li* or so, we come to the kingdom of *Po-fa-to-lo*[4] (Parvata). By the side of the capital is a great Sañghârâma, with about 100 priests, all of whom study the Great Vehicle. It was here Jinaputra, Master of Śâstras, formerly composed the Yogâchârya-bhûmi-śâstra-kârikâ. Here, also, the Master of Śâstras, Bhadraruchi, and the Master of Śâstras, Guṇaprabha, originally became disciples.

Because this country had two or three leading priests whose claims for learning might serve for guidance, the Master of the Law stopped here two years[5] and studied

1 何 for 河

2 I should think rather a Persian, than a Sanscrit word, is to be sought here.

3 The symbol in the text is doubtful. But I take it for "Jih," *the sun*.

4 For, *Po-lo-fa-to*.

5 Julien has *months*.

the Mulâbhidharma-śâstra and the Saddharma-Sampâri-graha-śâstra, and the Prasikshâ-satya-śâstra, as received in the Sammatîya school.

From this, returning again by a south-east[1] route to Magadha, the Master arrived at the Nâlanda monastery. There he paid his respects to the priest called Ching-fă-tsong, after which he heard that to the west of this place about three yôjanas there was a convent called Tilaḍaka, where lived a renowned priest called Prajñabhadra, a native of Fo-lo-po-ti (Bâlapati?), who had embraced the religious life in the school of the Sarvâstavâdins.

This man had distinguished himself by his knowledge of the three Piṭakas, and of the Śabdavidyâ and the Hetuvidyâ śâstras, and others.

The Master of the Law having remained here for two months, closely questioned him about matters on which he had doubts.

From this he went again to the hill called Yashṭivana, and stopped with a householder who was a native of Suratha and a Kshattriya by caste — his name was Jayaseṅa, a writer of Śâstras. As a youth he was given to study, and first under Bhadraruchi, Master of Śâstras, he had studied the Hetuvidyâ-śâstra; then under Sthitamati Bôdhisattva, he had studied the Śabdavidyâ śâstra (*and others*), belonging to the Great and Little Vehicle. Again under Śilabhadra, Master of the Law, he had studied the Yoga-śâstra.

And then again, with respect to the numerous productions of secular (*outside*) writers: the four Vedas, works on astronomy and geography, on the medicinal art, magic and arithmetic, he had completely mastered these from beginning to end: he had exhausted these inquiries root (*leaf*) and branch; he had studied all of them both within and without. His acquirements (*virtue*) made him the admiration of the period.

Purṇavarma râja, lord of Magadha, had great respect

[1] Julien gives *North*-East.

for learned men, and honoured those distinguished as sages: hearing of this man's renown, he was much pleased, and sent messengers to invite him to come to his court, and nominated him "*Kwo-sse*" (Master of the Kingdom), and assigned for his support the revenue of twenty large towns. But the Master of Śâstras declined to receive them.

After the obsequies of Purṇavarma, Śîlâditya râja also invited him to be "the Master (*of the country*)," and assigned him the revenue of eighty large towns of Orissa. But again the Master declined the offer. The king still urged him repeatedly to acquiesce, but he as firmly refused. Then addressing the king he said: "Jayasêna has heard, that he who receives the emoluments of the world (*men*), also is troubled with the concerns of life; but now my object is to teach the urgent character of the fetters of birth and death; how is it possible then to find leisure to acquaint myself with the concerns of the king?"

So saying, he respectfully bowed and went away, the king being unable to detain him.

From that time he has constantly lived on the mountain called Yashṭivana, where he takes charge of disciples, teaching and leading them on to persevere, and expounding the books of Buddha. The number of laymen and priests (*religious persons*) who honour him as their Master is always a large one, amounting to several hundred.

The Master of the Law remained with him first and last for two years, and studied a treatise on the difficulties of the Vidyâ-matra-siddhi śâstra, the *I-i-li-lun*, the *Shing-wu-wai-lun*, the *puh-chu-ni-pan-shih-i-yin-un-lun*, the *chwong-yan-king-lun*; and he also asked explanations of passages in the Yôga and the Hetuvidyâ śâstras which yet caused him doubt.

When this was done he unexpectedly dreamt in the night and saw all the chambers and courts of the

Nâlanda monastery deserted and foul; moreover, there were nought but water buffaloes fastened in them, with no priests or followers. The Master of the Law entering through the Western gate of the hall of Bâlâditya râja, beheld on the top of the four-storeyed pavilion a golden-coloured man, of a grave and imposing countenance, whilst a glorious light shone within the entire abode. His mind was overjoyed, and he wished to ascend to the top, but he found no way to do so; he then besought him to reach down and lift him up—but he replied: "I am Manjuśri Bôdhisattva; your *karma* does not yet admit of (*such a privilege*)"—and then pointing to the outside of the convent, he said: "Do you see that?" The Master of the Law looking in the direction indicated by his finger, saw a fierce fire burning without the convent, and consuming to ashes villages and towns. Then the golden figure said: "You should [1] return soon, for after ten years Śilâditya râja will be dead,[2] and India be laid waste and in rebellion, wicked men will slaughter one another; remember these words of mine!" After he had finished, he disappeared.

The Master of the Law when he awoke, filled with pleasurable emotion, went to Jayasêna and told him of his dream. Jayasêna said: "There is no rest in the entire world (*the three worlds*): it is quite possible it may be, as you have heard in your dream; but as you have received the intimation, the responsibility is yours: you must use your own expedient." From this may be gathered, that whatever good men (*great students*) do, all is watched over by Bôdhisattvas. When thinking of going from India—then it was told to [3] Śîlabhadra and he detained me. When still delaying and not going back, then I was told of the fact of death, by way of exhortation to return. If my conduct were not in agree-

[1] Kwei tsz' chü = go from here.
[2] For a full examination of this subject, *vide* Max Müller's *India*, p. 286.
[3] p. 146, Jul.—*Supra*, p. 108.

ment with the holy mind (*of the Bôdhisattva*) how could this have happened?

So towards the end of the Yung Hwei[1] period (*i.e.* about 654–5, A.D.), Śîlâditya râja died, and India was subjected to famine and desolation, as had been predicted. The imperial ambassador, *Wang-ün-tse*, was at this time making ready to be a witness of these things.[2] It was now the beginning of the first month.

It is in this same month, according to the rules of the Western country, they bring forth from the Bôdhi convent (viz., *at Gâya*) the Śarîras of Buddha. Both laymen and priests from all countries come together to witness the spectacle, and to worship. The Master of the Law, therefore, with Jayasêna both went to see the relic-bones. These are both great and small. The large ones are like a round pearl, bright and glistening, and of a reddish-white colour. There are also flesh-relics, large as a bean, and in appearance shining red. An innumerable multitude of disciples offered incense and flowers; after ascribing praises and offering worship they take (*the relics*) back and place them in the Tower (*stûpa*).

At the end of the first watch of the night, Jayasêna and the Master of the Law were discoursing about the inequality as to size of the different Śarîras. Then Jayasêna said, "Your disciple has seen in different places śarîras (*only*) as large as rice grains, how happens it then that these are so large? Venerable sir! have you any doubts on this point?"

Hiuen-Tsiang replied, "I share your doubts in this matter."

After a little while the light of the lamps in the building was suddenly eclipsed, and within and without there was a supernatural illumination produced. On looking out they saw the relic-tower bright and effulgent as the sun, whilst from its summit proceeded a lambent

[1] This period lasted to 656 A.D.

[2] That is, the embassy from China to India now being prepared.

flame of five colours, reaching to the sky. Heaven and earth were flooded with light, the moon and stars were no longer seen, and a subtle perfume seemed to breathe through and fill the courts and the precincts.

Then it was noised abroad, from one to the other, that the *śarîras* were exhibiting a mighty miracle. All the multitude, being cognizant of it, came together, and again offered their adoration, and spoke in rapture of the wonderful sight. By degrees the light grew less and less, and when at the last moment it was about to die out, it seemed to encircle the dome of the tower several times, and then it was absorbed (*as it were*) within (*the tower*). And now heaven and earth were again wrapped in darkness, and the different stars once more appeared. All who witnessed this miracle were freed from doubts.[1]

They then paid worship to the Bôdhi tree, and also to the sacred vestiges, and eight days having passed they returned once more to the Nâlanda monastery.

At this time the Master of Śâstras, Śîlabhadra, deputed the Master of the Law to expound to the congregation the Mahâyâna-samparigraha-śâstra, and comments on the difficulties of the Vidyâ-matra-siddhi-śâstra.

At the same time an eminent priest named *Siṁharasmi*[2] had been explaining for the sake of the fraternity (the *four classes*) the Prâṇyamûla-śâstra and the Śata-śâstra, newly arranged, the object of which was to refute the principles of the Yôga.

The Master of the Law had, in the best of spirit, opposed the Prâṇyamûla and Śata-Śâstra, and approved of the Yôga, with the opinion that the illustrious (*holy*) men, who founded these doctrines, each followed one thought, and were not mutually at variance, or opposed; and if they cannot be quite reconciled, he said, yet these are not contradictory, and the fault is with their successors, but this cannot bar the truth of the Law.

[1] It is curious to find from these accounts, the prevalence of such "pious frauds" in India at this time.

[2] I adopt this rendering from Julien; my copy has sz', "part of an army," and not sz', "a lion."

From a feeling of pity for the narrow views of this doctor, the Master of the Law frequently went to question and to correct his opinions. But he was unable to induce him to reply. From this circumstance his disciples gradually left him, and attached themselves to the Master of the Law.

Hiuen-Tsiang aimed by the assertions of the Pranyamûla and Śata-śâstras simply to overthrow the conclusions of the Sañkhya, but said nothing about a self-derived or external nature, or the perfectly complete true nature (*of Buddha*)—but yet Siṁharasmi could not grasp the argument nor consent to its truth. He affirmed only the proposition "*yih-tsai-wu-sho-teh*," ("*all things without attainment*"),[1] and he affirmed that the conclusion of the Yôga in reference to the complete, perfect, and true (*nature*), &c., was an error, and this was the uniform position he took up in argument.

The Master of the Law, in order to reconcile the two doctrines,[2] affirming that they were not contradictory, composed a śâstra which he called *Hwui-Tsung* in 3000 ślôkas. When finished he presented it to Śîlabhadra and the great congregation. All spoke approvingly of it, and it is generally accepted for study (*practice*).

Siṁharasmi, filled with shame, forthwith left the convent and went to the Bôdhi monastery (*at Gâya*). There he privately requested a fellow-student of his, one Chandrasiṁha of Eastern India, to come with him and discuss these difficult points of doctrine, and so relieve him from his former disgrace. But when this man came he was faint-hearted and silent, and did not dare to say a word. Thus the fame of the Master of the Law increased greatly.

Before Siṁharasmi had departed Sîlâditya-râja had

[1] *i.e.* "*that nothing is to be attained by effort;*" this proposition is the opposite of *yih-tsai-yeou-sho-teh.*

[2] Viz., 1st, that there is nothing to be attained by effort; and 2nd, that we may attain the one true nature [*by Yôga*].

constructed a Vihâra covered with brass plates by the side of the Nâlanda monastery, about a hundred feet in height. It was renowned through all countries.

The king after returning from the subjugation of Koṅyodha (Ganjam ?) came to Orissa. The priests of this country all study the Little Vehicle, and do not believe in the Great Vehicle. They say it is a system of the "sky-flower" heretics, and was not delivered by Buddha. When they saw the king after his arrival, they entered into conversation and said: "We hear that the king has built by the side of the Nâlanda convent a Vihâra of brass, a work magnificent and admirable. But why did not your majesty construct a Kâpâlika temple, or some other building of that sort ?"

The king answered: "What mean you by these words of reproach ?"

In reply, they said: "The Monastery of Nâlanda and its 'sky-flower'[1] doctrine is not different from the Kâpâlika sect: this is our meaning."

Before this a consecrated king of South India had a teacher, an old Brâhman, whose name was Prajñagupta, who was well versed in the doctrine of the Sammatîya school. This man composed a treatise in 700 ślôkas against the Great Vehicle. All the teachers of the Little Vehicle were rejoiced thereat, and taking the book showed it to the king, and said: "This represents our doctrine: is there a man of the other school that can upset one single word of it ?"

The king said: "I have heard of the fox, accompanied by the meadow rats, boasting he was able to contend with the lion, but as soon as he saw him, then his heart failed him and they were all scattered in a moment. You, sirs, have not yet seen the priests of the Great Vehicle, and so you firmly maintain your foolish principles. If you once

[1] The *sky-flower* doctrine is fully explained in the Śurañgama Sûtra. It was evidently a doctrine developed in the Nâlanda monastery, as this Sûtra was framed there. The doctrine is simply that all objective phenomena are only, like *sky-flowers*, unreal and vanishing.

see them—affrighted, you will, *I fear, then, be the same as that* (fox).

Then they answered: "If there be any doubt on the king's part about the matter, why not assemble a conference and let there be a close investigation, as to right and wrong?"

The king said: "And what difficulty is there in this?"

So on that very day he sent a messenger with a letter to the Nâlanda convent to Śîlabhadra, the Master of the Law, surnamed "the treasure of the true doctrine," (*Saddharma piṭaka?*), in which he said: "Your servant, whilst progressing through Orissa, met some priests of the Little Vehicle who, hampered by contracted views, adhere to a *śâstra* which abuses the principles of the Great Vehicle. They speak of the followers of that system as men of a different religion, and they wish to hold a controversy with you on this point. Now I know that in your convent there are eminent priests and exceedingly gifted, of different schools of learning, who will undoubtedly be able to overthrow them—so now, in answer to their challenge, I beg you to send four men of eminent ability, well acquainted with one and the other school, and also with the esoteric and exoteric doctrine, to the country of Orissa."

When Śîlabhadra had received the letter, he assembled the congregation, and after inquiry, he selected Sâgaramati, Prajñarasmi, Siṁharasmi, and the Master of the Law, as the four men in reply to the king's mandate. When Sâgaramati and the others were anxious about the result, the Master of the Law said: "Hiuen-Tsiang, Master of the three piṭakas, when residing in his own (or, *my own*) country, and also when he resided in Kaśmir, thoroughly examined all the schools of learning belonging to the Little Vehicle. Those separatists, if they purpose by their doctrines to overthrow the Great Vehicle, will not be able to do it. Hiuen-Tsiang, al though he were a man of slender ability and ordinary wisdom, would nevertheless be quite sufficient (*to overcome them*). Be not therefore anxious, venerable sirs! If he were to suffer defeat, he knows that the priests of China from this time would have no reputation!"

On this they were all filled with joy.

But Śîlâditya râja again sent a letter to this effect: "There is no immediate pressure for my former request: let them wait, and afterwards come here."

About this time there was a heretic of the "Shun-si" sect (*the Lôkâtiyas*), who came to dispute (*with the Nâlanda monks*), and he wrote out forty *theses* and hung them up at the Temple gate. "If any one within can refute these principles," he said, "I will then give my head as a proof of his victory."

Several days having passed without any response to this challenge, the Master of the Law sent an attendant (*pure man*) from within his quarters to go and pull down the writing (*document*), to tear it in pieces, and trample it under foot.

The Brahman in a great rage asked him and said: "Who are you?"

He said: "I am the servant of Mahâyânadêva."

The Brahman, who had long heard of the fame of the Master, was abashed, and dare not go in to dispute with him.

The Master of the Law therefore bade him come in and discuss the points. Then in the presence of Śîlabhadra he called on all the priests to be witnesses whilst he disputed with the Brahman. He then noticed in succession the various opinions of the different heretical schools, and said: The Bhûtas, Nirgranthas, the Kâpâlikas, and the Jutikas,[1] are all differently arrayed. The

[1] Or, *Chudinkas*, ascetics with matted hair. Cf. Eitel, *Handbook*, sub. *Djudingas*.

Saṅkhyas and the Vâiśeshikas[1] are mutually opposed. The Bhûtas cover themselves with cinders, and think this to be meritorious. Their skin of a livid white colour looking like a cat in the chimney corner. The Nirgranthas and their followers go without clothing, and so attract notice, making it a meritorious act to pull out their hair by violence; their skin dried up and their feet hard, and in appearance like the decayed wood on the river bank. The sect of the Kâpâlikas, with their chaplets of bones round their heads and necks, inhabiting holes and crevices of the rocks, like Yakshas who haunt the place of tombs. As for the Chingkias (*Chudinkas*), they wear garments soiled with filth, and eat putrid food. They resemble pigs that lie wallowing in the midst of a cesspool. And now, how can you regard these things as proofs of wisdom?—are they not evidences of madness and folly?

As to the heretics called Saṅkhyas (*sho-lun*), they establish twenty-five principles; from *prakriti* or *mûla-prakriti*, proceeds *mahat;* from *mahat* proceeds *ahankâra;* from this proceed the five subtle particles (called *tanmâtra*); from these proceed the five elements; from these the eleven organs (of sense and action). These twenty-four all minister to and cherish the *soul* (âtman), which accepting and using the help thus given, excludes and removes itself. This being done, then the "*soul*" remains pure and uncontaminated.[2]

As for the Vaiśêshikas,[3] they establish six predicaments, viz., "the true" (*substance*), quality, action, existence, the same and the different nature, the harmonious aggregate nature. These six are apprehended by soul, which by apprehending them, not being already liberated, is, by this apprehension, liberated, and by freedom from the six *lakshanas*,[4] it arrives at what is called Nirvâṇa.

[1] Formerly called *Wei-si-sse;* the expression used in the Text *Shing-lun*, probably refers to this system, as a *logical* school of philosophy.

[2] The difficulty of this translation is very great. I depend on the Chinese version of the Saṅkhya-Kârikâ (*Nanjio*, No. 1300).

[3] Colebrooke, p. 182.

[4] Chinese "*siang*."

But now, to rebut the principles of the Sâṁkhya-Sâstra; you say that in the presence of your twenty-five principles, the character of "*soul*"[1] is distinct and diverse, but by intermingling with the other twenty-four it becomes substantially and intimately one. And you say that Nature (*Prakriti*) is hypostatised by union with the three "*gunas*" of "Sattva," "rajas" and "tamas," and by intermingling of these three, there is perfected the "*Mahat*" and the other twenty-three principles; thus you affirm that these twenty-three principles are perfected by the three *gunas*. But if you constrain your "*Mahat*" and the others, to lay hold of the three, and so to become perfect, as in case of a crowd or a forest[2] and without this intermingling they are false,—how then do you say that "all things are true" (*substantially true*)?

Again, "Mâhat" and the rest, being each perfected by the three, then each one so perfected is the same as the whole; but if each is the same as the whole, then the office of each ought to be the same, and then, where is the force of the three forming the substance of all? Again, if one is the same as all, then the mouth and the eye functions, and so on, are the same as the functions of nature.

Again, if each function discharges the duties of all, then the mouth and the ear, and so on, ought to smell perfumes and see colours; for if not, what is the meaning of the assertion that the three "*gunas*" make one common substance? How can any sensible man formulate such principles?

But again, "*Prakriti*" and "*âtman*," both being eternal, ought to be in their hypostases identical; how, then, can one, in distinction from the other, by intermingling, produce Mâhat, and so on?

But again, with respect to the nature of "*âtman*," if it

[1] Personal existence.

[2] "*We speak of the qualities of Nature as we do of the trees of a forest,*' say the Sankhyas.—*Colebrooke*, p. 158.

is eternal, then it is the same as "*prakriti*"—but if they are the same, then what need of speaking of "*âtman*"?—and then the "*âtman*" is not able to accept the aid of the twenty-four principles, and so there can be no possibility of establishing the different offices of "*subject*" and "*object*."

Thus far, and in the same way, he discoursed, whilst the Brahman was silent and unable to reply.[1]

But at last, rising up, he respectfully said: "I am overcome; I am ready to abide by the former compact."

The Master of the Law said: "We who are Śâkyaputras do not propose as our end the destruction of the life of men. I now bid you act as my servant and follow my directions (*teaching*, or *doctrine*).

The Brâhman was overjoyed and immediately attached himself to his service. All who heard of this affair were filled with admiration and praise.

And now, the Master of the Law being desirous to go to Orissa, inquired about getting the essay of the "*Little Vehicle*" which proposed to destroy the principles of the "*Great Vehicle*" in 700 ślokas.

The Master of the Law after examination found several passages of a doubtful character.

He then addressed the Brâhman whom he had conquered: "Have you in former days studied these principles or not?"

He replied: "Yes! I have studied them five times."

The Master of the Law wished to make him speak to the point—on which he said: "How can I, who am your slave, venture to instruct you?"

Then the Master of the Law said: "These are heretical doctrines of which I know nothing: you may speak to me without any compunction."

[1] The foregoing section is omitted by Julien. I offer my translation as tentative only.

"In that case," he said, "let us wait till the middle of night, lest any of the public should suppose that you had aught to learn from me, your slave, and so lose confidence in your celebrity."

Accordingly when the night was advanced he dismissed all the rest, and caused him to go through the entire work.

Then having grasped the errors of the work, he wrote a refutation of it in 1600 ślokas, and called it "*The destruction of heresy*," taking up the doctrines of the Great Vehicle, point by point.

He presented the work to Śîlabhadra, and amongst all the disciples there was not one, on reading the work, but was consenting to it. "Who," they said, "can overturn such arguments?"

And now, not forgetful of the origin of this refutation, he said to the Brâhman: "You have been sufficiently humiliated as my slave, after conquest had in argument; I now liberate you; you may go where you will."

The Brâhman, filled with joy, went forth to Kâmarûpa, in Eastern India, and told Kumâra-râja about the high qualities of the Master of the Law. The king hearing of it was overjoyed, and immediately sent a message, bidding the Master of the Law to come to him.

BOOK V.

Begins with the prediction of the Nirgrantha relating to his return home, and ends with his arrival in China.

In the interval, before the arrival of the messenger of Kumâra, a naked Nirgrantha disciple, whose name was Vajra, unexpectedly entered the chamber (*of the Master of the Law*).

Now the Master of the Law had heard of old time that the Nirgranthas are skilled in divination (*divining by lots*). He asked this man therefore to be seated and opened out his doubts to him, questioning and saying: "Hiuen-Tsiang, a priest of China, has been here inquiring and studying for a year and some months. He now wishes to return home, but does not know whether his way is open to do so, nor whether it is better for his good fortune to stay or to go; he is in doubt, too, about the length or shortness of his life. I pray you, good sir, cast my horoscope and see." [1]

The Nirgrantha then took a piece of white stone and drew a figure on the ground, and after casting the lots, he replied: "It is very good for the Master to stay, all the clergy and laity in the five Indies have a profound respect for him; the time for going and successfully returning, with the respect of all, is also fortunate; but not so good as the other. As for the years of your life, you will have ten years added to your present age. But as for evidence as to the continuation of your present good fortune, there is nothing to be found out."

The Master of the Law again asked him: "My mind's

[1] This, in connection with other passages, is sufficient to show the superstitious character of the Pilgrim.

purpose is to return. but having a great number of images and sacred books, I hardly know if I shall succeed in arriving with them."

The Nirgrantha said: "Do not be anxious: Śîlâditya râja, and Kumâra-râja will themselves despatch men as escort; the Master will successfully return without accident."

The Master of the Law, in reply, said: "As to these two kings I have never yet seem them, how then can such a kindness befall me?"

The Nirgrantha said: "Kumâra-râja has already sent messengers to invite you to go to him, in two or three days they should arrive. After you have seen Kumâra you will also see Śîlâditya."

Having thus spoken he went away.

The Master of the Law forthwith making up his mind to return, paid especial attention to his books and images.

All the priests hearing of it, came to him in a body and begged him to remain, saying: "India is the place of Buddha's birth. The great Saint, although he has passed away, has yet left behind him many traces (*of his presence*); what greater happiness in life than to visit, and adore, and exalt these (*relics*)? Why then do you leave these, after having come so far? Moreover, China is a country of Mleććhas, men of no importance, and shallow as to religion, and so the Buddhas are never born there. The mind (*of the people*) is narrow, and their coarseness is profound, and hence neither saints nor sages go there from this country; the coldness of the climate, and the ruggedness of the country—these circumstances, also, are enough to cause you to think!"

The Master of the Law replied: "The king of the Law, *i.e. Buddha* (Dharmarâja), in establishing the principles of his doctrine, designed them for universal diffusion: how then can those who have received the benefit thereof, exclude those not yet enlightened. In that country of China the superior magistrates are clothed with dignity, and the laws are everywhere respected. The prince is regarded as sacred, the ministers are faithful, parents are loving, children are obedient, virtue and justice are highly esteemed, age and uprightness preferred in honour. Moreover, how deep and mysterious their knowledge! how divine the model of their wisdom! their rules in agreement with heaven. They do not regard the seven heavenly bodies as hidden from their literature,[1] they make instruments, divide the seasons, produce the six sharp-notes of music, and so are able to tame or drive away birds or beasts, subdue the spirits to their will, calm the influences of the *yang* and *yin* principles in Nature. From the time the bequeathed doctrine of Buddha penetrated to the East, they have highly venerated the Great Vehicle; in meditation, they are placid as the shining waters; in morals, their renown is like the perfume of opening flowers; in practice, they engage the heart; their earnest vow is to obtain the fullest degree of merit, and by quiet abstraction to prepare for the acquisition of the threefold body, and the highest condition of being.

"The great holy one descending spiritually (*into the world*), himself raised the standard of religious teaching, and proclaimed the excellent doctrine, he was exhibited in his golden features to the eyes of men, and still there is no check to the aim of his long career.

"How then can you say that Buddha did not go to this country (*of China*) because of its insignificance?"

They replied: "The Scriptures say that all regions are blessed with plenty or the opposite, according to their meritorious condition in point of religious excellence. It is better for the Master of the Law to live here with us in Jambudvîpa where Buddha was born than to go to

[1] That is, they are acquainted with the movements of the seven heavenly bodies (*viz.*, the sun, the moon, and five planets).

that country, inasmuch as that is a frontier and an evil country, without any religious merit, and for this reason we urge the Master not to return there."

The Master of the Law replied: "Vimalakîrrti, speaking to a disciple, said: 'Why does the sun travel over Jambudvîpa?' 'To disperse the gloom,' was the answer. This, also, is the reason why I purpose to return to my own country."

The priests having perceived that there was no agreement likely, besought him to go (*with them*) to Śîlabhadra, Master of the Law, and set forth his intention to him. Then Śîlabhadra, Master of the Law, addressing him, said: "Why, sir, have you come to this resolution?"

He replied: "This country is the place of Buddha's birth: it is impossible not to regard it with affection; only Hiuen-Tsiang's intention in coming hither was to inquire after the great law for the benefit of his fellow creatures. Since my arrival here, you, sir, have condescended, on my account, to explain (or, *recite*) the Yôgâchârya-bhûmi-śâstra, and to investigate doubtful passages. I have visited and adored the sacred vestiges of our religion, and heard the profound exposition of the different schools. My mind has been overjoyed, and my visit here, has, I protest, been of the utmost profit. I desire now to go back and translate and explain to others what I have heard, so as to cause others also to be equally grateful to you, with myself, in hearing and understanding these things; and for this reason I am unwilling to delay my return and remain here."

Śîlabhadra joyfully replied: "These are thoughts worthy of a Bôdhisattva; my heart anticipates your own wishes! I will give orders for your conveyance hence; and you, my friends, do not cause any trouble by delaying him."

Having said this, he retired to his room. After two days the messenger sent by Kumâra-Râja of Eastern India presented a letter to Śîlabhadra, to this effect:

"Your disciple wishes to see the great priest come from China. I pray you, respected sir, to send him and so gratify this imperial thought of mine."

Śîlabhadra, on receipt of the letter, announced to the congregation as follows: "Kumâra-Râja wants to invite Hiuen-Tsiang (*to go to him*), but we have already agreed to induce him to go to Śîlâditya-Râja's residence, to discuss with the (*doctors of the*) Little Vehicle. If he goes to that one (*Kumâra*), perhaps Śîlâditya will be expecting him, and then how will he be able to secure his presence? we ought not to send him." And so he told the messenger saying: "The priest of China is anxious to return to his own country and so is unable to comply with the king's request."

The messenger having arrived, the king again despatched another to renew the invitation, in these words: "Although the Master wishes to return home, yet for a little while let him come to your disciple. There shall be no difficulty about his departure. I pray you comply with my humble request, and do not again decline to come."

Śîlabhadra not having consented to the proposal, the king with great anger sent yet another messenger with a personal despatch for Śîlabhadra, the Master of the Law, to the following effect: "Your disciple like a common man has followed the way of worldly pleasure, and has not yet learnt the converting power residing in the law of Buddha. And now when I heard the name of the priest belonging to the outside country, my body and soul were overjoyed; expecting the opening of the germ of religion (*within me*). But you, sir, have again refused to let him come here, as if you desired to cause the world to be for ever plunged in the dark night (*of ignorance*). Is this the way in which your Eminence hands down and transmits the bequeathed law for the deliverance and salvation of all the world? Having an invincible longing to think kindly of and show respect to (*the Master*), I have again sent a messenger with a written request: if he does not come, your disciple will then let the evil portion of himself prevail. In recent times Śasaṅgka-râja was equal still to the destruction of the law and uprooted the Bôdhi tree. Do you, my Master, suppose that your disciple has no such power as this? If necessary then I will equip my army and elephants, and like the clouds sweep down on and trample to the very dust that monastery of Nalânda. These words (*are true*) as the sun! Master! it is better for you to examine and see (*what you will do*)."

Śîlabhadra having received the letter, addressed the Master of the Law thus: "With regard to that king, his better mind (or, *virtuous mind*) is fast bound and weak; within his territories the law of Buddha has not widely extended: since the time that he heard your honourable name, he has formed a deep attachment for you; perhaps you are destined to be in this period of your existence his 'good friend.'[1] Use your best diligence then and go. You have become a disciple in order to benefit the world, this then is perhaps your just opportunity: and as when you destroy a tree you have only to cut through the root, and the branches will of themselves wither away, so when you arrive in that country only cause the heart of the king to open (*to the truth*), and then the people will also be converted. But if you refuse and do not go, then perhaps there will be evil deeds done. Do not shrink from this slight trouble."

The Master of the Law, leaving his teacher, went with the envoy, and arrived there. The king seeing him was greatly rejoiced, and met him with his great officers, and paying him reverence with much ceremony, conducted him within his palace. Every day he arranged music and banquets, with religious offerings of flowers and incense,

[1] For this expression *vide* Haug's Essays on the Parsees (*Trübner's Edition*), p. 209.

and requested him to follow the ordinary rules of religious fast days.

Thus passed a month and more, when Śîlâditya-râja, returning from his attack on Kongyôdha, heard that the Master of the Law was residing with Kumâra. Being surprised, he said: "I frequently asked him to come here before this—and he did not come, how is it that he is now living there?" Sending a messenger, therefore, he bade Kumâra-râja to send the priest of China to him at once.

The king replied, "He can take my head, but he cannot take the Master of the Law yet." The messenger returning gave this answer, on which the Śîlâditya-râja was greatly enraged, and calling together his attendants, he said: "Kumâra-râja despises me. How comes he to use such coarse language in the matter of a single priest?"

Then he sent another messenger who said, in an abrupt manner: "Send the head, that I may have it immediately by my messenger who is to bring it here."

Kumâra, deeply alarmed at the folly of his language—immediately ordered his army of elephants, 20,000 in number, to be equipped, and his ships, 30,000 in number. Then embarking with the Master of the Law they passed up the Ganges together in order to reach the place where Śîlâditya-râja was residing. When he arrived at the country of Kie-shu-ho-ki-lo (*Kajûrgira*), there was a conference held, and Kumâra, being about to depart to explain matters, first ordered some men to construct on the north bank of the Ganges a pavilion-of-travel, and then on a certain day he passed over the river and coming to the pavilion he there placed the Master of the Law, after which he himself with his ministers went to meet Śîlâditya-râja on the north bank of the river.

Śîlâditya seeing him coming was overjoyed, and knowing his respect and love for the Master of the Law, he did not repeat his former threatening words, but simply asked him where the priest of China was stopping.

In reply he said: "He is staying in a certain pavilion-of-travel."

The king said: "And why did he not come with you?"

"Replying, he said: "Mahârâja has respect for the virtuous, and loves religion; why not send for the Master to come to confer with the king?"

The king said: "It is well; but for the present you may depart to your residence, and to-morrow I myself will come."

Kumâra returning spoke to the Master of the Law, saying: "The king, although he says he will come to-morrow, I suspect he will come to-night; and we must attend him when he comes—but if he arrives, let not the Master be moved (*with anxiety*)."

The Master of the Law replied: "Hiuen-Tsiang will conduct himself according to the directions of the Law of Buddha."

About the first watch of the night the king did in effect arrive. There were some men who reported that on the river there were several thousand lighted torches, and that they heard the sound of beating drums.

The king said: "This is Sîlâditya-râja approaching."

He immediately ordered them to take torches in hand, whilst he himself, with his ministers, went forth a long way to meet him.

As Śîlâditya-râja marched, he was always accompanied by several hundred persons with golden drums, who beat one stroke for every step taken; they called these the "music-pace-drums" (*tsieh-po-ku*).

Śîlâditya alone used this method—other kings were not permitted to adopt it.

On his arrival the king bowed down at the feet of the Master of the Law, then scattering flowers before him he regarded him with respect, and uttered his praises in verses innumerable; this done, he addressed the Master thus:

"Your disciple invited the Master in former days to come,—why did you not comply with my request?"

Answering, he said: "Hiuen-Tsiang came from far in search of the law of Buddha, and for the sake of hearing the Yôga-bhûmi-śâstra. When your order arrived I had not finished examining this *sâstra,* and so did not immediately come to meet the king."

Again the king asked, as follows: "The Master comes from China; your disciple has heard that that country has a king of Ts'in, whose fame is celebrated in songs and airs set for dancing and music; I never yet knew who this king of Ts'in was, or what his distinguished merit was, that led to this distinction." [1]

The Master of the Law said: "In my country when there is a man observable for the quality of protecting the good, capable of averting evil from the people, and able to nourish and cherish with fostering care all living things—then they sound his praise in songs and chants arranged to music, in the first place, for the ancestral temple; and then for the use of the distant village folk. The king of Ts'in is the same, now, as the reigning Emperor of China—but before the highest authority of the Emperor (*i.e. She-wong-ti*) was established, then he was but invested as prince of Ts'in. This was a period of disorder in heaven and earth; the people had no ruler, the fields and plains were covered with the bodies of men, the streams and valleys were full of their blood; during the night ill-omened stars shed their pestilent light, vapours rose with the day, the three rivers were infested by voracious toll-collectors, and the four seas were afflicted with the poison of monstrous snakes.

"The Prince, as the next of kin to the supreme ruler (*ti*), obedient to the call of Heaven, filled with noble ardour, rallied his troops, put down the oppressors (male and female, *k'ing i*) by force; seizing the battle-axe and the lance, he quickly calmed the sea, the villagers were

[1] The reference is presumably to the Emperor She-wong-ti, B.C. 221.

profoundly quiet, and the districts restored to order as before. The sun and moon and stars shone out again, and the world was filled with gratitude for his care. For this reason we sing his praises."

The king said: "Such a man is one sent by heaven to be the Lord of the world."

Again addressing the Master of the Law, he said: "Your disciple must now return; to-morrow I will escort the master (*to our palace*)—I trust he will not suffer from fatigue."

Thus taking leave, he departed.

On the next morning the messenger came, and the Master of the Law with Kumâra went together to Śîlâditya's palace, on arriving near which the king with some twenty attendants came forth to meet them. Entering they sat down, when choice viands were set before them, accompanied with music and strewn flowers.

The entertainment being over, the king said: "I have heard that the Master has composed a Śâstra with a view to restrain wicked doctrine—where is this work?"

The Master of the Law replied, "It is here," and then he caused the king to take it and look at it.

Having examined it the king was much pleased, and addressing his attendants and the rest, he said: "I have heard that when the sun rises in its splendour the light of the glow-worm is eclipsed, and when the sound of heaven's thunder is heard, then the noise of the hammer and chisel is silenced: so with regard to the doctrine which the Master defends, all the others have been destroyed, and in discussing the method of right deliverance, the priests have not dared to offer a word."

The king said (*moreover*), "The chief Sthavira of the priests, Dêvasêna, said of himself—that in the explanation of doctrine he was superior to all his rivals, and in his studies embraced all branches of science. But in advancing his strange opinions he ever opposed the 'Great Vehicle.' Hearing, however, that the stranger priest had come he forthwith went to Vâiśalî, to pay reverence to the sacred vestiges—from this I gather that all these priests are without ability in discussion."

The king had a sister of great intelligence who was distinguished for knowledge of the Sammatîya-school doctrine; she was sitting behind the king, and as she heard the Master of the Law extolling the doctrine of the Great Vehicle, and exposing the extreme poverty of the Little school of Doctrine, she was filled with joy, and could not cease her praises.

Then the king said: "The treatise written by the Master is very good; quite enough to convince both your disciple (*i.e. himself*), and all these teachers, and the faithful generally; but I fear there are other sectaries belonging to the Little Vehicle, of other countries, who will still cling to and defend their foolish doctrine. I propose therefore to call a grand assembly in the town of Kanyâkubja, and command the Śramans and Brâhmans and heretics of the five Indies to attend, in order to exhibit the refinements of the Great Vehicle, and demolish their abusive mind, to make manifest the exceeding merit of the Master, and overthrow their proud thought of 'self.'"

The same day he sent an order throughout the different kingdoms that all the disciples of the various schools should assemble in the town of Kanyâkubja to investigate the treatise of the Master of the Law, of China.

Then the Master of the Law, at the beginning of winter, in company with the king, advanced up the river (*Ganges*) and in the beginning of the last month[1] of the year arrived at the rendezvous.

[1] In the *Records*, i. 218, we are told they were ninety days in their progress towards the rendezvous. I should be inclined, therefore, to consider the symbol "La" in the text as equal to *Varsha.*

There were present kings of eighteen [1] countries of the five Indies; [2] three thousand priests thoroughly acquainted with the Great and Little Vehicle, besides about three thousand Brâhmans and Nirgranthas and about a thousand priests of the Nâlanda monastery. All these noted persons, alike celebrated for their literary skill, as for their dialectic, attended the assembly with a view to consider and listen to the sounds of the Law; they were accompanied with followers, some on elephants, some in chariots, some in palanquins, some under canopies. Each was surrounded by its own peculiar attendants, like the clouds for multitude, which in the winter time spread through many scores of miles, and if we said that they were like the standards [3] of the rebellious tribes of the three "*Wu*," or like the drops of rain which fall from the clouds, even this would not be an exaggeration.

The King had previously ordered two thatched halls to be constructed at the place of the assembly for receiving the figures (*of Buddha*) and the body of the disciples. When he arrived they were both finished; they were lofty and spacious, each capable of seating a thousand persons. The travelling palace of the king was some five *li* to the west of the place of assembly; he had in this palace cast a golden statue, and now, ordering a great elephant to be equipped with a precious daïs on its back, he placed thereon (*the statue of*) Buddha. Then Śîlâditya râja, under the form of Lord Śakra, with a white chowrie in his hand, went on the right, and Kumâra-râja, under the form of Brâhma-râja, with a precious parasol in his hand, went to the left. They both wore tiaras like the Dêvas, with flower wreaths and jewelled ribbons.

Moreover, they harnessed two other great elephants and laded them with jewels and flowers (or, *precious*

[1] The *Si-yu-ki* states that there were twenty kings present, *vide Records*, i. 218

[2] Julien says: "eighteen kings of Central India;" but it is not so in the text.

[3] The passage in the original is defaced.

flowers) to follow behind the image of Buddha, and each step they took they scattered these flowers abroad.

The Master of the Law and the chief servants of the king were directed severally to mount a great elephant, and to follow the king in order; moreover, there were other 300 great elephants appointed for the princes, great ministers, and chief priests of the different countries, on which they rode in double file on each side of the procession course, chanting laudatory verses as they went. The procession began at early dawn from the travelling palace (*of the king*). As they drew nigh the gate of the outer court of the place of assembly, each one was directed to dismount whilst they conducted the figure of Buddha within the hall. There they placed it on a precious throne, whilst the king and the Master of the Law, in succession, presented it with offerings.

After this the king ordered the princes of the eighteen countries to enter the Hall; then, of the most renowned priests celebrated for learning he selected about one thousand to enter the hall; of celebrated Brahmans and followers of heretical doctrine he selected five hundred to enter the hall, and about two hundred of the great ministers of the different kingdoms. The unbelievers and secular persons (*who were not able to be admitted*) he ordered to be seated outside the gate of the entrance hall.

The king then sent to those within and without, alike, food to eat. This done, he presented as an offering to Buddha[1] a golden dish, a golden cup, seven golden ewers, one golden staff, three thousand gold pieces, and three thousand vestments of superior cotton-stuff.

The Master of the Law and the other priests each offered according to their different ability.

This being over, the king caused a precious couch to be arranged, and invited the Master of the Law to sit upon it as Lord of the discussion.

The Master then began to extol the teaching of "the

[1] Julien translates this passage very differently, *Vie*, p. 244.

Great Vehicle," and announced a subject for discussion, and he commissioned *Ming-hien*, a Shaman of the Nâlanda monastery, to exhibit it to the members of the great Community. He also caused a placard to be written and hung outside the door of the place of assembly, exhibiting the same to the whole people, and adding, "if there is any one who can find a single word in the proposition contrary to reason, or is able to entangle (*the argument*), then at the request of the opponent, I offer my head as a recompense."

Thus until night there was no one who came forward to say a word.

Sîlâditya-râja, very well pleased at the event, adjourned the assembly and returned to his palace; whilst the princes and the priests all returned to their resting-places. So also Kumâra-râja and the Master of the Law retired to their resting-places.

On the morrow they again escorted the image, the king and the others, as before.

After five days had passed, the unbelievers of the Little Vehicle, seeing he had overturned their school, filled with spleen, plotted to take his life.

The king hearing of it, issued this proclamation: "The seething of error obscuring the truth, is the experience of ages. (*The followers of false doctrine*), hiding the true, deceive the people; if the world were without superior sages, how could their falsehood be discovered? The Master of the Law of China, whose spiritual power is so vast, and whose power of explanation is so grand and deep, with a view to rebut the errors of the people, has come to sojourn here, to exhibit the character of the great Law, and to rescue the foolish and the deceived. But the followers of delusion and falsehood, not knowing the way of repentance or the forsaking of error, have conceived a murderous purpose against his person; this intention must inspire every one with resentment. If, then, any one should hurt or touch the Master of the Law, he shall be forthwith beheaded; and whoever speaks against him, his tongue shall be cut out; but all those who desire to profit by his instruction, relying on my goodwill, need not fear this manifesto."

From this time the followers of error withdrew and disappeared, so that when eighteen days had passed there had been no one to enter on the discussion.

The evening before the dispersion of the assembly the Master of the Law again extolled the Great Vehicle, and sounded the praises of the religious merit of Buddha, by which a vast number of men were converted from error and entered on the right path: forsaking the Little Vehicle, they found refuge in the Great Vehicle.

Śîlâditya-râja, reverencing him more than ever, bestowed on the Master of the Law 10,000 pieces of gold, 30,000 pieces of silver, 100 garments of superior cotton, whilst the princes of the eighteen kingdoms each presented him with rare jewels. But all these the Master of the Law declined to accept.

The king then ordered his attendant ministers to place a howdah upon a great elephant, with the request that the Master of the Law would mount thereon, whilst he directed the great Ministers of state to accompany him; and as they passed through the throng he directed the proclamation to be made that "he had established the standard of right doctrine, without gainsaying."

This is the custom of the Western kingdoms whenever any one has obtained the victory in discussion.

The Master of the Law desired to waive this mark of distinction and not to go in procession, but the king said: "It has ever been the custom, the matter cannot be passed over"—and so, holding the Master of the Law by his kashâya garment, they everywhere proclaimed, "The Master of the Law from the kingdom of China has established the principles of the Great Vehicle and overthrown all opposing doctrines; for eighteen days no one has dared to enter on the discussion. Let this be known everywhere, as it ought to be!"

The whole multitude were filled with joy on account of the Master's success, and all wished to fix for him a name in connection with his principles.

The congregation of the Great Vehicle called him Mahâyâna Dêva, that is, the Dêva of the Great Vehicle, whilst the followers of the Little Vehicle called him Môksha Dêva, *i.e.* the Dêva of deliverance. Then they burnt incense and scattered flowers, and paid him reverence and departed.

From this time (or, *circumstance*) the report of his eminence (*virtue*) spread abroad everywhere.

To the west of the king's travelling palace there was a Sañghârâma under the patronage of the king. In this building there was a tooth of Buddha about an inch and a half long and of a yellowish white colour. It ever emits a sparkling light.

In old days when the Kritya[1] race in Kaśmir had destroyed the law of Buddha, and the priests and their disciples were scattered everywhere, there was a Bhikshu who travelled (*from there*) afar through India. His follower, the king of Himatala, of Turkhâra, was enraged that this despicable race should destroy the law of Buddha, disguised himself as a merchant, and with a company of 3000 men of might, he took with him many valuable jewels, under the pretext, as he gave out, of offering them (*to the king*).

[1] Rubruquis calls the Kirais, *Crit*, *vide* also Crindle's *Ptolemy* (Indian Antiq.), p. 400. The Kirais, according to Howorth, were a Turkish race, descended from the Uighurs. *Ind. Antiq.* Nov. 1880, p. 276.

The king, who was of a covetous disposition, was overjoyed when he heard the news, and sent some messengers to escort him on the way.

But the king of Himatala, who was of a disposition fierce and haughty, and dignified in his carriage like a god, when he arrived at the throne of the king, took off his bonnet and denounced him. The Kritya king seeing him thus, was terrified, and forthwith in rising fell to the ground.

The king of Himatala cut off his head which he had seized, and then addressed the body of his ministers and said: "I am the king of Himatala; bearing in mind that you slaves had destroyed the law of Buddha I have come to punish you. But as the fault lies with one man, it would be wrong to involve you in it. You may therefore rest in peace; I shall, however, banish the chief of those who incited the king to his wicked conduct to a distant land; as to the rest I exact nothing." Having exterminated the odious race, he founded a Sanghârâma, and assembling the priests he gave it to them, and returned.

The Bhikshu before alluded to who had gone to India, hearing that his country was restored to quiet, began to return there, staff in hand. On the way he encountered a herd of trumpeting elephants approaching him. The Bhikshu, when he saw them, climbed into a tree to hide himself. The elephants forthwith began to pour water on the tree from their trunks, and then with their tusks they underdug it, and after a while it fell. The elephants then lifted the Bhikshu on the back of one of the herd with their trunks, and went off with him.

They arrived at the middle of a great wood, where there was a sick elephant suffering from a wound and lying on the ground.

The elephant then drew the hand of the Bhikshu to touch the place of his suffering. Looking at the swollen part he saw that a bamboo splinter had pierced it—drawing this out he washed away the blood, and tearing up his robe, he bound up the wound, so that the elephant got gradual ease.

Next morning the herd all went away to seek for fruits, which, when found, they respectfully offered to the Bhikshu. The Bhikshu having eaten thereof, an elephant with a golden casket came to the wounded elephant and offered it to him. This one, having received it, offered it to the Bhikshu. The Bhikshu having taken it, all the herd took him out of the wood to the original spot where they found him, and placing him on the ground, paid lowly reverence, and departed.

The Bhikshu opening the casket, lo! there was the tooth of Buddha. Taking it back (*to his country*), he devoted himself to its worship (*culture*).

In recent times Śîlâditya-râja, hearing that Kaśmir possessed a tooth of Buddha, coming in person to the chief frontier, asked permission to see and worship it. The congregation, from a feeling of sordid avarice, were unwilling to consent to this request, and so took the relic and concealed it. But the king fearing the exalted character of Śîlâditya, set about digging here and there till he found the relic, and having found it, presented it to the king. Śîlâditya seeing it was overpowered with reverence, and exercising force, carried it off to pay it religious offerings. This is the tooth spoken of.

After breaking up the assembly the king handed over to the Saṅghârâma the golden image he had cast, and the garments and money, warning the priests to take care of them.

The Master of the Law, first taking leave of the priests from the Nâlanda convent, having taken his books and images, on the 19th day, the conference being ended, paid his respects to the king with a view to his departure home.

The king said: "Your disciple, succeeding to the royal authority, has been lord of India for thirty years and more: I have constantly regretted the small increase to my religious merit, resulting from a want of previous good deeds. In consequence of this I have accumulated every kind of treasure and precious substance in the kingdom of Prayâga, and between the banks of the two rivers,[1] I have established a great religious convocation every five years, to attend which all the Śramans and Brahmans of the five Indies are invited, and besides these the poor and the orphans and the destitute; on this occasion during seventy-five days the great distribution of alms called the Moksha is attended to; I have completed five of these assemblies and am now about to celebrate the sixth: why does not the Master delay his departure till then, and so, by witnessing the spectacle, rejoice with us?"

The Master answered, "Bôdhisattva by meritorious conduct and by wisdom prepared himself (*for enlightenment*); the wise man having obtained the fruit (*of his conduct*), does not forget the root (*of his happiness*); if your Majesty does not grudge his treasure for the good of others, how can Hiuen-Tsiang grudge a short delay (*in his departure*). I ask leave, therefore, to accompany your Majesty on your journey."

The king hearing this was delighted, and on the twenty-first day he went forward, conducting him to the kingdom of Po-lo-ye-kia (Prayâga), and proceeded to the great-distribution arena. This was bounded on the north by the Ganges (*King-kia*), and on the south by the Jumnâ (*Yen-mu-na*). These two rivers coming from the north-west and flowing eastward, unite their stream in this kingdom.

On the west of the place of junction of the two rivers there is a great plain some fourteen or fifteen *li* in circuit. It is flat and even like a mirror. From days of old the various kings have frequented this spot for the purpose of practising charity: and hence the name given to it, the "*Arena of Charitable Offerings.*" There is a tradition which says that it is more advantageous to give one mite in charity in this place than a thousand in any other place: and therefore from old times this place has been held in honour.

[1] *i.e.*, the Jumnâ and Ganges.

The king directed them to portion out on this space a square enclosure for distributing the charitable offerings, enclosed by a bamboo hedge 1000 paces each side, and in the middle to erect many scores of thatched buildings in which to deposit all the treasures (*intended for distribution*); to wit, gold, silver, fine pearls, red glass, the precious substance called the *Ti-tsing-chu* (the Indranila pearl), the *Ta-tsing-chü* (the Mahânila pearl), &c. He constructed, moreover, by the side of these, several hundred store-houses (*long buildings*) in which to place the silk and cotton garments, the gold and silver money, and so on.

Outside the enclosing hedge, he caused to be made places for partaking of food. In front of the various depositories for treasure, he, moreover, erected some hundred or so long buildings arranged like the market-places of our capital, in which some thousand people might sit down for rest.

Some time before these preparations the king had summoned by decree, through the five Indies, the Śramans, heretics, Nirgranthas, the poor, the orphans, and the solitary (*bereaved*), to come together to the Arena of Charity, to receive the prepared gifts.

As the Master of the Law had not yet returned from the assembly at Kanyâkubja, he now hastened to the place of the distribution of charity. The kings of eighteen kingdoms, moreover, followed in the suite of the royal monarch with a like purpose. Arrived at the spot they found a body of people amounting to 500,000, or so, already arrived.

Śîlâditya-râja pitched his tent on the north bank of the Ganges. The king of South India, *Tu-lu-po-pa-ćha* (Dhruvabaṭṭa or Dhruvabhaṭa), located himself on the west of the junction of the rivers. Kumâra-râja occupied the south side of the river Jumnâ, by the side of a flowering grove. All the recipients of bounty occupied the ground to the west of the position of Dhruvabaṭṭa râja.

On the morrow morning the military followers of Śîlâditya-râja, and of Kumâra-râja, embarked in ships, and the attendants of Dhruvabaṭṭa-râja mounted their elephants, and so, arranged in an imposing order, they proceeded to the place of the appointed assembly. The kings of the eighteen countries joined the cortège according to arrangement.

On the first day of the first period, they installed the image of Buddha within one of the thatched buildings on the field of charity. They then distributed precious articles of the first quality, and clothing of the same character, and offered exquisite meats, whilst they scattered flowers to the sound of music. At the close of the day they retired to their tents.

The second day they installed the image of Âditya-deva, and distributed precious things and clothing in charity, to half the amount of the previous day.

The third day they installed the image of Iśvara-deva, and distributed gifts as on the day before.

On the fourth day they gave gifts to 10,000 of the religious community, arranged in a hundred ranks. Each received 100 pieces of gold, one pearl, one cotton garment, various drinks and meats; flowers and perfumes. After the distribution they retired.

The fifth arrangement was the bestowal of gifts to the Brahmans, which lasted for twenty days.

The sixth turn related to the heretics, which lasted ten days.

The next occasion was the bestowal of alms on those who came from distant spots to ask for charity: this lasted for ten days.

.The eighth distribution was to the poor and the orphans and destitute, which occupied a month.

By this time the accumulation of five years was exhausted. Except the horses, elephants, and military accoutrements which were necessary for maintaining order and protecting the royal estate, nothing remained. Besides these the king freely gave away his gems and goods, his clothing and necklaces, ear-rings, bracelcts, chaplets, neck-jewel and bright head-jewel, all these he freely gave without stint.

All being given away, he begged from his sister an ordinary second-hand garment, and having put it on he paid worship to the Buddhas of the ten regions, and as he exulted with joy with his hands closed in adoration, he said: "In amassing all this wealth and treasure I ever feared that it was not safely stored in a strong place; but now having bestowed this treasure in the field of religious merit, I can safely say it is well bestowed. Oh that I (*Śilâditya*) may in all my future births ever thus religiously give in charity to mankind my stores of wealth, and thus complete in myself the ten independent powers (*daśabalas*) [of a Buddha]."

The two magnificent convocations being finished the kings severally distributed among the people their money and treasure for the purpose of redeeming the royal necklaces, hair-jewels, court vestments, &c., and then taking them, restored them to the king; and then after a few days these same things were again given away in charity, as before.

But now the Master of the Law requested the king to let him return home, as he desired.

The king replied: "Your humble disciple, in common with yourself, desires to spread far and wide the knowledge of the bequeathed law of Buddha; why then do you so hastily return home?"

On this he remained yet another ten days.

Kumâra-râja also was courteously affected towards him, and addressed the Master thus: "If the Master is able to dwell in my dominions and receive my religious offerings,

I will undertake to found one hundred monasteries on the Master's behalf."

Hiuen-Tsiang, perceiving that the kings' purpose was not to let him go, afflicted with grief, addressed them as follows: "The country of China is very far from this, and has but recently heard of the law of Buddha. Although it has received a general knowledge of the truth, yet it has not accepted it in its entirety. On this account therefore have I come to inform myself how to put an end to differences. And now having completed my aim, (*I remember*) how the learned men of my country are longing to fathom to their depth the points I have ascertained. Therefore I dare not delay a moment, remembering the words of the Sûtra:—'Whoever hinders men from a knowledge of religion shall, for generation after generation, be born blind;'—if then you hinder my return you will cause countless disciples to lose the benefit resulting from a knowledge of the law; how then will you escape the dread of being deprived of sight?"

The king replied: "Your humble disciple admires and values the virtue of the Master; and I would ever look up to and serve him; but to stand in the way of the benefit of so many men would truly cause my heart to be filled with fear: I leave the Master to his choice, to go, or to stay; but I know not, if you prefer to go, by what route you propose to return; if you select the Southern Sea route [1] then I will send official attendants to accompany you."

The Master replied: "When I left China and arrived at the western limits of the country, I reached a territory called Kau-chang; the king of this place was an enlightened man and passionately attached to the Law. When he saw me, in my search after the truth, come to his kingdom, he was filled with profound joy, and freely

[1] That is, by way of Java, or Sumatra.

provided me with every necessary, praying me on my return to visit him once more; my heart is unable to forego this duty; I will therefore return by the Northern road."

The king answered, "I pray you, then, let me know what provisions you stand in need of."

The Master replied: "I require nothing."

The king said, "It is impossible to permit you to go thus."

On this the king ordered them to offer him gold coins and other things; Kumâra-râja also bestowed on him every sort of valuable. But the Master would take none of them, except from Kumâra-râja he accepted a cape called *ho-la-li* (Hâri ?), made of coarse skin lined with soft down, which was designed to protect from rain whilst on the road.

Thus he took his departure. The king with a large body of attendants accompanied him for several ten *lis*, and then returned. On their final separation they could none of them restrain their tears and sad lamentations.

As for his books and images, the Master confided them to the military escort of a king of North India called Udhita, to be carried on horseback, but the advance being slow King Śîlâditya afterwards attached to the escort of Udhita-râja a great elephant, with 3000 gold pieces and 10,000 silver pieces, for defraying the Master's expenses on the road.

Three days after separation the king, in company with Kumâra-râja and Dhruvabaṭṭa-râja, took several hundred light horsemen and again came to accompany him for a time and to take final leave, so kindly disposed were the kings to the Master. Then he commissioned four Ta-kwan (*official guides*) to accompany the escort: they call such officers Mo-ho-ta-lo (Mahâtâras ?) The king also wrote some letters on fine white cotton stuff and sealed them with red wax (or, *composition*), which he ordered the *Ta-kwan* officers to present in all the countries through which they conducted the Master, to the end that the princes of these countries might provide carriages or modes of conveyance to escort the Master even to the borders of China.

From the country of Prayâga he went south-west, through a great desert waste for seven days, when he arrived at the kingdom of Kauśâmbî. To the south of the city is the place where the lord Goshira presented a garden to Buddha.

Having adored the sacred traces again, he proceeded with Udhita-râja north-west for one month and some days, passing through various countries. Once more he paid adoration to the sacred traces of the heavenly ladder, and then proceeding north-west three *yojanas*, he came to the capital of the country of Pi-lo-na-na (Vîrashana).[1] Here he halted two months, during which time he met with two fellow students, Simhaprabha and Simhachandra, who discoursed with him on the Kôsha-samparigraha-Śâstra, the Vidyâ-mâtra-siddha-śâstra, &c. He was met and escorted by all the people with great rejoicings.

When the Master of the Law had arrived, he took up his discourse on the Yoga-śâstra-kârika, and the Abhidharma-śâstra. At the end of the two months he took his leave of them, and continued on a north-western route for one month and some days. Passing through various countries, he arrived at the kingdom of Che-lan-ta (*Jâlandhara*), the royal city of North India. Here he halted one month.

Udhita-râja now sent with him an escort, with which, proceeding to the west for twenty days or so, he came

[1] *Vide Records*, vol. i. p. 201, n. 107.

to the country of Siṁhapura. At this time there were about 100 priests belonging to the North, who were in charge of sacred books, images, &c.; these, relying on the escort accompanying the Master of the Law, returned in his company. And so they went on for about twenty days through mountain defiles. These spots being much frequented by robbers, the Master of the Law feared they might be spoiled in an encounter with them, and so made a rule to send on a brother in front, who if he met any robbers, was told to say, "We have come from a long distance searching for the Law, and now we are carrying with us nothing but the sacred books of our religion, and images and holy relics. We pray you, therefore, to be our patrons (*dânapatis*), and protect us without exhibiting a hostile mind." The Master of the Law with his companions and followers brought up the rear. By these means they escaped any harm from the brigands whom they encountered.

Thus travelling on for about twenty days, they reached the country of Takshaśilâ, where the Master again did reverence to the spot where Chandraprabha-râja gave for a thousand times his head in charity.

To the north-east of this country fifty *yojanas*, is the kingdom of Kaśmir.

The king of this country sent messengers to invite the Master of the Law to come to him, but on account of the heavily laden elephants, he was unable to go.

After a delay of seven days, he again set forward in a north-westerly direction, and after three days, reached the great river Sindhu. This river is five or six *li* wide. The books, images, and fellow travellers were embarked on board a boat for the passage across, but the Master of the Law crossed the stream mounted on an elephant.

He had deputed one man to accompany the boat for the purpose of looking after and protecting the books and all the different flower-seeds of India. And now when the boat was in the mid-stream, all at once the winds and the waters commingling, caused the waves to rise, and the boat, violently tossed, was almost swallowed up. The guardian of the books, filled with terror, fell into the water, but was finally rescued by the passengers; but there were lost fifty manuscript copies of Sûtras, and the flower seeds of various sorts. With these exceptions, all else they managed to save.

At this time the king of Kapiśa, who formerly dwelt in the town of U-to-kia-han-ch'a (Uṭakhâṇḍa), hearing that the Master of the Law had come, himself went to the river-side to pay his respects and escort him. Then he said: "I have heard that the Master has lost many sacred books in the middle of the river. Did you not bring with you here from India flower-seeds and fruit?"

"I did so," he replied.

"That is the sole reason," the king said, "of the storm that damaged the boat. It has been so from days of old till now, whoever attempts to cross the river with seeds of flowers is subject to similar misfortunes."

The Master then returned to the city with the king, and took up his abode in a temple-convent for fifty days or so. In consequence of losing his copies of the Sûtras, he despatched certain persons to the country of Udyâna, for the purpose of copying out the Tripiṭaka of the Kâśyapîya school.

The king of Kaśmir, hearing that the Master was gradually nearing his kingdom, in spite of the distance, came in person to pay his respects, and, after some days, returned.

The Master of the Law, in company with the king of Kapiśa, proceeding for a month in a north-west direction, came to the frontiers of the country of Lan-po (*Lamghân*).

The king sent his son, the heir to his throne, in advance, to direct the people of the capital and the body of priests to prepare flags and banners, and with them to march from the city to escort (*the cavalcade back to the city*).

And now the king and the Master of the Law gradually approached—and on their arrival they found several thousands of clerics and lay people with flags and banners, a vast concourse, awaiting them.

The people, on seeing the Master of the Law, were overjoyed, and paid him reverence, after which they went before him and in the rear, surrounding him as they advanced, sounding his praises. Arrived at the capital they lodged in a temple of the Great Vehicle. At this time the king held a great assembly for bestowing charity (*Moksha-mahâdâna*), during seventy-five days.

Once more, going right south for fifteen days, he halted in the country of Fa-la-na (*Varaṇa*) for the purpose of adoring the sacred traces.

Again, going north-west, he stopped in the kingdom of *O-po-kin* (Avakan). Again, advancing to the north-west, he stopped in the country of *Tsau-ku-ch'u* (Tsaukûṭa).

Again, going north 500 *li*, he reached the country of Fo-li-shi, and the country of Sa-tang-na (perhaps a mistake for *Fo-lo-shi-sa-tang-na*, i.e. *Vardasthâna*). From this, going east, they emerged on the frontiers of Kapiśa. Here the king again held a great assembly for distributing gifts during seven days, after which the Master of the Law requested to be allowed to take his leave and advance homewards. Going north-east one yojana they came to Ku-lu-sa-pang (Kroṣapam ?); here he separated from the king and proceeded northward.

The king sent with him a great officer, accompanied

by a hundred men, as an escort, whilst he crossed the Snowy Mountains, and to convey fuel, provisions, and other requisites for the journey, which the king provided.

After seven days they reached a great mountain top; this mountain is marked by its sharp-pointed peaks and dangerous crags, which mount upwards in different and strange forms. Now and then there is a flat surface, and then a high sharp peak; there is no uniformity. It would be impossible to narrate the difficulties and fatigues to which they were exposed in crossing these heights.

From this point they were no longer able to ride on horseback: the Master therefore advanced, supported by his staff.

After seven days more they came to a lofty mountain pass at the foot of which there was a village of about 100 houses. The people feed flocks of sheep which are as large as asses. Here they stopped for the day and set off again at midnight, having induced a villager to precede them on a mountain camel as a guide.

In this land there are numerous snow-drifts and glaciers (*crevasses*). If travellers do not carefully follow the steps of their guide, there is great danger of falling and perishing.

They went on thus from dawn till sunset crossing these frozen peaks. At this time the company consisted only of seven priests, twenty followers, one elephant, and ten asses, and four horses.

On the morrow they reached the bottom of the pass. Tracing their way through a tortuous road they now directed their march towards a ridge which seemed as if covered with snow, but when they got to it they found nothing but white stones. This ridge is very high, so that, although cloud-wrapped, the flying snow does not reach its summit. It was towards sundown when they got to the mountain top, but the freezing wind was so icy cold, that not one of the travellers dared pause on the top.[1]

This mountain affords no trace of vegetation, but only stones heaped up in confusion, and peaks and slender pinnacles, like a forest of trees devoid of leaves. Beyond this spot the mountain is so high, that when the wind suddenly rises the birds on wing cannot pass it in their flight. From the south of the ridge to the north of the ridge, there is a distance of several hundred paces—this passed, then one can find a little ease.

Throughout Jambudvîpa we shall not find among the mountain peaks, a higher one than this.

The Master of the Law having descended some *li* to the north-west, found a small level space where he spread his tent for the night. In the morning he again advanced, and after descending the mountain for five or six days he came to the country called *An-ta-lo-fo-po* (Antarava, Andarâb); this country is the old territory of *Tu-ho-lo* (Tukhâra).

There are here three Saṅgharâmas and some scores of priests. They belong to the Mahâsaṅghika school. There is one Stûpa built by Aśôka-râja.

The Master stopped here five days, and then going north-west four hundred *li* or so, still descending the mountain, he reached the country of *Kwoh-sĕh-to* (Khost), which again formed a part of the old territory of *Tu-ho-lo* (Tukhâra).[2]

Proceeding north-west from this place, and still continuing along the mountains for 300 *li* or so, he reached the kingdom of *Hwoh* (Kunduz) which lies along

[1] Cf. *Records*, ii. 286.
[2] Or, the old *Turanian* territory; cf. *Records*, i. p. 37, *n.* 121.

the side of the Oxus river (*Po-tsu*); this is the eastern boundary of Tukhâra. The capital is situated on the southern [1] bank of the river.

The Master, because he saw that the nephew of She-hu-khan, was ruling over Tukhâra, calling himself She-hu (*i.e. chieftain*) he repaired to his encampment and remained there one month. The She-hu having sent a guard of soldiers to accompany him, he, and the merchants in his train, went to the east two days and arrived at Mung-kin (*Munjan*). Connected with this territory is the country of O-li-ni (*Ahreng*), the country of *Ho-lo-hu* (Roh), the country of *Ki-li-sse-mo* (*Krishma*, or, *Kishm*), the country of *Po-li-ho* (Parika); all these countries formed a part of the old territory of Tukhâra.

Again going east from *Mung-Kien*, entering the mountains and travelling for 300 *li* or so—we come to the country of *Hi-mo-ta-lo* (Himatala); this also was a part of the old Tukhara territory. The habits of the people are in general like those of the Tuh-kiuch (Turks). There is one difference, however, which is, that the married women wear in their head-dress a wooden horn about three feet high. It has a division in front signifying the father and the mother of the husband. The higher division signifies the father—the lower, the mother—and as either of them dies the division (or branch) corresponding to that one, is removed; when both are dead, then the horn is entirely removed.

From this, again going eastward 200 *li* or so, they arrived at *Po-to-na* (for, *Po-to-chang-na*) [Badakshân], which also was a part of the old Tukhâra territory. Here they remained, on account of the frost and snow, for a month and some days.

Again going south-east through the mountains about

[1] Julien has "the *eastern* bank."

200 *li*, they arrived at the kingdom of *Ki-po-kin* (Yamgân).

Still going south-east through a mountainous and precipitous district for 300 *li*, they arrived at the kingdom of *Ku-lang-na* (Kurân).

Going north-east from this, across the mountains, for 500 *li* or so, they came to the country of *Ta-mo-si-tie-ti*[1] (Tamasthiti). This country is placed between two mountains bordering on the Oxus. It produces excellent (*shen*) horses, small in growth but very strong. The people have no manners, and are of a passionate temperament and unseemly appearance. Their eyes are chiefly of a bluish-green tint,[2] different from all other people. There are ten Saṅghâramas here. The capital of the country[3] is named *Hwăn-t'o-to*, in which there is a Saṅgharâma which a former king of this country built. In this Saṅgharâma is a stone figure of Buddha, above which is a gilded copper circlet, ornamented with various gems; it hangs unsupported over the head of Buddha, and when men worship the image and invest it, the canopy also moves with them, and when they stop, it stops. No one can explain this spiritual prodigy.[4]

North from this country, across some great mountains, there is the country of *Shi-k'i-ni* (Shikhnân).[5]

Again crossing from *Ta-mo-si-tie-ti* we come to the country of *Shang-mi* (Śâmbhî).

From this country, again going east across mountains 700 *li*, we reach the valley of Pamir. This valley is about 1000 *li* from east to west, and 100 *li* or so from north to south. It lies between two ranges of the Snowy Mountains. Moreover, this valley lies as it were in the

[1] Called also *Hu-mi*.—Ch. Ed.

[2] Like the *pih* stone, the colour of the deep sea.

[3] Either my text is defective or that of M. Julien was redundant, cf. *Julien*, p. 270.

[4] *Vide Records*, ii. 295.

[5] This passage is wrongly placed in the French translation.

midst of the T'sung-Ling Mountains, so that the wind and snow tempests fly to and fro during the spring and summer incessantly. The soil is always frozen, vegetation is scanty and rare, the seeds sown do not fructify, the whole district is desert and without inhabitants.

In the middle of this valley is a great lake, 200 *li* from east to west, and fifty *li* from north to south. It lies in the centre of Jambudvîpa, at an immense height. Regarding its watery expanse it extends beyond range of sight. The animals that dwell in it are of infinite variety; the noise of their ten thousand cries is like the tumult of a hundred workshops.

We see here, moreover, birds ten feet or so in height; eggs as large as a round water-jar, probably the same as were formerly called the Ku-koh (*big shells*)[1] of the Tajiks (*Tiu-chi*).

From the western division of the lake proceeds a river, which, flowing to the west, reaches the eastern frontier of *Ta-mo-si-ti* where it unites with the Oxus, and flowing westward, enters the sea. All the rivers on the right, moreover, unite together in the same way.

From the eastern division of the lake a great river proceeds in the direction of the Kie-sha country (*Kashgar*), and on its western frontier unites with the Sitâ river, and flowing to the east enters the sea. All the streams on the left, likewise, unite in the same way.

Beyond the mountains which are to the south of the valley is the country of *Po-lu-lo* (Bolor) where there is much gold and silver; the gold is the colour of fire. This lake, moreover, is one with the Anavatapta lake, in its north and south direction.

Proceeding from the eastern side of this valley, scrambling over crags and precipices, and along roads

[1] That is, the *egg-shell*; probably of the ostrich.

covered with snow for 500 *li*, they then reached the kingdom of *K'ie-p'an-to.*[1] The chief town of this country is flanked by a high mountain peak, whilst on the north it is backed by the Śitâ river. This river on the east enters the sea. Passing through the salt lake (Lake Lob) it flows underground, and emerging at the *Tsih-shi* mountain, it is the origin of our (*Yellow*) river.

The king of this country, from whom a long succession of rulers arose, was remarkable for his wisdom; it is said (or, *he professed*) that he took his origin from *Chîna-dêva-gotra* (*i.e.* the offspring of the God of China). In the old palace of the king there is the Saṅghârâma of the old Master Kumârajiva:[2] this Master was a man of the Takshaśilâ country. He was of great spiritual discernment and brilliant reputation. Each day he repeated 32,000 words and also wrote others down. He delighted in pursuing his religious studies, he was elegant in composition, and was the author of many scores of *Śâstras*, which gained a wide-spread renown. He was the first master of the Sâutrântika school.

At this time Aśvaghosha flourished in the East, Deva in the South, Nagârjuna in the West, Kumârajiva[3] in the North; these were called the four suns, able to enlighten all that lives. The renown of Kumâralabdha had reached such a height that a former king himself attacked his country (*Takshasilâ*) that he might honour and cherish him.

South-east of the city 300 *li* or so, there is a great (*rock like a*) stone wall with two stone chambers in it, in each of which there is an Arhat sitting in a profound (*extinct*) state of ecstasy; each of them sits upright and without movement: they look extremely emaciated, but

[1] For some remarks on this name, *Vide Records*, ii. 298.

[2] For Kumâralabdha.

[3] Read Kumâralabdha.

without any appearance of bodily decay, although 700 years and more have passed *(since they arrived at that condition)*.

The Master of the Law remained in this country for twenty days or so, and then going north-east for five days he fell in with a band of robbers; the merchants, his companions, were panic-stricken and made for the mountains; the elephants being driven about in the pursuit, were engulfed in the water and perished.

The robbers having passed by, they all proceeded slowly to the eastward, over crags and across mountain gorges, descending the heights and patiently enduring the cold. After 800 *li* they emerged from the T'sung-ling mountains and reached the kingdom of *U-sha* (Och).

To the westward of the capital about 200 *li* there is a great mountain covered with crags and precipices; on the top of a very high peak is a Stûpa. The old story goes, that many hundred years ago, the thunder having shivered a mountain, in the midst of one of the denuded crags there was seen the body of a Bhikshu of an extraordinary size, who sat there with closed eyes, and his matted hair descending over his shoulders and his face. Some woodcutters having seen the sight, went and told the king; he went in person to witness it and to offer his adorations.

The news being spread abroad the people from far and near flocked together, all intent on offering him their religious devotions and heaping up flowers. After this was done, the king said: "What man is this?"

A certain Bhikshu answered and said: "This is an Arhat who, having left his family, entered on (*a condition of*) complete ecstasy. Since this occurred many years have elapsed, and therefore his hair has grown to such a length."

The king replied: "If you know how, cause him to arouse himself."

In reply he said: "In the case of one who has long gone without food, when he awakes from his ecstasy his body would decay, so that first you must anoint him with cream, which being rubbed into his body will lubricate and soften his muscles; then afterwards you must sound the *ghantâ* (a metal gong): when he is stirred up and awakened he will perhaps rise up (*from his seat*)."

The king answered: "Well spoken!" and according to the directions he anointed him with cream and then sounded the *ghantâ*.

The Arhat, then opening his eyes and looking around him, said: "What sort of men are you, clothed with religious vestments?"

They replied: "We are Bhikshus."

He answered: "Where now dwells my master Kâś-yapa Tathâgata?"

Again they said: "He has passed into Nirvâṇa."

Hearing this he uttered a cry, and then rejoined: "Has Sâkya-Muni yet accomplished 'the unequalled condition of perfect enlightenment'?" (*i.e. become a Buddha*).

"Yes," they said, "and having procured benefit to the world, he too has passed into Nirvâṇa."

Having heard this he lowered his eyelids, and after a time, having with his hand raised his locks, he ascended from his place into the air and by his great spiritual power having caused his body to consume itself with fire, which appeared at his will, his bones fell to the ground as his bequeathed relics.

The king and the great congregation collected the

bones, and raised over them a Stûpa—and this is the one we are noticing.

Going north from this place 500 *li* or so, we come to the country of *Kie-sha* (Kashgar).[1]

Going south-east from this place 500 *li* or so, and crossing the Śitâ river, they passed over a great mountain range and reached the kingdom of *Cha-kiu-kia* (Yarkiang ?).

To the south of this country there is a high mountain in which there are a number of niches like chambers; many men of India who have arrived at the fruit (*of Bôdhi*) by their spiritual power, transport themselves here to rest in peace, and a great many of these who have died here (*obtained Nirvâṇa*).

At present there are three Arhats who dwell in a mountain cavern here, and have entered into the ecstasy of complete forgetfulness. As their hair and beards gradually grow longer, the priests from time to time go to the spot to cut them.

In this country are many Sûtras of the Great Vehicle; this literature includes many tens of works amounting to 100,000 ślokas.[2]

Going east from this 800 *li* or so, we come to the country of Kustana (Khotan). This district is a great flat covered with sand and stones. The soil, however, is fit for the cultivation of cereals and is very productive. They manufacture carpets (*rugs*) from wool, fine haircloth, and silken taffeta; the soil produces much white jade and dark jade. The climate is temperate, and the

[1] The old name was *Su-li* (*Syr ?*) and so the city was called. The right sound, however, was *Shi-li-ki-li-to-ti* (Śrihritati ?); the way of writing it—*Su-li*, so commonly adopted—is wrong—*Ch. Ed.*

[2] It would seem from this (as I have remarked elsewhere) that the *Great Vehicle* system found its way into India, from Baktria.

common people understand politeness and right principles; they esteem learning and are fond of music. They are upright in their conduct and truthful, and in these respects differ from other Tartar tribes (*Hu*). Their literature (*letters*) resembles that of India with some slight differences. They greatly esteem the law of Buddha.

There are 100 monasteries here and about 5000 priests. They mostly study the Great Vehicle. The king is a polished and learned man, brave and versed in the arts of war. He is well affected towards virtuous people. He professes to be descended from *Pi-sha-man* (Vaiśravana).

The great ancestor of the king was the eldest son of Aśôka-râja, who dwelt in Takshasilâ. Afterwards, being banished from the kingdom, he[1] went forth to the north of the Snowy Mountains. As he went looking for grass and water for his herds, he came to this place and built his chief residence here.

After a while, because he had no son, he went to worship in the Temple of Vaiśravana Deva. The forehead of the god bursting open in front there came forth a male child, and the ground, fronting the temple, at the same time produced a wonderfully sweet-scented (*substance like milk from the*) breast; taking this for the nourishment of the child he grew up to maturity.

At the king's death he mounted the throne and established his rule in righteousness, and brought many countries under his power. The present king is his descendant. As his ancestor had been nourished by a breast of the earth, the name of *U-tien* (for *Kustana*) was given to it, meaning an earth-pap.[2]

[1] Or, should it not be, *they*, *i.e.* the accusers of the royal prince?

[2] Pausanias also speaks of a fountain near which is a stone, *mammis muliebribus persimile*, p. 778. I have often thought that the celebrated *Gomati* Temple at Khotan was so called from "mother earth." In fact, the entire account both here, and in Fa-hien, of the character of the Khotan people and their civilisation, seems to point to a non-Indian origin.

When the Master of the Law entered the frontiers of this kingdom, he came to the city of *Po-kia-i* (Bhagpa ?). In this is a sitting figure of Buddha about seven feet high; on its head is a precious jewel-crown, and its appearance is perfect and complete (*for majesty*). The old people gave the following account of it.

The image originally belonged to Kaśmir and came to this place by invitation.

There was formerly an Arhat who had a Śrâmaṇêra (*as a disciple*) whose body was afflicted with leprosy. When he was near death he desired to have a cake of *tsoh-mai* (sour meal ?). His master by means of his divine sight saw that such food could be got in Kustana. Accordingly he transported himself there by his power of Irrdhi, and having begged some, returned and gave it to the Śrâmaṇêra. Having eaten it he was filled with joy and desired to be born in that country. His earnest prayer could not be abortive, and so after his death he was born in the royal family.

After he had come to the throne, being sharp-witted and brave, he purposed to make a foray and seize some neighbouring territory. Crossing the mountains therefore he attacked the old country of his birth.

The king of Kaśmir accordingly chose his generals and marshalled his troops in order to repel the attack.

And now the Arhat said: "Do not attempt to use force: I myself will go to him."

Forthwith he went to the place where the king of Kustana was, and told him about the loss caused by the covetousness and violence of the head-born (Mûrdhaja) king; and then he showed him the garment he had worn when in his former person he had been a Śrâmaṇêra.

The king seeing it, and arriving at a knowledge of his former condition, was deeply ashamed, and forthwith formed an alliance with the king of Kaśmir, and renounced his purpose of conquest. Returning to his country, he was accompanied by (or, *he received as a guest*) the image which he had formerly worshipped, and which now followed the army. When the image arrived at this spot it stood still and would go no farther. The king and all his army tried to move it forward by force, but it would not move. Accordingly the king raised above the image a little chapel, and invited the priests and their companions to come and worship it. Moreover he placed on the head of Buddha (*i.e. the image*) his own much-valued and magnificent head-dress. This head-dress is still to be seen, and is of priceless value on account of the jewels; all beholders are filled with exultation at the sight.

The Master of the Law remained here seven days.

The king of Khotan hearing that the Master was entering his territories, went forth in his own person to meet him, and the following day he conducted him on his way.

The king, arriving at his capital in advance, left his son to attend (the Master).

After proceeding thus for two days the king further despatched an official guide (*ta kwan*) to conduct him on his onward way.

When forty *li* from the town he rested for the night. The next day the king, with a number of clerics and laymen, taking with them sounding music, perfumes, and flowers, accompanied him along the road on the left side; on his arrival he invited him to enter the city, and located him in a temple of the Little Vehicle, belonging to the school of the Sarvâstivâdins.

About ten *li* to the south of the city, there is a large Saṅghârama which was built by a former king of this country in honour of Vâiróchana Arhat.[1]

Formerly, when this country had not yet received the

[1] For an original and compendious account of the history of Khotan, *vide* Rockhill, "*The Life of the Buddha*," cap. viii.

benefit of the teaching of the Law, an Arhat came here from Kaśmir, and sat down in silent meditation in the midst of a forest.[1]

Some persons who saw him were frightened at his appearance and clothing.

Having told the king about it, he came in person to examine his appearance.

He then asked him who he was, living thus in the midst of a solitary wilderness.

He answered: "I am a disciple of Tathâgata; his law enjoins on me this solitary abode."

The king replied: "When you speak of Tathâgata, whom do you mean?"

He answered and said: "Tathâgata is the distinctive title of Buddha. He was in former days the eldest son of Suddhódana-râja, his name being Sarvârthasiddha; moved by tenderness for "all flesh" engulfed in the sea of sorrow, without a teacher and without any refuge, he rejected the seven gems belonging to a *Chakravarttin,* and the 1000 sons, and the sovereignty over the four continents (*quarters,* or *islands*), and in the solitary forest earnestly sought after wisdom (*Bôdhi*); having obtained the fruit of his six years' discipline, his body yellow as gold, he reached the law which is acquired without a Master. He scattered sweet dew (*i.e., preached on the deathless condition of Nirvâṇa*) in the garden of deer, and caused the brightness of the Mani-gem to shine on the summit of the Ghṛidrakûṭa (*i.e.,* declared the *highest* truth). For eighty years he published his doctrine for the profit and happiness (*of all creatures*). His connection with (*conditioned*) life being now broken, he peacefully passed away to the true condition of being, leaving his image and his body of doctrine as a perpetual legacy, and these still survive.

[1] The *Tsu-la* grove, *op. cit.*, p. 237. The word in our text, however, may mean "*the wilderness.*"

"And now the king by his meritorious conduct in previous states of life has established himself as a ruler of men; he ought therefore to take charge of and enjoin obedience to, this religious system (*wheel of the law*), that those who understand its purport may find in it their salvation (*refuge*). But why are you so dumb, as though you heard me not?"[1]

The king replied: "My sins, accumulated and overflowing, have prevented me from hearing the name of Buddha. But now, thanks to the downpouring virtue of the holy man, what remnant of merit I have, has accrued to my benefit. May I be allowed to adore his image and obey the doctrine he has bequeathed to the world?"

The Arhat replied: "You must seek the joy of fulfilling your vows. First then build a Sañghârama, then the divine image will of itself descend."

On this the king returned, and with his various ministers having selected a suitable site, and having summoned his workmen, he asked the Arhat for a plan of the building to be raised. He then proceeded with the work.

When the temple was finished, the king further inquired, "The Sañghârama is completed, but where is the statue of Buddha?"

He replied: "Let the king only seek the fullest assurance (*insight*) and the image will come forthwith."

On this the king and all the great ministers and the gentry and people, lighting their incense and scattering flowers, stood still in profound meditation; in a moment the image of Buddha came down from space with its

[1] This may also be translated, 'What can be said (of your wisdom) if you turn a deaf ear to my (or, *his*) words."

precious daïs, glittering and bright, and of a majestic appearance.

The king seeing it, was filled with joy, and congratulated himself on his extreme good fortune. Moreover, he requested the Arhat to preach the Law for the benefit of the people. Then, because he instituted for the people (or, *among the people*) a festival of dedication, this Sañghârama is (*remembered as*) the very first foundation in the country.

The Master of the Law, since he had previously lost his books in crossing the river, when he came here, immediately sent messengers to go to Kuchi and to *Su-li* (Kashgar), to seek for others; and now, notwithstanding his delay with the king of Khotan, as they had not obtained the books, he sent forward a young man of Kau-chang with a written memorial, desiring him to follow in the train of the merchants, and to present it at court, with the tidings that he who had formerly gone to the country of the Brâhmans to seek for the Law, had now returned so far as Khotan.

The memorial was couched in these words: "The words of the Śramaṇa *Hiuen-Tsiang*: Hiuen has heard say of *Ma-yung*,[1] *Ki-chen*, and *Ching-Huan*,[2] that they were teachers of public morals: *Fuh-sing*[3] was illustrious for his eminent talent: Cho-T'so[4] himself (*founded*) the schools to the south of the Tsih. Here we see the character of these learned men But if we admire these ancient masters for thus going afar in search (or, *support of*) learning, how much more those who search into the secret traces of the profit-bringing religion of the Buddhas, and the marvellous words of the three Piṭakas, able to liberate from the snares of the world? How can we dare to undervalue such labours, or not regard them with

[1] *Vide* Mayers' *Manual*, No. 479.
[2] *Op. cit.*, No. 59.
[3] *Op. cit.*, No. 147.
[4] *Op. cit.*, No. 97.

ardour? Now I, Hiuen-Tsiang, long since versed in the doctrine of Buddha, bequeathed by him in the Western world, the rules and precepts of which had reached the East in an imperfect form, always pondered on a plan for searching out the true learning, without any thought for personal safety. Accordingly, in the fourth month of the third year of the period Chêng-Kwan (630, A.D.), braving dangers and obstacles, I secretly found my way to India. I traversed over vast plains of shifting sand: I scaled precipitous mountain-crags clad with snow: found my way through the scarped passes of the iron gates; passed along by the tumultuous waves of the hot sea. Beginning at the sacred city of Chang'an, I reached the new city of Râjagṛiha.

"Thus I accomplished a journey of more than 50,000 *li;* yet, notwithstanding the thousand differences of customs and manners I have witnessed, the myriads of dangers I have encountered, by the goodness of Heaven I have returned without accident, and now offer my homage with a body unimpaired, and a mind satisfied with the accomplishment of my vows. I have beheld the Ghṛidrakûṭa Mountain, worshipped at the Bôdhi tree: I have seen traces not seen before; heard sacred words not heard before; witnessed spiritual prodigies, exceeding all the wonders of Nature; have borne testimony to the high qualities of our august Emperor; and won for him the high esteem and praise of the people. In my travels through successive kingdoms I have passed seventeen years, and now, having come from the country of Prayâga; passed through Kapiśa; surmounted the precipices of the T'sung-Ling, traversed the valley of Pamir, I have reached Khotan.

"And now, because the great elephant (*which I had*) is perished in the waters, I have not yet succeeded in obtaining transport for the numerous books which I have brought back. On that account I have remained here a little while; but not having obtained (*even here*) the necessary mode of conveyance, I purpose at once to go forward and visit your majesty. With this view I have sent forward a layman belonging to Kau-Chang, whose name is *Ma-huan-chi*, in the company of certain merchants, respectfully to present this letter, and to announce my purpose."

After this, during a day and a night, he explained to the priests of Khotan the principles of the *Yôga*, the *Abhidharma*, the *Kosha* and the *Maháyâna-samparigraha-Śâstras*.

The king with the clergy and lay-people all sought to do honour to his teaching, and many thousands embraced the faith daily.

Seven or eight months having elapsed, the messenger returned with a gracious message from the king, to this effect: "When I heard that the Master who had gone to far-off countries to search for religious books, had now come back, I was filled with joy without bounds. I pray you come quickly, that we may see each other. The priests of this kingdom who understand the *Fan*[1] language and the explanation of the sacred books, I have also commanded to come and pay you greeting. I have ordered the bureaux of Khotan[2] and other places to send with you the best guides they can procure, and conveyances as many as you require. I have commanded the magistrates of Tun-wang to conduct you through the desert of shifting sands, and I have desired the Shen-Shen (*government*) to send to meet you at Tso-moh."

[1] The sacred language of India (*Julien*). But it cannot be confined to the *Sanscrit*, as Mr. Alwis supposes (*Lecture* ii. p. 50), because Fa-hien speaks of the Buddhist books in Ceylon, as written in the *Fan* language. *Records*, i., lxxx.*

[2] From this, as Rockhill remarks, (*op. cit.* p. 231, *n.*) we may gather that Khotan at this time was subject to the king of Kau-chang.

* Unless indeed, as Mr. Foulkes seems to suppose, the books which Fa-hien procured in Ceylon were written in *Sanscrit* (vide *Indian Antiq.*, May 1888, p. 124, c. 1).

The Master of the Law having respectfully received this letter of instructions, forthwith set forward. The king of Khotan provided him with a large store of provisions.

Having gone 300 *li* or so from the capital, eastward, he reached the town of Pi-mo.[1] In this city is a sandal-wood image of Buddha in a standing position. It is thirty feet high, and is of a grave and majestic appearance. It has great spiritual virtue, insomuch that men who are afflicted with any bodily hurt, if, according to the place so affected, they place some gold leaf on the corresponding part of the image, they are immediately restored. Those who pay their vows to this image and make request for any favour are mostly successful. The old tradition goes that when Buddha was formerly alive in the world, Udâyana-râja, of Kauśâmbî, made this image. After the Nirvâṇa of Buddha it came flying of its own accord to the north of this country, and located itself in the city of *Ho-lo-lo-kia* (Râgha or Urgha?); after this it again transported itself to this place. The saying is, that according to tradition, when the religion of Śâkya is destroyed, this image will enter the Dragon palace.

Leaving the town of Pi-mo and proceeding eastward, we enter the desert of sand and stone. Going 200 *li* we reach the town of *Ni-jang*.[2] Eastward of this again is the desert of drifting sand, without water or vegetation, burning hot, and subject to the evil of poisonous fiends and imps. There is no road, and travellers in coming and going have only to look for the deserted bones of men and cattle as their guide. We have before described the arid and toilsome character of this desert journey.

Again going 100 *li* or so, we reach the old country of Tukhâra. Six hundred *li* further on we come to the old country of *Che-mo-t'o-na*,[3] which is the same as the Ni-mo territory.

[1] Pimâ, *vide Records*, ii. 322.

[2] *Records*, ii. p. 324.

[3] *Records*, ii. 325, *n.* 75.

Again going north-east 1000 *li* or so we come to the old country of Na-fo-po, which is the same as the territory of Leu-lan.[1]

From this, after various détours, we arrive at the borders of China. Having obtained conveyances the Master then sent back to Khotan the messengers and their horses and camels. They returned therefore, having declined to accept the recompense awarded them for their services.

Having reached Sha-chow, he forwarded a memorial (*to the Emperor*). The Emperor was then residing in his palace at Lo-yang. On receiving the letter he learned that Hiuen-Tsiang was gradually approaching: he then commanded Fong-huan-ling, duke of the kingdom of Liang, of the titular rank Tso-po-she, who had been left as governor of the western capital (Si-gan-fu), to despatch proper officers to go forth and conduct (*the Master of the Law*).

The Master, understanding that the Emperor desired to question him as to his fault in leaving the country without permission, wished to avoid any delay in his arrival, and therefore pressed forward on his march with haste, and arrived by way of the canal.

The magistrates not knowing the routine of polite reception and escort, were unable to make the necessary preparations; but the news spreading fast, the people came together of their own accord in vast numbers to behold and pay their homage to the Master. The streets were so crowded that when he wished to disembark, he could not advance for the crush, and so he passed the night on the canal.

[1] That is, Shen-shen.

CONCLUSION.

HAVING disembarked, Hiuen-Tsiang was escorted to the western capital (Si-gan-fu), where he arrived in the spring of the year 645 A.D.[1]

On the day following, the members of the various monasteries conducted Hiuen-Tsiang, with flags and banners, to the convent called Hong-fu (*extensive happiness*). He here deposited the treasures he had brought from India, viz. :—

1. One hundred and fifty particles of flesh *śarîras*, of the Tathâgata.

2. One golden statue of Buddha (*according to the pattern of*) the shadow left in the Dragon cave of the Pragbôdhi Mountain in the kingdom of Magadha; also a glittering pedestal 3 ft. 3 in. high. This figure resembles the image of Buddha as he is turning the wheel of the Law[2] in the deer-park at Bânâras.

3. A sandal-wood figure of Buddha with a shining pedestal 3 ft. 5 in. high, after the model of the sandal-wood figure made according to the likeness drawn by the desire of Udâyana, king of Kauśâmbî, when he was longing for (*the return of*) Tathâgata.

4. A figure of Buddha with a shining pedestal 2 ft. 9 in. high, after the model of the figure of Tathâgata,

[1] The nineteenth year of the period of Chêng-kwan, 646 A.D. (Mayers).
[2] That is, *preaching*.

when he descended on the jewelled ladder from the heavenly palace to the country of Kapitha.

5. A silver figure of Buddha with a translucent pedestal, 4 ft. high, after the model of Buddha delivering the *Saddharma-puṇḍarîka* and other Sûtras on the Ghrĭdrakûṭa Mountain, in Magadha.

6. A figure of Buddha with a translucent pedestal, 3 ft. 5 in. high, after the model of the figure of his shadow, which he left in the country of Nagarahâra, in the place where he subdued the poisonous dragon.

7. A sandal-wood figure of Buddha with a translucent pedestal, 1 ft. 3 in. high, after the model of a similar figure representing Buddha as he went round the city of Vaiśalî on his work of conversion.

He also deposited in this temple the books of the Great Vehicle, which he had brought from the West, including 224 Sûtras,[1] 192 Śâstras,[2] 15 works of the Sthavira[3] school, including Sûtras, Vinaya, and Sâstras; the same number belonging to the Sammatiya school; 22 works of the same character belonging to the Mahîsâsaka school; 67 books of the same character belonging to the Sarvâstîvâdin school; 17 works of the same character belonging to the Kâśyapîya school; 42 works of the same character belonging to the Dharmagupta school; 36 copies of the Hetuvidyâ śâstra; 13 copies of the Śabdavidyâ śâstra; altogether 520 *fasciculi*, comprising 657 distinct volumes, carried upon twenty horses.

After having visited the chief officers of the western capital, the Emperor being at Lo-yang, the Master pro-

[1] Julien has 124.

[2] Julien (whose copy appears here to have been defective) has *lun-i-yen*, where the symbol *yen* is evidently a misprint for *pih*, the number being 192 instead of 92.

[3] Julien has throughout his translation substituted *Sarvâstivâdas* for *Sthaviras*.

ceeded to that town, and had an interview with the sovereign. He was received with the greatest attention in the I-lwan[1] palace. Being seated, the Emperor asked him why he had gone from home without consulting him. He replied that he had sent three requests for permission to leave the country previous to his departure; but having received no answers he was unable to restrain his desire, and accordingly left without the desired permission.

After a lengthened conversation, Hiuen-Tsiang having declined to accept a secular life, retired to the monastery of Hong-fu in Si-gan-fu, and there began his work of translation.

At the conclusion of the year 647 A.D. he had completed the translation of the (1) Bôdhisattva-piṭaka-Sûtra, (2) Buddha-bhûmi-Sûtra, (3) Shaṭmukhî-dhâraṇî, and others.

By the end of the year 648 he had completed in all fifty-eight books, including the Si-yu-ki (*undertaken at the Emperor's express command*).

In the year 649 the Emperor caused Hiuen-Tsiang to take up his residence in the Sse-'en Temple.[2] Here he continued the work of translation until his death.

In the year 650 A.D. the Emperor T'ai-Tsung died and was succeeded by Kao-Tsung.

From this time the Master of the Law devoted himself with earnest resolution to the work of translation. He rose every morning at dawn of day, and after a slight repast devoted four hours to the explanation of the Sacred Books. And being in charge of the Monastery he had regard to the discipline of the resident monks.

[1] The Palace of the Phœnix.

[2] This is the Temple of "Great Benevolence," from which the Chinese title of the work we have before us is taken.

Upwards of 100 disciples daily attended his lectures; and notwithstanding his manifold occupations, he showed the same energy in his work as he had exhibited from the first. He discoursed largely on the various systems of the schools and the distinguished Masters of the West, so that the princes and ministers who came to listen to his discourses, frequently expressed their admiration and respect for his eminent talent.

In the year 652 A.D. the Master of the Law caused a pagoda (*Feou-to*) to be constructed at the southern gate of the Hong-fuh temple, in which he finally deposited his sacred books and images for safety. The total height of this structure was 180 ft. It was built after the model of the Indian Stûpas, and had five stages—surmounted by a cupola. In the highest storey on the southern side, there was a chamber constructed, in which were preserved copies of the two prefaces composed by the former Emperor and the Prince Royal, to the volumes translated by Hiuen-Tsiang.

In the year 654 a deputation from the Mahâbôdhi Temple in Central India visited the Master and conveyed to him the assurances of the high esteem in which he was held. Hiuen-Tsiang replied, acknowledging the honour conferred upon him, and requesting that the books he had lost in crossing the Indus might be replaced by others from India.

During the years 655 A.D. and 656 A.D. the Master continued the task of translating his books: he suffered from an old malady contracted in crossing the mountains of India, but by the help of the physicians sent to him from the court he partly recovered. In the year 658 the Master returned from Lo-yang to the western capital, the suite of the Emperor, and took up his residence in the newly constructed temple called *Si-ming*. Here he remained until signs of advancing age caused him some anxiety lest he should be unable to translate the Prajñâ (*pâramitâ*) works. With the view of entering on this task he requested the Emperor's permission to retire to the *Yuh-fa* (gem flower) palace, and there in quietness to prepare for this translation. In 659 he moved into this palace, and in 660 began the new translation. The Indian copy of the Mahâ-prajñâ-pâramitâ Sûtra consisted of 200,000 *ślôkas;* he purposed to produce an abridged translation, but was warned by a dream not to do so. The Master had procured three copies of this work in India, and he at once proceeded to collate these with a view to correct the text from which he translated. He was now sixty-five years of age, and feeling that his end was near he worked without interruption in order to finish his task before he died.

He completed his labours in the 10th month of the year *Lung So* (661 A.D.). The entire work of the Mahâ-prajna-paramitâ Sûtra consists of 600 chapters, in 102 vols.

Having declined to undertake the translation of the Ratna-kûta Sûtra, he composed himself to await his end. He had now finished the translation of seventy-four distinct works, in 1335 chapters. He had, moreover, made a vast number of pictures, and written out with his own hands copies of various Sûtras. When the recital of all these works was finished, he closed his eyes and lay perfectly still. Having now repeated some verses in adoration of Mâitreya,[1] he gradually sank until the day of his death, in the 10th month, 13th day, of the year 664.

[1] The earnest desire of Hiuen-Tsiang was to behold Mâitreya and dwell with him in the Tuśita heaven. Mâitreya, of course, is the future Buddha, and represents the character of Love.

He was buried in the Western capital, but in the year 669 his remains were removed by order of the Emperor to a space situated to the north of the valley of Fan-chuen, where a tower was constructed to his memory.

THE END.